ESOTERIC PRINCIPLES OF
VEDIC ASTROLOGY
A Treatise on Advanced Predictive Techniques

ESOTERIC PRINCIPLES OF
VEDIC ASTROLOGY
A Treatise on Advanced Predictive Techniques

BEPIN BEHARI

A Sterling Paperback

STERLING PAPERBACKS
An imprint of
Sterling Publishers (P) Ltd.
A-59, Okhla Industrial Area, Phase-II,
New Delhi-110020.
Tel: 26387070, 26386209; Fax: 91-11-26383788
E-mail: mail@sterlingpublishers.com
ghai@nde.vsnl.net.in
www.sterlingpublishers.com

Esoteric Principles of Vedic Astrology
A Treatise on Advanced Predictive Techniques
© 2003, Bepin Behari
ISBN 978 81 207 2560 7
Reprint 2006, 2010

Printed in India

Printed and Published by Sterling Publishers Pvt. Ltd.,
New Delhi-110 020.

PREFACE

Serious students of Hindu astrology have recently become concerned about the status of this ancient subject. There is considerable scepticism about astrology and astrological predictions. Occasionally there occurs vehement outbursts from ill-informed and misguided physical scientists against this ancient occult science.

During the Vedic period, the people were clear about their goal in life and lived in harmony with Nature. They lived a life which was in harmony with the seen and unseen powers regulating and guiding human development. In Indian scriptures when stellar configurations were mentioned on important occasions such as births of sovereigns, avatars, and wars between the *devas* and the *asuras,* the basic objective was to show that every event in our life takes place according to a divine plan, which could be deciphered by those who already knew the language of the stars. The knowledge of this science was given out to make the people conform with their inner nature and ultimate destiny and beneficent natural forces. Presently, we have slipped away from this spiritual goal, so even the ancient science of astrology lost some of its ancient shine. But nowadays, some serious students are coming up who desire to revive the pristine glory of this occult science, retrieve this esoteric knowledge and reinstate its original status.

The basic principles of Hindu astrology which prevailed during the Vedic civilisation, disappeared during the last thousand years or so but some of its superficial aspects remained with the public, to remind of its past glory and vast possibilities. Since the middle of the last century, there has been a revival. Vedic astrology is an ancient science and a subject with great possibilities. It is considered a system of knowledge which could unveil a bit of our future. It is also felt that it has a great potential for providing an impetus for pious living. The impetus thus received made many self-effacing volunteers search for ancient manuscripts, bring them to light, translate them into modern languages and disseminate them for wider consumption. This great efflux of predictive rules increased the popularity of the subject. Books on astrology began to appear in public. Many astrologers began to make remarkable predictions. This was indeed a very encouraging comeback.

Temptation to make use of the subject for undesirable objectives, however, could not be checked. During the Second World War, each side began to recruit astrologers to read the charts of army generals and to seek their help in destroying the enemy's manoeuvres. The revelations of the hidden messages of Nature became a means of acquiring personal glory and to destroy mankind. The cessation of armed hostilities brought to the fore the emergence of many new political parties and a new brand of industrialists. They became regular customers of this new commodity. Every street corner became full of 'astrologers' who could predict the fluctuations in the stock exchange, the fate of political parties, and the behaviour of other countries. It was a period of great expansion of the astrological market. This deflected the gaze of serious students from the basic objectives of the occult science and in competition with the newly emerging brand of astrologers, they could not succeed in retrieving the earlier grandeur of the subject.

There are two main reasons for serious concern. First, the growing technological advancement along with its social and psychological fall-out made the new physical scientists much against astrology. Second, the ancient seers had emphasised the need for austerities and spiritual code of life for those who practised this subject for revealing future to others. This was a very difficult requirement which very few persons could or were prepared to practise. Thus there has been a revolt against the revival of ancient astrology in the new world. It required that those who delved in this subject acknowledged the reality of the unseen forces and the unseen deities. Those who did not have occult *siddhis* and clairvoyance, vehemently denied such possibilities. Yet they liked to experiment and assess the validity of astrological predictions. They are the persons who present the greatest hindrance against the propagation of ancient astrology.

A new factor relevant in the present context has been the approach of the present day (serious) astrologers. There are many pious astrologers who are practising the subject in right earnest, but they think that the astrological knowledge is concerned only with predictions of one's future and suggestion of palliatives. But there is a positive aspect of the subject as well. Astrology is not concerned with maladies, afflictions, child births, promotions, marriages and sorrows of life. Presently, many thoughtful persons have begun questioning the purpose of life, meaning of death, the basic causes of their adverse conditions of life and such other matters. They are concerned with fundamental questions of sorrows, anomalies of life-conditions, and the best-suited course for them. These are some of the questions with which astrology is, in fact, vitally related. This is a new dimension in the emerging scenario of astrological counselling. The present study aims at showing the relevance of astrology in this context.

The present study throws some new light atleast on the five aspects of astrological counselling. First, the emerging attitude to astrology does not require silencing the opponents and the psuedo-scientists who are increasingly becoming impatient with (and even afraid of) growing popularity and new proofs of the validity of astrological predictions and its rationale. There are some astrologers who think that the so-called 'scientists' must be silenced otherwise their (astrologers') profession, earnings and sustenance would be jeopardised. But in case, new scope of astrological counselling is accepted and the astrologers reorient themselves to new dimensions of astrology and wean themselves away from sensationalism, their apprehensions could to a great extent be eliminated.

Second, the new astrological science should take into consideration the wisdom-base of world religions in deeper understanding of astrological principles. *An Introduction to Esoteric Astrology* aimed at showing that the ancient religions of the world have much to contribute to the understanding of zodiacal signs and the planetary disposition. Later, *A Study in Astrological Occultism,* tried to show that astrology is a part of the science which tries to understand deeper impulses. It also tried to indicate that astrological principles could be helpful in one's yogic practices. *Myths and Symbols of Vedic Astrology* discussed in depth how zodiacal signs, planets and *nakshatras* are parts of extensive occult forces working behind human evolution and how the ancient seers explained these laws in mystery languages which could be studied with advantage by us. In the present study, we have devoted a major portion of the study in giving certain basic principles of this line of research which can be effectively pursued further by those who wish to do so.

Third, the study attempts to discuss the goal of one's evolutionary course which could, to some extent, be discovered on the basis of astrological principles already available with us in classical texts. Every event of our life is directed towards accomplishment of our goal in life. Modern psychology has already explored this aspect to a great extent. On the basis of astrological principles, this line of study can be pursued further, taking individual uniqueness into consideration in counselling and study. Thus making astrology related with brighter aspects of life and a confident living despite various sorrowful and difficult conditions of existing situations.

Fourth, it solves some of the enigmas of astrological laws which one finds in classical treatises. The various planetary combinations, as well as descriptions of wrong planetary position, needs to be understood in the changing situations of modern society. The effects of exalted planets, *Pancha Mahapurusha Yogas, Kala Sarpa Yoga* are some of the planetary combinations which often baffle astrology students. Principles like *Bhavat Bhavam* which have been indicated in classical texts but not well explained, have been discussed in this study to clarify and guide its utilisation in a better and more meaningful way.

Fifth, and the most important contribution of this study is to indicate the manner in which some of the sorrowful events in one's life could be traced back to one's previous birth and how they could be effectively counteracted. The palliatives such as gems, mantras, charities, etc., usually practised by many astrologers and found helpful by many individuals, in the long-run do not absolve the individuals from their karmas. Generally, these maladies appear to them at a later stage and in some cases with greater virulence. An effective remedy against them lies in psychological reorientation of oneself and initiating counterveiling forces. The lessons from adverse forces have to be learnt and life-pattern suitably altered in order to align oneself with one's inner impulsions. A deeper study of patterns in one's horoscope unveils some of these features.

This study in fact is not meant to be exhaustive. It only aims to show and suggest some new angles from which to approach the ancient Indian astrology which could operate as a guide to one's everyday life. Many persons have helped in its evolution. Many editors and astrologers have cooperated and supported the concretisation of this volume. *The Astrological Magazine,* Bangalore, with its erudite editor and pioneer in Indian astrology, Dr. B.V. Raman, enabled me to share my early thoughts on some of these subjects with his readers. Interaction with many of the serious readers helped me immensely. The encouragement accorded by Dr. B.V. Raman helped me to propose the ideas more ardently. Late R. Santhanam, the founder of *The Times of Astrology,* New Delhi, and its discerning editor from its inception provided me valuable facilities for giving vent to my emerging ideas. Without his help and assistance, many of these ideas would have died in absence of proper nourishment. Many overseas publications have also rendered their cooperation in this undertaking. Spanish version of "Intergration of Personality" and of "Profession and Marriage" appeared in *Revista Astrologica Mercurio,* Barcelona, Spain, and "Shadow Planets: Rahu and Ketu" appeared in *The Mountain Astrologer,* California, USA. The author is very much thankful to all these editors for their cooperation and assistance.

In the end, I would like to thank and express my gratitude to a large number of friends and well-wishers without whose constant encouragement, this publication would not have been possible.

The reader will often find an unusual aroma of influences pervading throughout the study. I felt this influence myself many a time. It makes me feel that I have merely been a mouthpiece of invisible thought-currents circulating these days in the astrological world. I am extremely grateful to these unseen powers which have enabled me to articulate them. The real test of the usefulness of this effort however lies with readers. If they feel aroused to new thought currents, whether in conformity with these or at variance with them, I will consider my efforts successful.

I am also thankful to the readers for their perusal and study of this book. It makes me immensely satisfied that the effort is rewarded. There is much in this publication which new as well as advanced students will find useful and if they consider it worthwhile to send me their comments, I shall be very appreciative of their responses.

C-505 Yojana Vihar   BEPIN BEHARI
New Delhi - 110092

CONTENTS

PART-I

Astrological Counselling

SCOPE OF
ASTROLOGICAL STUDIES

Astrology is accepted as an ancient occult science, widely known and believed as a subject of tremendous importance by all great civilisations of the world. Every ancient society recognised it as a divine science and practised it in many forms. But H.P. Blavatsky, the greatest occultist of the nineteenth century, very truly affirmed that "astronomy and physiology are the bodies, astrology and psychology their informing souls; the former being studied by the eye of sensual perception, the latter by the inner or 'soul-eye'; and both are exact sciences."

The growing interest in occult sciences such as astrology, psychometry, psychic perception, dream analysis, and so on, almost in all the parts of the world, specially in the so-called materialistically advanced countries, proved that the teeming billions have been eagerly trying to develop their 'soul-eye'. The growth and development of their physical senses and organs has presently been almost stagnant. But the scientists have collected much evidence to show that the consciousness of man is limitless and immense scope exists for its development. Psychology is now accepted as a science which opens a vast panorama of human psyche. This science is enabling modern man to take a radically different view of life. In many ways, psychological knowledge has begun to help the individuals in understanding their fellow-beings and their environment in a radically different manner.

A similar change in outlook is imminent with regard to astrology, if this subject could be properly comprehended and its deeper principles well explored. It reveals many universal forces operating on the growth and development of our consciousness and relationships. Their knowledge and understanding could alter our life and social intercourse; it may affect our aspirations towards and confidence in divinity of man. The modern man is not in touch with his ancient heritage and he is still learning to appreciate the wider ramifications of this science. But, occasionally, we find persons who are led by their inner voice or by their intellectual insight to feel that astrology has a legitimate place in our life and for personal guidance in many areas of our existence, it is very effective. The progress of our society to a great extent depends on such enlightened rational individuals.

The classical astrological texts have given very abstruse principles for the prognostication of intricate and complex occurrences in our daily life. But these have been practised by many astrologers to such an exactitude that many have often been baffled. The special areas of the experts cannot be usurped by the novice. However, there are many other ways in which the common man could take advantage of astrological knowledge. Most importantly, man is primarily interested in knowing his basic attributes on the basis of which he could decide his course of life specially in areas such as vocational choice, financial possibilities, proneness to different malignant diseases and accidents. This may be discovered with the help of astrology. All these are necessary and helpful, but in order to assess the nature and grade of his horoscope, on the basis of which, the chances of occurrences of the events are predicted, the astrologer should be aware of certain intricacies of planetary influences. In this connection, one should know the inherent characteristics of one's Ascendant, Moon and the Sun, Jupiter, Saturn, Rahu and Ketu apart from astrological phenomena such as combustion, retrogression etc. Without some idea of the lunar mansions, or *nakshatras,* which exercise immense power and were very well recognised for their importance even by the Vedic seers, finer appreciation of one's horoscope would not be possible. The exposition of directional astrology is necessary and that could be easily found by working out the degree of the natal Moon and then applying the result to any good ephemeris. More important than this, however, is the influence of transits which very easily mar or help the effects of the ruling planets. These technical details would be helpful in order to evaluate the astrological effects on one's life. One may not remain contented merely by such knowledge and would like to see the working of God in his special case: how the Supreme is shaping him towards his archetype. This would require the individual to have a knowledge of his ray and how developed are his various "principles". These are very complex subjects, but the common man should at least try to grasp this knowledge which would reduce much of his frustrations. The soul unfolds the consciousness of the individual by gradually energising and vitalising his various "principles" and "rays".

Every individual progresses on his individual ray which has much deeper implications than superficially appreciated. Astrologically we are told that the Sun is the soul of this universe and it sends specialised rays. These are seven in number and have been named as Sushumna, Harikesh, Visvakarman, Visvatryarchas, Sannaddha, Sarvavasu, and Svaraj. The Sushumna is said to energise the Moon. One does not know the detailed working of these rays, but Varahamihira has been very clear in enunciating that all the planets, the *nakshatras* and the signs of the zodiac are dependent on the Sun. Limiting ourselves only to the Sun's seven rays and linking them to the planets, when we analyse them further we find that the seven rays of the Sun produce special temperamental conditions for the human individuals. At early stages of the soul's growth, the characteristics of these rays are not very specialised and much mixed up effects are present, but gradually these are differentiated. Finally, the Sun would produce the ray of power working on *atmic* level and expressing itself in a highly specialised administrative skill evolving on which the individual could become a great emperor. It is on this ray that Manus are born. The second ray is that of the Moon on which greatly developed *buddhic* principle leads the individual to reflect Divine Wisdom and propound them for human goodness and their salvation. Lord Buddha and Jesus Christ exemplify incarnations at the apex of this ray. This is the ray of wisdom. The third is that of intellect, of the great thinkers whose mind or *manas* are highly energised. They are logical persons who work in a specific way because they have been intellectually satisfied with that course of action. Such people are under the influence of Mercury. The Sun,

Moon and Mercury are thus considered to function on the
consciousness side of life. They are very active in the realm of
subjective or the inner side of life. Mars is the scientist; the
temperament concerned with this planet is engaged on the physical
side of life, but it is very much concerned with working out its
inner elan, and to utilise it on the external plane. The scientists
discovering these latent principles try to manipulate them for
external or physical advantage. Such persons are generally skilled in
their handiwork. The sixth ray is associated with Jupiter and
exoteric religions consisting of much rituals and strict adherence to
religious observances. The seventh ray under the influence of Saturn
specialises in concretising grand ideas and thus they are highly
skilled in arts, architecture and other similar activities. Venus, which
is unique in many ways and much misunderstood as well, produces
harmony among different types. Venus is concerned with individuals
who apparently do not contribute anything special from their own
side but synthesise the ways of living, thoughts, and differences
expressed in different departments of life. Such a synthetic approach
to life is the special gift of Venusian harmony. These specialised
rays go so much deeper to the very core of individual's life that his
mode of shopping, type of books he reads, the nature of people he
associates with and the vocation he adopts, are all influenced by
these rays. Even when the individual has begun to be differentiated,
at early stages, two or more rays get suffused and it is only
gradually that the primary and secondary rays emerge. Any
professional astrologer would find it difficult to identify the special
ray of the individual because it requires much inward search in the
mental state of an individual. It is an exploration in one's
psychology, which not even a psychologist can do effectively. But
once the individual is able to establish a rapport with one's own
inner being, with one's own inner working of the mind and is able
to relate that with different planets, it would give immense power in
his hand for rebuilding his own life and shaping it in the destined
manner.

On this path of exploration, the individual should be able to
identify even the nature of his various sheaths or *koshas* of which
various occult literature have discussed. Adi Guru Shankaracharya
described the various human sheaths in great detail. An
identification of these sheaths with different planets has not so far

been exoterically given out. Based on scattered hints, one speculates that the physical or the *Annamaya Kosha* is linked with Saturn. Jupiter is connected with that aspect of one's body which absorbs solar globules and imparts health and vitality to the human constitution. On the effective circulation of this energy in his health, aura, depends the physical well-being of the person. It provides an effective shield against invasion from different maladies. Mars is connected with astral or emotional nature of the person. How much of the instinctive reaction or involuntary impulses control the person is indicated by this planet. The capacity to sympathetic vibration and the power to identify one's feelings with others result from the nature and development of this sheath.

Selfishness, self-centredness, cravings of different kinds and ruthlessness of temperament are expressions of an impure body, but once impurities are purged out, philanthropy, martyrdom, susceptibility to other persons' sorrows replace the earlier qualities. The healthy growth of an integrated personality depends upon well-formed emotional body. Personality defects, specially of the psychological kind, arise when there is some impediment to the free flow of pure energy in this sheath. Mind is divided in two parts — the lower mind is concerned with logical and rational or intellectual perception, whereas the higher levels of it are concerned with abstract, intuitional, and spiritual perception. The lower mind is linked with Mercury and the higher one with Venus. Then comes the *buddhic* level linked with the Moon and the highest principle known as *atmic* one is connected with the Sun. The triad consisting of *Atma-Buddhi-Manas* represented by the Sun, Moon and Mercury, contains within itself the eternal component of the individuality which in essence is the quintessence of all experiences and all understanding of life. That is what one ordinarily calls the soul. This triad is linked with the lower quaternary consisting of Venus, Mars, Jupiter and Saturn. They are the progenitors of the material counterpart of the being, which dissolves and incarnates at each birth. The relationship between these seven planets gives the clue regarding the harmony prevailing at various levels of the individual. By understanding this harmony, it is possible to know the health or otherwise of the specific sheath which could enable combing up operations leading to cleansing of the sheath so that the hints and suggestions coming from the *atmic* level could flow smoothly.

Often one comes across many inexplicable problems confronting the individual in his everyday struggle. Some traits of character or some happenings may not be the usual characteristics based on the rule of normalcy. These are the occurrences about which the individual enquires from astrologers. He wants to know as to why such things happen to him. In a general way, all the planets influence the individual according to the law of karma, but there are two planets in Vedic astrology which are considered particularly significant in this regard. The importance of Rahu and Ketu is great. Some illness, misfortune, temperamental difficulties, marital unhappiness, vocational upsettings and great psychological sorrows result from the impact of these two planets. Sometimes other planets, like Mars and Saturn also come into play in this regard, but they are mainly the acting agents while the basic karmic causes are indicated by Rahu and Ketu. Their placement in the horoscope indicates the areas which are liable to have karmic afflictions. A knowledge of this situation would enable the native to take proper care to counter the tendency so that harmony is achieved in his life and the karmic impediment is removed for ever. Without a knowledge of the conditions and the direction in which countervailing efforts are needed, the individual would be buffeted by the circumstances occurring in his life for which he has no explanation and which would continue troubling him immensely. Rahu and Ketu show the areas where special care is needed for the permanent happiness of the individual.

Equipped with such knowledge given by the planets, the individual can study his horoscope to assess if his particular life is important or not. In this regard, one has to consider whether affluence is the most important aspect of one's life or the so-called unhappy events have a greater value in orienting his life to his soul-ward direction. This assessment could impart to the individual a sense of fulfillment and would also give him self-confidence. The significance of illness and misfortune coming to his life would also change. The choice of profession and adjustment problems in service may become easier with this kind of information. But the most important contribution of astrological knowledge is, the discovery of the path of return generally known as yoga, which the individual could practise for achieving his end result.

One of the special outcome of astrological studies, apart from knowledge of the self, is an insight into the metaphysical basis of cosmogenesis. Generally, questions related to the origin of the universe, the beginning of the earth cycle, the advent of man on this earth and the course of spiral growth of human civilisation are all speculative when one studies them as a part of philosophy. But when astrology is studied in its deeper aspect, the knowledge about God, evolution, creative intelligences, the septenary principles in life, the trials or crucifixion and the stories relating to mystery schools prevalent in almost all ancient esoteric religions become more real. What is still more important is the advance indications of the future course of events, whether for the individual, society, or the world. With this kind of knowledge, one could consider them rationally and if found justified, the intelligent men could take up those hints and suggestions and begin working for either their own unfoldment and orientation, or for working towards a new society. What more useful subject could there be than that which helps unfoldment of one's latent potentialities, forewarns the coming events and reveals the future?

2

ASTROLOGICAL
COUNSELLING

Presently, interest in astrology has become so universal that one has
to open any international journal to find extensive advertisements for
providing astrological services. These advertisements refer to
cartomancy, mediumship, unique method of Egyptian fortune-telling,
psychometry, tarot method of foreseeing, clairvoyance, etc. These
methods are expected to yield effective results even from a distance
in delicate matters of personal life, return of affection, marital
problems, predictions related to horse races and professional
difficulties. In every metropolis of the world, there are reputed
crystal gazers to whom the customers of all levels of the society
flock to get 'predictions' made. There is, however, a possibility that
these very customers in public utterances would denounce such
professions as superstition and primitive but, privately would seek
their advice on urgent personal matters. So to disregard these public
utterances of the so-called rational and scientifically oriented
intellectuals and to assume that the interest in a positive way is
growing very fast in the present-day world, are realistic assumptions.

This belief is shared by a large number of individuals in
different countries. Though in India, this movement is yet to gather
momentum, in the West it has almost become a craze to learn
astrology. As a result of this popularity, many schools of doubtful
character have sprung to cater to the mass curiosity. In the name of
Hindu astrology, Egyptian method of fortune-telling, Chinese system

of divining future and of such other ancient civilisations, the popular interest in the subject is being exploited and there is none to protect the unwary individuals and to guide them in the right direction. It is important that the state of astrological science is carefully assessed by serious-minded persons and if necessary, correctives at right places applied.

The present trend makes it apparent that there is a growing desire among the people to understand the occult world and to mobilise the forces arising and operating in this realm of our existence to advantage. In this process, they have consciously or unconsciously begun to believe that there are non-physical forces which are operating on the affairs of men. They may not be aware of the exact mechanism by which the physical conditions of the individuals are influenced by the future, which may be epitomised as God, Nature, or by any other name, but there is a growing belief in a possibility of altering the course of likely events. They are also aware of the fact that the future can be comprehended, the human mind can overcome the time-barrier. Growing psychism of the modern world is an offshoot of this tendency.

Another important deduction from the present trend is related to the human belief in the powers of the stars. Those who seek to decipher the messages from them, secretly hope that the various stars are somehow capable of causing successful love affairs, remove illnesses and other human maladies, or influence the possibility of their professional preferment. If delays in marriages or the recurrent destruction of pregnancies could be avoided by planetary propitiation, the tiny stars must be highly powerful. By such interrelationships, man has extensively, though vaguely, begun to realise that the extra-terrestrial influences on him are quite powerful. He not only believes in such a relationship, but also that these forces work in accordance with certain principles. These principles can be known and are known to some persons. They have established certain harmonious relationships between certain human acts, such as, offerings, sound vibrations of mantras, wearing of certain metals and gems, and warding off of certain maladies based on some kind of relationship between planets and certain categories of persons, such as Jupiter with brahmins and Saturn with foreigners as well as due to some relationship between certain planets and some identified function of these stellar influences. To every imaginative person it would therefore become clear that the physical world of ours and everyday events in it are believed to form a part of the wider cosmic interrelationship.

Our life is greatly exposed to the influence of non-physical forces. The individual is no longer confined to himself and to his immediate environment. His relationship with the stars goes so deep that his thoughts and emotions, capacity to learn and to express himself, scientific or artistic talents, approach to life and to religion, dictatorial or submissive attitudes, are all connected with the planetary disposition. This being so, it is logical to consider that man basically consists of various "principles" each of which has very intimate links with the distant stars. Moreover, astrology is proving to be very effective in prognosticating mundane events and these events have very closely followed the predicted course. It implies that the society is closely connected with the distant stars. In such a relationship, it is not justified to consider man as an atomistic individual. The metaphysical statement that man is the cosmos in its totality, not necessarily only a reflection of it or constituting all the ingredients of which the cosmos is built, makes it imperative that he cannot be conceived in isolation of others. In such a case it is necessary to reassess the role of man in the world. Even if this question is not presented now in its deeper metaphysical aspect, the contemporary movement towards the occult will necessarily lead the common man to ask these questions very soon. The philosophers of the modern age have already begun moving in this direction. They have started challenging the already well-established attitudes of life and its problems which led to serious crises in human affairs. These are not merely theoretical questions but are intimately linked with our everyday life. Those who are involved in astrological movement have presently a tremendous responsibility arising from the serious upheaval in human thinking.

There are many areas in which astrologers are greatly interested. Here we are not considering the psuedo-astrologers who indulge in it to gain some kind of personal benefit, but those who are practising astrology for its own sake with prognositications made on scientific principles and not just in order to pamper the psychological weaknesses of the clients. Some of these practitioners are serious students whose main objective is to understand the various facets of the science and to rightly comprehend the laws which govern this cosmos. Others are intimately involved with predicting the future so that they could be cautioned of impending dangers and be properly oriented to meet the likely situation. One could classify the former as the research scientist and the latter as the physician. In the actual discharge of their responsibilities, they may differ to some extent but basically both of them are concerned with human life and welfare. Therefore, it is very important that society should bestow appropriate consideration on them. If presently it is not so, one need not cry for it because sooner or later it will be done. Meanwhile it is necessary that the astrologers must equip themselves for their future responsibilities which would be greater than those of the nuclear scientists or international economists.

Presently there are a few departments of human life regarding which the astrologers' help is normally sought. Generally, when an individual consults an astrologer, he is suffering either from some actual problem or from some anxiety. Under such circumstances, if the astrologer himself loses his balance and the general prospective of events, he cannot be an effective help. His first task, whatever the problem of the consultee, is to put him at rest and to be at peace with himself. This is a difficult task, but it has to be done. In doing so, he may use his astrological advice or he may just begin firstly by giving personal counsel as a sympathetic friend and guide. Having done so, when he looks at the actual subject matter of the enquiry, he may find that the questions may relate to problems pertaining to health, education, marriage, spells of ill-luck and dogged failure, professional and job problems, financial setback or problems pertaining to power, prestige, humiliation or social relationships. All these will have to be tackled differently, but the basic astrological principles related to them must never be lost sight of.

While dealing with the various aspects of life, firstly it is important to consider whether the problem is permanent or of short-term. The former will have to be examined in relation to the general strength of the chart and the latter by the calculation of the ruling planetary period. If the ascendant lord is in strength, according to classical texts, the temporary setbacks will not be serious and the palliatives will work very easily. In this context, it is worth remembering that there may exist a connection of the afflicting planets, whether in the case of temporary setbacks or in the case of permanent damages, with the sixth or eighth houses because they are very deep-rooted houses bringing the causes of the affliction from past lives, and these should be handled very carefully. If such afflictions are foreseen before the occurrence of the event, it is advisable that proper medical care should be taken at the most appropriate time. The malady may not be an ordinary one and it could require utmost attention in order to reduce its intensity. If the trouble has already started, the astrologer should advise the person regarding different ways of minimising the adverse effect of the planet. Every physical affliction of a permanent or deep-rooted nature is caused because of certain undesirable karmas of the person concerned. It is caused for karmic retribution and cosmic counterbalance. Both these can be considerably reduced and the desired purpose achieved, if the person begins to work out the countervailing activities. There is every possibility of thus reducing the pain. For example, if the individual suffers from anaemia, it is said that by his immersion in helpful activities and by inspiring others in humanitarian acts, the danger of anaemia is greatly reduced. One has to assess the malady, the personality structure of the questioner, and then suggest a line of effort, which radically alters his living pattern. That is generally required besides medical assistance, in the case of physical maladies.

As far as educational counselling is concerned, the task of the astrologer is very significant from another standpoint. In many western countries, presently the industrial management and even educational institutions are taking recourse to what is considered bio-rhythmic studies. The lessons and holidays are being arranged in such a way that the harmonious rhythm chart of the student synchronises with the work programme in the school. Industrial relations are also being organised in keeping with the same principle. This makes one feel that shortly the aid of astrologers will be greatly mobilised for educational and industrial welfare. Presently, people in India are very reticent in accepting astrological couselling on a large scale or on an organised basis, but almost every astrologer sometime or the other is confronted with such problems specially brought in by traditional guardians. Even the students themselves, at an advanced stage of their career, come for such advice. In such cases, it is important to distinguish between the natural talents of the individual, the career pursued by him and the line of his success. All these are predicted differently. The astrologer must at the very outset recognise that the individual may have talents in one line, while he may have to undertake a profession which is radically different from it. Intellect, schooling and profession are determined by three different houses such as the fourth, fifth and the tenth houses. Often it is considered that the fourth rules the intellect, the mind while the schooling and related subjects are ruled by the fifth house. Opinion may differ in this regard, but the association of different planets and the other rules of astrological predictions may be clearly distinguished for determining the subject in which the student may have proficiency and natural aptitude, while the success or the line which he will have to take in order to earn his livelihood would depend on different planets. The astrologer should make it clear that the student may have proficiency in one line of learning but he may have to take up another for his profession. This kind of prediction would depend upon the differences between the fourth, fifth and the tenth houses.

Professional counselling, though very closely connected with educational career, is very difficult to prognosticate. In advising about one's profession, it is necessary to distinguish three aspects of the problem, namely, the line of activity, the level attained and the amount of money earned.

An individual may earn much money but he may have neither social prestige nor a very high level of achievement in his trade. For example, there may be a smuggler or a pick-pocket who may be getting much money, yet in his own trade he may be quite ordinary. On the other hand, there may be a lecturer, which is deemed quite a respectable occupation, and he may be a very ordinary lecturer but by giving private tuitions he may earn quite a large amount of money. Often, a confusion regarding these three aspects of one's life creates frustration. In classical texts, it is considered quite elementary to predict the line of profession. The disposition of the tenth house is mainly the basic house in this regard. The nature of the planets involved, the signs of the zodiac and the usual rules of astrology apply, but this house is much more significant and enigmatic than it appears on the surface. It is important to examine this house very carefully.

The interpretation of the tenth house in an astrological chart is one of the most difficult tasks and it requires all the skill of the astrologer. To interpret only professional matters from this house is to take a limited view of it. Kalidasa in *Uttara Kalamrita,* while describing the various significances of the tenth house, gives two very meaningful phrases. Inter alia, it says that *aswa gamanam,* i.e. riding on a horse, as well as *nidhi nikshepa,* i.e. spending of the treasure, should be divined by the tenth house. These two terms in their deeper import suggest some of the implications of this house. In view of the fact that the tenth house is considered the *karmasthana* or the house of activities, the whole of one's life is connected with this house. During the life period, the individual gets involved in this world in various ways and that is how the vast reservoir of the vital energy is spent. It is the indicator of the ways of human involvement in this world. In this process of involvement the individual gets power, prestige, money, honour or humiliation. All these are important, but merely as a consequence of the individual's involvement in this world of activities.

When we try to consider the profession of an individual, it is important to consider this as the main house for examination. But the tenth house has a much wider significance than merely the service career. The astrological treatises mention that the first attention of the astrologer should be directed to the tenth house and in case of no planet being vitally connected with this house, the individual may not be worth much attention. A large number of human egos have yet to get differentiated and specialised before forging towards their ultimate goal. Unless any planet is significantly connected with this house, the person under examination, no matter how other aspects of his life are indicated, will have an ordinary ego undifferentiated, one in the multitude. The light in him will still burn very dimly. His profession will be non-descript. But when the planets begin to show special relationships with the tenth house, the astrologer has to be careful.

The individual has begun to move towards his destined assignment in a much more purposeful manner. On this path, such differentiated individuals do not necessarily have only one line of activity. For example, the world-famous Ramanujan was already delving in the deeper and abstruse mysteries of mathematics, while working as an ordinary low-paid office clerk. Einstein was one of the greatest scientists of the modern age, but as a violinist also he was not insignificantly skilled. Winston Churchill was a great strategist as well as a politician, but even his skill as a painter was not ordinary. B.V. Raman, who is a celebrated astrologer in India, has his proficiency as a Vedantic scholar and an astute publisher not of the ordinary kind. This should clearly imply that the tenth house which is intimately connected with the manner of one's involvement in the world of matter need not be considered exclusively to indicate the profession by which one earns one's livelihood.

The tenth house indicates the quality and the channels through which the creative faculties of the individual flow. Recognition of this fact makes the astrologer careful in indicating the line of profession that the individual is likely to adopt. This recognition is helpful in professional counselling. This house clearly shows the level of stature the individual would attain in this world, which need not necessarily be connected with his professional or money-earning career. Honour from the sovereign, name, prosperity, honourable living, prominence and repute are all the things which must be assessed from this house. There are many persons who have great repute, scholarship, and money, but those who know them closely do not rate them very high. Moral merits may be lacking in them. These qualities should be assessed with the help of planets in the ninth house. The influence of Jupiter on this house, no matter what the other characteristics are, would make the individual a religionist and a moralist. On the other hand, those who have Saturn's influence on this house, will find their involvement in the world full of negative influences. They may not be always welcome everywhere. People will be a little reluctant to be friendly with them. Under Ketu's influence, the world of activity would be more in the realm of thoughts and ideas, than in the world of matter and action. Often persons with this characteristic suffer from excruciating pain and experience humiliation. With the association of Sun, there must be some association with royalty, administration and flashes of spark in life. Often such individual will feel that they deserve much more than what has been given; he is likely to have much more latent faculties than he has been able to express. With Rahu, one is bound to be mean and lowly. Such pointers relate to the personality and have no relationship with his precise means of money-earning job or profession.

About general affluence, it is important to consider the various houses with caution. The accrual of money is judged on the basis of astrological principles, but there are some combinations which have great relevance in this context. The relationship between the *trikona* (fifth, ninth or first house) and the *kendras* (first, fourth, seventh or the tenth house) is of great merit. This is because the trines bring karmic forces from the deep past while the *kendras* relate to the present activities. A relationship between the two is very auspicious. If the tenth house is connected in this way, the individual will have his involvement with the world of matter in a powerful manner. The vast forces of the past would be at his back as a result of which he may make much headway in this world. He would be affluent. Thus, when the astrologer is confronted with questions relating to profession, prestige, honour and affluence, he should carefully direct his attention to the tenth house and assess the general strength of the horoscope and the directing factors which give the status of the individual in this world.

The temporary setbacks are like clouds indicated by the transits of the different planets, and the planetary rulership of the period would indicate the sequence of the unfoldment, whereas the strength of the house would indicate the heights which the individual would attain. The astrologer should, in such a case, be like a moral preceptor or at least a guide to indicate the course of the voyage meant for the individual in this world, for which he should unhesitatingly prepare himself, no matter whatever be the temporary setbacks and sufferings.

An important aspect of astrological responsibilities is related with the question of matrimonial relationships. It is an area in which Vedic astrology has much to contribute. The great disharmony in family life all over the world and difficulties between married partners rampant at large, can be effectively tackled by Vedic astrology. A harmonious relationship between the two individuals which is very difficult to attain, depends upon many diverse factors. Among the differing individuals when marital relationship is established, it cannot (and should not) be taken very casually. When a relationship is like that of a husband and a wife, it is a *karmic* relationship associated with many difficult problems. It is not merely a question of sexual adjustment. Therefore, the growing disharmony among the married partners with its consequential repercussions on family life and the psychology of the growing children is immense. If the astrologers are alert and watchful, there is a possibility that the Indian astrology could be a great help to the world peace and harmony.

Vedic astrology has worked out various rules on the basis of which the compatibility between two persons specially for the purpose of marriage can be worked out. The "modern" society which considers these rules as superstitious and lays greater emphasis on "love" marriages, has been reaping the consequences of the same. It is important that these rules are well understood and every astrologer engaged in marriage counselling should carefully understand the various considerations on the basis of which the marriage compatibility is determined. Prior to the marriage, the prospective partners should be warned against sexual infatuation. The inevitable would, however, happen and there would be various other problems which the astrologer will have to tackle. Thus, there would be marriage delays and disharmony. In these matters astrological texts have given some methods of overcoming delays; these advices should be treated like those from the medical profession. In many cases, the affliction of Mars, Saturn and Rahu will be quite severe. The inevitable consequences of these planets should be explained to the partners. There are certain psychological preparations which may help in enduring and meeting the misfortune when it occurs. As far as Mars is concerned, inspite of everything, the adverse consequences of sudden and rash action will have to be borne. The only precaution is that the partners will have to be careful all the time for any tendency towards such reactions. Saturn creates the problem of lack of warmth, psychological disharmony leading to sexual coolness. There is no mingling of life-currents between the married partners. A careful understanding by the partners of their psychological constitution and enlightened approach and understanding of their problems would go a long way in their mutual adjustment. When Rahu afflicts, they should be careful of certain complications which would be very difficult to decipher. The problems arising due to these three planets, viz., Rahu, Saturn and Mars must be understood and discussed with the partners rather than suggesting certain remedial measures – the gems and mantras and the like, will have very limited effects on these planets.

The scope of astrology in the future will be immense. The growing interest in the subject is a great opportunity. There is' a need for opening the frontiers of astrology and trying to synthesise it with philosophy, psychology, politics, meteorological forecasts and economic fluctuations. This would be the theoretical approach to the subject, but presently, there is need for establishing astrological predictions, not merely to satisfy the idle curiosity of individuals, but to aim at counselling, so that different individuals who wish to take advantage of astrology may be properly guided and real professional and enlightened guidance provided. But for this responsibility, the astrologers must reorient and open themselves to the great wind of intellectualism blowing all over the world.

3

ASTROLOGICAL IMPULSES

Every event is an important part of the general pattern of existence. We cannot deny its interrelationship with others. But life, whether for the individual human being or for the society as a whole, is immensely vast and full of mysterious depths and innumerable ramifications. Astrological science, specially Vedic astrology which is considered a limb of the Veda, *Vedanga*, is capable of providing an opportunity for delving deep into the immensity of each event and therefrom obtain a glimpse of the divine plan being unfolded for the individual. For example, an individual in his sixties, after completing his official career and most of his family responsibilities like getting his children well settled in life, suddenly meets with an accident from which he is miraculously saved without even a scratch on his body, except the great psychological trauma. He comes home to find that his wife has been greatly upset, because the Ganapati idol which they had placed at the entrance and to which they were greatly attached, was stolen. Such individual events even when accurately forecasted by astrological charts, do not reveal the whole story. There is much more in these single events than ordinarily predicted.

Generally, the consultee's reaction to these predictions, if they are 'inauspicious' is to find out ways and means to avoid, eliminate, or reduce the impact of such occurrences and know their propitiatory and other remedial measures. But, the responsibility of the Vedic astrologer is much greater than merely indicating the possibility or otherwise of the occurrence of any specific event, auspicious or inauspicious. It is in such circumstances, that the uniqueness of Vedic astrology comes out predominantly. It reveals the spiritual significance of every situation through which the individual passes in his life's journey. In understanding the deeper significance of every event, one understands the Divine Plan for himself much more clearly and thereby cooperates with Nature (in this case Nature represents the Divine Mother, Aditi, who very carefully and affectionately takes care of each of her child).

The most important event in one's life is his or her birth. One recognises that there are many methods of prediction, such as numerology, crystal gazing, clairvoyance, western system of prediction, Mayan method of prediction and so on, but Vedic astrology is entirely different from all these. Every practitioner of this system is reminded that accurate prediction of the future is possible only for Brahma, the astrologer merely ventures to intuit the future. One finds that in other systems, infallibility of astrological predictions is almost postulated, whereas in Vedic astrology every prediction is considered only probable and the degree of probability depends upon the spiritual attainments of the astrologer. It does not depend only on the acquisition of various astrological tools on the basis of which he attempts to peep into the Divine Plan. It also relies on his own yogic perfection. The birth epoch is merely a peep-hole through which one tries to see the immensity of the individual, his possibilities and the journey through which his ultimate goal is attained. Unless this comprehensive view is received, each individual event will only be uncoordinated, sporadic and meaningless incident without much significance to the individual in his long journey. Only when an integrated view is taken that the significance of every single event is understood and necessary lessons learnt from it.

The classical texts have given various hints, suggestions and principles for predicting the future. An important aspect of this exercise is to find out where does the individual stand in his evolutionary journey. Is he still on the lower rungs of the ladder, or has he individualised sufficiently to proceed further in his specially earmarked direction? But very few consultees are interested in such enquiries. One finds that persons come to enquire whether their marital life would be happy, or when would they be 'blessed' with a child. Sometimes even political aspirants consult astrologers to know the possibility of their being a minister or some such important being. No one ever enquires whether these successes or failures would enable one to attain one's destined goal. It is primarily because of this reason that the real values of Vedic astrology have so far not been appreciated. Each event, whether it is marital happiness or unhappiness, success or failure in profession, becoming a minister or a prime minister, is related with the main goal of the ego, the soul. Such an enquiry will really make an individual's life purposeful, and he would be able to react to various events of his life much more confidently. So the important point for a deeper study of a horoscope is to discover the purpose of one's life.

The tenth house in a natal chart is very mysterious and it has many layers of impulses affecting the individual. One therefore has to study it very closely. This house shows the goal of one's present incarnation. All successes and frustrations in life have to be studied in relation to this house. The basic strength for achieving this goal depends upon the power of the Ascendant, but the importance of the fourth and seventh houses cannot be overlooked. It is only on the strength of one's emotional nature, one's relationship with one's near and dear ones, one's likes and dislikes, one's intelligence and the power to understand, and such other qualities that the possibility of attaining one's goal can be assessed. But one's basic nature (ascendant) and marital relationship and all that is deciphered from the seventh house will produce the limiting conditions beyond which the individual will not be able to proceed.

An important point to note is the cause for these limitations or helpful conditions. Here comes the necessity of understanding the hidden laws of existence which cannot be indicated from the chart, but once the astrologer has understood the scheme of life's evolutionary course and the working of the Law of Karma, the chart may enable him to corroborate or refute his conclusions. The disposition of planets and their impact on the permanent nature of the individual, his nature, his family conditions, professional situations and other relationships should be related with the individual's main goal, tenth house. From these discoveries, the individual would know the pshychological orientation necessary to enable him to permanently and effectively remove the basic limitations in his long-run journey of the soul.

Such an approach to horoscopy takes us to many interesting aspects of one's inner exploration. An interesting digression of astrological studies is to understand the basic structure of one's multi-dimensional personality. Now that the importance of single events has been dropped out for the moment and we are enquiring about the real stature of the person, we have to understand and apply the astrological principles differently. Probably the consultee is not interested in this kind of knowledge, and many times even 'big' personalities feel disappointed and even disillusioned with the new discoveries about his own-self. Simply because one has been positioned at a very high position in the official hierarchy, or has acquired much eminence and fame, or even if he is considered a very 'religious' person, he does not necessarily possess an evolved soul. The development and maturity of a soul depends upon several special factors. In a horoscope if the astrologer finds that there are individual events in the chart, such as big money, high status, much education and learning, etc., but these are not well related with one another, then one may infer that the individual is still one of the common beings and the process of individualisation has not so far begun for him. In the evolutionary process, every spark at first moves indiscriminately, without any special direction. They are like water-bubbles of the ocean. They do not move in any special direction, their uniqueness is still latent. Only when the streams begin to seek a direction, ultimately all of them will have to flow in seven channels, then the process of differentiation begins, and the individuals begin to take a definite course. This is reflected in the emergence of patterns in horoscopes. The patterns in a chart are different from planetary combinations about which we often read in astrological texts. There are many kinds of patterns emerging in a chart which may be interesting to study for understanding the differentiation that begins in the individual's life.

For example, take the case of a baby born on 18 August 1993. He was born with Libra as the Ascendant. Rahu is in Scorpio, Saturn in Aquarius, Ketu in Taurus, Venus in Gemini, Mercury in Cancer, Sun and Moon in Leo and Jupiter and Mars in Virgo. This chart is a very good example of pattern formation. The Sun and Moon together, Sun and Saturn in opposition, Sun flanked by auspicious and important planets, Venus placed second from its own sign Taurus, Mercury second from its sign Gemini, Moon second

		Ketu	Venus
Saturn	CHART I 18 August 1993		Mercury
			Sun Moon
	Rahu	Ascdt	Jup Mars

from its own sign Cancer, Jupiter seventh from its own sign Pisces and so on. There may or may not be any special planetary combinations in such horoscopes, but the point to note is that every planet in this horoscope has taken a special position and is mutually related to another in a special manner. It shows that the birth of the individual occurred when every planet was very much concerned to bestow its special influence to the child. From such indications, one would draw the inference that the child is not a common one. He is on the path of differentiation. Beginning with such a process when the individual begins to work out his special mission, the life and its individual events would make a different significance.

The next enquiry relates to the discovery of one's special qualities for attaining one's destined goal. It involves the study of the special nature of the stream in which he is moving, and secondly, whether he is fully equipped to receive the free flow of various planetary radiations so that he moves confidently and effectively towards his goal. This problem relates to the seven channels of human development very little discussed in exoteric astrological texts. The question of the free flow of Divine Energy which could lead the individual to his ultimate goal is discussed under the title "Foundations of an Integrated Personality*" and it was also mentioned in *Brihad Parashara Hora Shastra*.

The question of fulfilling one's goal requires that there is no impediment in the free flow of the Divine Energy, while the individual is involved in his everyday life. It implies that all the

---

*See *Chapter 8.*

Energy Centres, the *Chakras* as these are mentioned in the yogic literature, function in their natural manner. It will enable the Divine Energy entering the body of the individual through his *Muladhara Chakra* to move unimpeded towards his *Crown Chakra* and all the intervening *chakras* will help the Divine Energy in proper manner till it reaches the *Crown Chakra*. When this happens, the Moon will be able to reflect without any distortion the specific message (Ray, Spark) coming from the Sun (*Crown Chakra*) and transmit the same to *Vishudhi Chakra* (Mercury) so that the intelligence in the individual is able to grasp the Divine intonations and make his sociability (Venus) harmonious with the world around him (Mars, Jupiter and Saturn). It is in this context, that the relationship between the planets and the *chakras* becomes important. It is important for the astrologers to carefully analyse the relationship as it pertains to the individual chart. The exaltation, ownership and friendly signs are important indications of this relationship. How far a *chakra* is functioning effectively depends upon the nature of various planets connected with the same. Knowing it, the consultee has to involve himself in producing counteracting impulses, so that the impeding factors are removed. The specific events that happen in one's everyday life are the natural and slow-producing processes for producing this change, which is required for the free flow of the Divine Energy.

Karma plays an important role in one's life. Each individual tries, consciously or unconsciously, to remove the various impediments and psychological blocks, which is not always a very pleasant task. Once a person is able to understand the compulsions of karma as they operate on his life, it is possible to face them without wasting much of one's energy. It is very difficult to understand these forces which are not very pleasant and many of the consultees are not willing or capable of facing them. But from the natal chart, it is possible to get a view of the past karmic impulsions constantly impinging upon one's life. From various such impulses, in each specific life some of these forces are taken out and allotted to the individual for setting the account. In this regard, the importance of Rahu and Ketu is considerable. Each incarnation revolves around certain problems represented by the two houses tenanted by the Nodes. All major events of the individual's life will somehow or the other, be connected with these two houses. The two houses thus involved, are also positive and negative to each other – the forces generated in one will have to be worked out through the other. The nature of forces generated in the chart will also be related with the nature and planetary disposition of these shadow planets. This axis relates the individual events of one's life with the main goal for which the individual is given the present birth. All major twists and turns of one's life must be related to the disposition of Rahu and Ketu in one's horoscope. They are the great karmic agents whose power is beyond the individual to overcome.

One karmic factor which is often overlooked, though the ancient seers had emphasised it, is the relationship between the individual and his family members. In traditional Hindu families, there was a belief that each individual was under the guardianship of the *Kula Devata*, the family deity who was watching and leading the family members towards the fulfillment of their destiny. The modern intellectuals treat the belief as a pure fabrication of one's imagination. If one examines the family horoscopes in a bunch, all together, one may find a unique planetary relationship between the various horoscopes.

Every family has a specific aura through which the Divine Energy radiates to different members of the family. The nature of radiation indicates the specific line on which each individual in that family will progress. It does not imply uniformity or identity of life patterns. In this connection, one finds that certain planets, or certain houses, certain signs, or sometimes certain planetary combinations (in the classical sense) persist in many members of a family. These characteristics will have to be related to the various religious doctrines (of the occult nature) given for understanding the life process. On the basis of such a study, one will be able to understand the inherent impulsions of the individual and the repercussions of working out his karma on the other members of the family. There has to be a common bond between all of them, at the same time, there will inevitably be differences between them. An artist in a businessman's family, a not-so good looking girl in a chief justice's family so as to prevent her marriage and bring some sadness to the family, a pious family with a studious girl not finding a suitable match for her, and similar incongruities make the study of family relationship very interesting. It is on the basis of these differences among the family members that one can find out the working of the laws of evolution.

This kind of approach will necessarily be very time consuming. It will also require much close cooperation between the astrologer and the consultee. A professional astrologer may not be able to devote so much time for a single consultation of an individual, unless he is suitably compensated. But even then, this study will involve several sittings before a well meaning and some useful direction about any one's life is worked out. Psycho-analysts do the same, and there is no reason why the astrologers cannot adopt this practice. It will also open out a new aspect of astrological consultation. So far, generally speaking, individuals consult an astrologer during periods of difficulties, their deprivations, their sorrows, non-fulfillment of their desired goal and so on. Very few persons want to understand the karmic forces impinging upon them and the specific goal to which all the individual events are guiding them. By relating the individual events with the general pattern of one's life, it is possible to realise new areas of usefulness of astrological prognostications.

PART—II

Nature of Man

4

BASIC MOTIVATION
OF THE INDIVIDUAL

An important contribution of astrological approach to human problems is to lay bare the hidden forces operating on them. Many a time, the real intentions of a person are camouflaged by external pretensions. An ordinary individual is unable to penetrate them and is therefore duped. Sometimes the person himself is unable to understand his own basic motivations. It makes him run away for the mask, though it lies latent in his own navel. Such difficulties can be removed very easily by a careful understanding of astrological impulsions. We should approach astrology not for mere physical level prognostications but for understanding our real selves. The physical level predictions may be necessary only to point to the central direction in one's true mission.

The subject of self-discovery is a very elaborate one. It consists of detailed examination of several aspects of the problem. Any conclusion in this respect by the astrologer will necessarily be tentative in nature. The individual concerned will himself have to arrive at any final conclusion.

In this context, it is necessary at the outset to clearly understand the nature of one's basic motivation. Ordinarily, it means understanding the psychological make-up of the person. But the concept of basic motivation has a much wider and deeper connotation. We can only try to approach the problem indirectly. It may enable us to see the inner nature or the core of one's basic being. In many popular folklores, it is said that the hero of the tale had to vanquish his adversary but no one knew where the latter kept his 'heart' which contained his 'life'. Sometime it used to be kept in a pigeon on a distant unknown tree, sometimes in a fish under the bed of a river, or sometimes within the heart of a pet kept unknowingly in the custody of the king's military chief. Unless the 'heart' thus kept was retrieved and destroyed, the individual adversary could continue to thrive no matter howsoever powerful be the weapon of the invader. The heart in these folklores represents the primary essence of the individual. Astrologically, it is different from the tenth house which represents the 'Karma' of the individual on the basis of which the individual's avocation is predicted. But this house is not a sure indicator of one's basic motivation. It is evident from the fact that the individual does not feel contented whatever may be his achievement, unless he achieves the fulfillment of his basic urge. This basic goal is different from desire, status, position etc. It is something that the psychologists call by their term 'libido', yet it is not exactly that. It is something very vague, at the early stages of one's egoic growth. It is indistinct inner impulsion which is undefined, but the individual feels its presence at the core of his being all the time. Even then he may be unable to identify it. Only later on, when he has proceeded further and is capable of having an insight in his inner self, that his basic motivation begins to take shape before his inner-eyes. Till that position is reached, the enquiry into one's basic motivation will necessarily remain vague and unarticulated. One will have to proceed in his exploration, at the initial stages with this vague realisation of the basic motivation of his life and the direction towards which, his soul is constantly guiding him.

In such explorations, one has also to distinguish between one's psychological nature as popularly understood and the basic motivation. For example, the basic nature of Rama and Ravana, in both the cases, was religious. Rama was deeply devoted to Lord Shiva and he dedicated all his endeavours and actions to him, but Ravana was also able to achieve the highest benediction of Lord Shiva. His penance as well as understanding of the methods of pleasing the supreme god were of the highest order. Both of them could be considered as religious persons, but Rama was concerned with being a beneficent force in the world, whereas Ravana wanted everything for himself. The difference between the two can be summarised between two phrases – for Rama, it was 'In His Name', while for Ravana, it was 'For My Satisfaction'. The basic motivation of Rama was to help the world, or establish spiritual order, while for Ravana it was acquisition for one's own sake.

In ordinary life, we often come across persons who have (apparently) happy family life, children are well placed and helpful, wife is very faithful and caring. He himself is well honoured in the society and enjoys a good professional position, yet is not happy. There is something missing in his life. This missing factor is sometimes related to the affliction of Moon, but it may not thus be explained in all the cases. The basic cause arises from the fact that the individual attached greatest value to something else in his life. If it is so, he may not have external trappings of life, yet he could be extremely well-at-ease in his life; he may not have any grumblings about it. This kind of difference lies at the root of the basic motivation, the basic core of one's being. Even when it is indicated to him, he may not always be willing to accept it. Once the discovery becomes real, and the individual begins to see the truth of the discovery, the purpose and direction of his life may not change, but he would begin to observe a pattern in his reactions to external stimuli. It will be a permanent gain for his evolutionary efforts. This basic element is not necessarily what should be pursued and nurtured, but it must be known and influenced in order to attain one's mission in life.

The first step in the discovery is to observe the ascendant lord and its placement. The nature of the ascendant lord is not so important as its placement. In case the ascendant lord is in the ascendant itself, the person will be very self-centered. He will consider that the happiness in his life can come only when he attains something unique, something not attained by anyone else. The nature of the object obtained will depend upon the nature of the planet concerned, the planets aspecting it and the general disposition of the horoscope. But these are secondary considerations. The very placement of the ascendant lord in ascendant makes all other conditions of life move around his personal self; he will not feel satisfied unless he feels that he has acquired – something pristine, something new and not already possessed by someone else. It must be something for which he has persevered, struggled and won. The thing received is not that important as its being received by him for his being uniquely qualified to receive it. Such a tendency is sometimes expressed as 'crankiness,' often as egotism, but basically, the individual projects his role in the world and the response of the world to him from his personal (often prejudiced) point of view. These external symptoms indicate the basic unsatisfied urge, the foundation of his life, and in being uniquely qualified to receive the special gifts – respect, acceptance of opinion, anything which was not tarnished by others. Examples of such an element can be seen from the horoscopes of the Mughal emperor Akbar, Karl Marx, Mahatma Gandhi and Jawaharlal Nehru. The nature of the ascendant, aspects on it and the general delineation of the horoscope may introduce interpersonal differences in their external approaches, but none of these were willing to consider themselves second to anyone else (inspite of their sometimes affirming otherwise). Each of them thought, consciously or unconsciously, as gifted persons qualified to receive special gifts of gods which when denied, brought immense sorrow and frustration. If they had realised this unconscious element in their life, (probably) their reaction to external stimuli would have been different.

When the ascendant lord is in the second house, the life of the person is radically different from the previous one. The second is a house which links the individual with the Sea of Immutability, with some karmic relationship. Such a placement could make a person parochial, missionary, or deeply universal. These external symptoms express the basic urge of identifying onself with a group of persons, irrespective of the size and nature of the group. In the case of Ramana Maharshi, his heart was with the humanity-at-large; his happiness, success or failure, rested not with his personal achievements, but with the retrieval of something useful for the humanity in general. In the case of Margaret Thatcher, it is her country while in an ordinary person, such a placement could make him more concerned about the welfare of his family members, his caste, or the group of people to which he belongs. Such individuals do not delight in their personal glorification; they measure their success or otherwise according to what they have achieved for others. Even the content of the achievement is immaterial in the present case; that would depend upon the nature of the ascendant lord and other considerations but here one should emphasise the basic or the primary concern of the individual with some group of people with whom he is linked karmically.

The placement of ascendant lord in the third house is different from the previous ones. In this case, the individual is concerned with himself but not in the manner as in the first house. Here, the primary interest of the individual which could provide him enduring satisfaction would be provision of something tangible for his brothers, kith and kin, or in the display of his valour and courage. The third house is an important base of the Material Triangle in the chart. When the ascendant lord is in the third house, the individual may deceive himself with all kinds of justifications, but basically he will be concerned with providing something material to his own kith and kin in which act there should be some display of his own valour. Nothing else would satisfy the inner promptings of the individual. An example of this placement in its sublime form is evident in the case of Lord Krishna whose basic element was to secure physical wealth (Kingdom) for his people by vanquishing Kansa for which he gave up (or jilted) his beloveds. He secured the kingdom for the Pandavas who were his near relatives, for which he participated in the most bloody war that was ever fought. In all these he got something material, something for his people, and something which he did with his own prowess. Alexander was also in search of similar pursuits. Another example has been of an international president of a religious society professing universal brotherhood. His lord of the ascendant was placed in the third house. But it was neither Venus as in the case of Lord Krishna, nor Mars as in the case of Alexander, but it was Moon with Mars. Unknowingly and without being aware of it, he appointed his own relations at important positions, provided them with material support though it brought decay of the organisation and much dishonour to himself. Oblivious of the obvious, he was impelled by his inner compulsions which gave him greater satisfaction than the philosophical ideal of universal brotherhood which he preached.

The fourth house is still more difficult to decipher, but the basic principle holds good even in this case. The confusion arises primarily due to the mysterious nature of the fourth house. It has much in common with the second house, but in the present context certain other elements have affected the result. The connection of this house with one's emotion is very strong. Whatever the emotional upsurge, whether it is self-sacrifice for the salvation of the humanity and acceptance of the blame of the entire world, and thereby undergoing all the punishments for the same, or it is the conquest of the world including brutal murder of those who defied the person, the individual is not concerned with what happens in the process. As long as he is working for the satisfaction of his 'heart', he will feel satisfied. Such persons are missionaries not necessarily in the sense of doing good to others; they may even inflict immense pain to others which is inconsequential to them. Whatever they consider right, not necessarily intellectually but emotionally, they will be happy to accomplish that. Gautam Buddha, Jesus Christ, Chengiz Khan as well as Guru Nanak are some examples of this kind. Such varied personalities have one thing in common; all of them were moved by what they emotionally felt right irrespective of the troubles and difficulties it caused to others or to themselves.

In the case of ascendant lord being placed in the fifth house, the individual feels utmost happy in seeing the fruits of his own creativity. Such activities may involve personal sacrifice, it may even imply that they have to forego much of their personal comforts. But as long as what they have produced or are producing are being appreciated, they will feel greatly delighted, thus minimising their sorrows in other aspects of life. Fifth is an important base of the Spiritual Triangle in a horoscope. When the ascendant lord is placed there, the individual finds happiness in creative efforts. Those artists who are oblivious of their personal inconveniences but are greatly attached to their artistic creations, belong to this category. An example of this category is Rabindranath Tagore. His ascendant lord Jupiter was placed in the fifth house which made him attuned to his artistic attachments more than any material reward or physical comforts.

The sixth house is again one of those houses where the enormous powers of Nature are stored. When the ascendant lord is placed in the sixth house, the individual takes delight in activities which are connected with hidden sides of Nature. Unless the individual is spiritually developed, he will find happiness in destroying the happiness of others which may cause much difficulties even to himself. Such individuals do not wish to follow the straight line of evolution or social activities. They must challenge, they must provoke Nature, society and other individuals so that something unusual comes out of them. If they are spiritually evolved, they will venture into religious occultism and try to challenge their own personality and will feel happy when they are able to externalise their own hidden powers. An example of this type is that of Sri Aurobindo whose happiness was in unfolding his own latent faculties. Such traits occur even in ordinary persons who have this combination.

When the ascendant lord is placed in the seventh house, the individual is never satisfied with ordinary existence. The seventh house represents the field which the individual-labour tills, or, it is the arena where the individual-actor plays his role. Simultaneous occurrence of detachment and attachment found in the psyche of an individual in this category makes it extremely difficult for him to feel happy. He always pines for that which is not available to him. He is like the Tantalus; he is capable, he has many conveniences of life and has much success to his credit. But nothing satisfies him. He pines for that which is not there, which is slightly away from him; he wants the whole world for him to enjoy and to conquer. He rises from a mean position to a great height, but whatever the height, he feels that the unscaled height should also belong to him. Such a person may be so lustful that his sexual appetite will induce him to change his partners as frequently as it is possible. In his official career, he will always remonstrate and grumble that his promotions have been less than what he deserved; in his military conquests, he will always feel that there are more countries to conquer. His happiness rests in the region beyond the known horizon, in the area beyond one's reach, in securing that which one lacks. As these are not well-articulated identified regions of acquisitions, such individuals are bound to feel inwardly unhappy howsoever great be their achievements. Such examples are of Shivaji with his ascendant lord Sun in the seventh house with Aquarius, while Hilter had Venus as his ascendant lord placed in seventh house Aries. They had been powerful persons, but always wanted to possess that which was beyond their reach.

The eighth is a mysterious house in the same sense as second, fourth or the sixth. It has however a few additional attributes. It is a concealed house; it provides impetus for delving deep in mysterious laws of Nature; it also throws open its rewards for the individual. The sixth may be barren to some extent, but the eighth leads the individual to the bosom of Nature's secret. When the ascendant lord occupies the eighth house, the individual takes delight in the unknown, mysterious, secret, hidden and the occult side of life. That which is known is not satisfying to him. Such a person is not so much satisfied with his higher levels of income and right flow of money as much as with black money, bribes and secret deals. Such activities that are open and generally known to everybody do not give happiness to the person. This does not imply that the individual is necessarily engaged in surreptitious operations. That which is hidden is not necessarily dishonourable. For example, Jagdish Chandra Bose never wanted to share his life and work with any one else. The man was extremely religious, highly sensitive, but he always lived in a world which was unknown to others. His discoveries about life in plants and metals are merely an outer expression of the fondness of his inner self with that which is hidden, concealed, esoteric and still lying in the bosom of Nature.

The ninth house is important for the unfoldment of spiritual nature of the person. In actual life, this aspect is represented in many different ways. It is known as *Poorva Punya;* it represents the spiritual quests indicated by religious studies, philanthropic activities and renunciation of material affluence. When the lord of the first house occupies the ninth house, the individual's inner core forms an intimate link with his past proclivities and the future goal. In pursuance of this relationship, the whole life of the individual becomes unworldly. His heart, consciously or unconsciously, is fixed to the world which is not appreciated by the materialistic people. But the individual is not interested in such persons or in the approbation of the world. He wants to transform his life according to his inner dictates irrespective of the price he may have to pay for it. Ramakrishna Paramahamsa had his ascendant lord Saturn placed in the ninth house occupied by Libra; and the Duke of Windsor had his Saturn, the lord of his ascendant sign Capricorn in Virgo occupying the ninth house. One does not have to labour hard to show that all these persons valued their inner conviction and the sense of righteousness more than what the world considered 'worldly wisdom'.

In the tenth house, there is a unique synchronisation of the actual involvement of the person and his inner happiness. The tenth house represents the individual's involvement in the world of his existence. When the ascendant lord is placed in this house, the unconscious desire of the person is unified with what he does in actual life. This identification does not always appear as external happiness; the unconscious motivation of the person does not always lead to physical delight of sensual gratification. But it does not necessarily deny the same. It only suggests that the inner core of the individual does not feel that what he does is great, or that he should have been doing something else than what he is doing. Examples of this category of persons are Abraham Lincoln whose ascendant lord Saturn being the ruler of Aquarius is in Scorpio, H.G. Wells with Capricorn as his ascendant sign has his Saturn in Libra. Even if we study a general case, we find that an IAS Officer with Cancer ascendant, having his Moon in Aries in the tenth house takes to his office as duck takes to water; not because his performance was always exceptional, but because there was no conflict in his mind. He never thought that anything else would have been more satisfying to him.

The eleventh house once more presents an enigmatic situation. It represents the important base of the Material Triangle. Through the activities of this house, the individual is immersed in material conditions. This relationship is expressed by individual's attachment to worldly ways of socialisation, womanisation, drinks, monetary carvings, and comparison with others. Such persons attach great significance to themselves and they want that the world should move around them. They may have great achievements to their credit, but that is not the aspect of their life which satisfies them inwardly. What is satisfying is their recognition, and achievement. There is always some material core about their activities which only could provide some satisfaction to them; otherwise the activities and their results were very inconsequential to them. Even Swami Vivekananda's greatest satisfaction was not so much in philosophical discourses or in spiritual (personal) attainments as in the establishment of an organisation, which even today is necessarily a material base in the national regeneration programmes, which also has a tinge of politicisation of religion. Even in the case of Einstein, his achievements of scientific laws of relativity and the rest of it did not give him as much happiness as it brought to him the sorrow, because of its material application in the manufacture of the atom bomb. He was more concerned with his own personal reputation and social relationships.

The twelfth house is the life beyond the portals of death. All those persons who have their ascendant lord in the twelfth house are very unworldly in their inner life. Their unconscious attachment with life after death, the theory of karma, altruism, and the rest of it, is much deep as a result of which they often fail in their worldly life. But what matters to them is their 'ultimate destiny.' Only that is of some enduring value and could provide some inner satisfaction to them. Everything else is superficial. Shankaracharya is a glaring example of this condition. He did many things in life. But even sanyasa was not of that importance to him as his own concept of his ideal, his mission, his goal. All his ideals were based on those laws which operate in the realm extending beyond the portals of death, the life which is everlasting. That is the real enduring interest of those who have their ascendant lord in the twelfth house.

Here, we have tried to elaborate only one of the superficial principles leading to the discovery of one's hidden motives and proclivities which in actual life will have to be interpreted very carefully. However in the task of self-discovery, this is an important step which if objectively followed could reveal certain inner aspects of one's unconscious motivations. In one's astrological self-discovery programme which could analyse one's life in its wider perspective, there are many revealing hints available which might completely revolutionise the life of an individual. This is the first step in the pursuit of self-awareness.

5

EXTROVERSION AND INTROVERSION OF PERSONALITY

Modern psychology often categorises a person either as an extrovert or an introvert. It assigns several characteristics to these terms. Generally, the term extrovert means a person who is not given to introspection whereas introvert means mind or thought of the person turned inward upon oneself. In common parlance, these are not considered very respectable traits in an individual. Presumption is that the individual with such features is abnormal. Such characteristics of a person, however, should not be considered derogatory.

They merely refer to the attitude of the person and to the operation of his thought process. The mind of a person may be centripetal implying that it is turned towards the centre from which everything that one perceived has been reeled off. As the individual is always the centre for himself, such a mind always brings to it all the various perceptions and experiences. Selfishness has nothing to do with introversion or with relating every experience with one's own self. Selfishness is wanting everything for oneself whereas introspection is a way of observation. Such a person generally thinks as how everything affects him. Similarly, an extrovert person is not necessarily generous. He is not necessarily charitable. He is merely looking without concerning himself with the thought or the relationship of the external thing or the event with his own self, such a mind has centrifugal tendency. An awareness of the working of his mind helps him in his social relationship and in sorting out the various repercussions of the conditions of life on his individuality.

There are some persons who are quite contented with every given situation. Such individuals are generally very good family persons, enjoying their blissful existence with their family members. Such individuals are not unduly concerned with others or with themselves. They do not attach so much importance to the thinking principle in life as much to the feeling component of it. Astrologically, one could classify humans in three categories namely, extroverts, introverts and well-balanced. Even these three categories of persons will have marked differences in their character traits.

The four zodiacs which make an individual extrovert are Aries, Gemini, Leo and Sagittarius, while Virgo, Scorpio, Capricorn and Aquarius make an individual introvert. Those persons who are primarily family-men, well contented within their narrow acquaintances and friends, are mainly influenced by Taurus, Cancer, Libra and Pisces. Within these broad categories, one finds marked characteristics of other signs of the zodiac as well.

Aries is an extrovert in the sense that it cannot pause to examine its own shortcomings and failures. It will make the individual always active. The person may have many types of activities in which he would be interested. Further the thing or the person, the more interested in them will be the Aries born individuals. In all his reactions and relationships, there will be an undercurrent of helpfulness. He feels greatly delighted when he can make some sacrifice for someone. But his personal life will not be very orderly. He will easily fall under the influence of the opposite sex. His prime interest may not be sexual relationship but he will be accused of such intentions. There will be an attitude of nonchalance in him specially when the matter is connected with his individual life or his personal convenience.

Those who are affected by Gemini, will not be as forceful as the Aries born persons, but they will also be interested in the world around him. They will be extremely capable of understanding the personal foibles of others, on which they would generally act to control and influence them. Such individuals will be strong in their intellect which they will consider their valuable asset. Guided by their intelligence, they will move with different kinds of people and places. They will observe them objectively. They will however find altruism difficult for them to cultivate. Their understanding of the environment and the people with whom they move and mingle will be used for making the information useful to themselves. Thus, there could be some trace of selfishness in their extroversion.

Leo is a very enigmatic sign. Such persons who are under the influence of Leo are very powerful. They rise very high in their social setting by apt handling of their problems and relationships. They will always desire to work for the society, for others and for some ideals. But knowingly or unknowingly, the interest of these persons in social problems and ideals springs from a deep-rooted concern for their own self-improvement, self-power and personal status. These individuals are aware of the influence of the society on them and their role in the society, but they will always like to make others believe that they are interested in others for the welfare of the society. In many cases they often succeed. Those who can see through their attitude and inner compulsions, will incur their displeasure and may even be subjected to their wrath.

Sagittarius makes the individual extrovert of a markedly different kind. Impelled by the inner sense of righteousness and the fear of the other world, such a person will instinctly move towards acting for others. They are interested in action. Their prime concern is helpfulness and will not be much interested in enjoying pleasure for themselves. They will be engaged in such activities which in the long-run, according to their own understanding, will be good for others. A unique kind of fire burns in their life and arouses their enthusiasm for dedicating themselves for the spiritual upliftment of the society.

Among the introverts, Virgo born persons will be noticeably different from others in the group. Under this sign, the individuals are so much concerned about their personal responsibilities that they try to adapt themselves to the needs of others. In most of these persons there is strong selfishness because they are always comparing themselves with those who are luckier. They will burn with an idealism, they will endeavour to do good to others, but in all these relationship, they will evaluate the outcome of these actions from their own standpoint of the personal (little) self. They are extremely self-centred which greatly accentuates their sorrow and touchiness. They are good-intentioned sorrowful persons.

Scorpio-influenced introverts are in a way the very embodiment of vindictiveness, self-seeking persons concerned primarily with their own sensuous pleasures. They are helpful to others, only if they feel that these actions will bring to them much increased dividends. Their approach to others is to exploit their companionship as much as it is possible. They are not very susceptible to higher feelings and sentiments of life. They could, under the exaggerated influence of this sign, be vampire-like persons. They finally suffer and often become suicidal. Their heightened self-seeking urge when foiled, which in fact is bound to occur some time or the other, will completely throw them out of gears. Salvation of Scorpio persons lies in the the company of some family type permanent company who though suffering himself may be concerned with cooling the boiling passion of personal gratification of these persons. Scorpio represents the condition under which introversion becomes often pathological. If interested in undergoing psychoanalysis, these individuals may benefit much from it.

Capricorn also makes an individual introvert but the traits of this sign are different. In this case, the individual tries to mould his personal life to gain the virtues of spiritualism. They are not very happy in their own personal life, but they do not wish to take vengeance for it. They think that by involving themselves in the service of others, they could probably be happier. They endeavour to improve their own personal lifestyle and mould their own attitudes. But being extremely rigid about themselves, adaptability is not their forte. They could be successful self-seeking politicians.

When Aquarius sways the life of a person, it makes the individual self-centred. Under its impulse the individual feels that life should have treated him better. He compares himself with those who are in better placed situations. This comparison is important in his case. He does good to the society and engages himself in many laudable social activities. In all these, there is the basic desire that he should be recognised as important. Such a person need not be selfish, but he is certainly self-centred. He is quick to react to any slight to his personal vanity. He is not forgiving, though he may like to pay back any good deed done to him. Aquarius impulse generally makes a person ethical, and all his self-centredness is directed to attain these ethical ideals.

Some individuals are well balanced and take a normal view of life. These persons with moderate ambition, caring for family affection, peaceful home and respectable social status within their immediate surroundings are the persons who are influenced by Taurus, Cancer, Libra and Pisces. When Taurus is important, the individual is sensitive, pleasant, loving and very fond of his family and other social relations. He is a connoisseur of food, dress, music and pleasant family surrounding. Often such persons may come in contact with aggressive, self-seeking and very ambitious persons from whom they may like to shirk away though greatly attracted to them. Such persons will like to take active interest in social events, but these will generally be for socialising with others and entertainment for their family members and friends.

With Cancer as the predominant influence, the individual will always feel homesick. His mind will be active, he will be thinking, reading, and often discussing his ideas about social regeneration with others, but will not be interested in his own active involvement in them. Such individuals may like to enjoy the presidential position in a public function, he may like to be the final arbitrator, but in any situation where his personality seems cramped, he will try to refrain from it. Many persons of undesirable character will try to come in his contact, yet he will like to forgive them. In his hearts of the heart the memory of such misdemeanour will linger. Inspite of seemingly forgiving nature and charitable disposition, he may take revenge. Cancer will bestow a very pleasing external, pliable nature, reserved temperament, yet the person under its influence will be very parochial, more concerned with their own family members' welfare, than with that of the society, though they may like to give an impression otherwise.

Libra by its influence makes the individual very balanced. Under its impact, the individual may become ambitious and covet affluence of others but basically he will remain a family man. His main object in life will be to see his children well placed, a good and prestigious house constructed and an important social status for the family secured. Libra influence will make the individual down to earth. He will not be basically honest, but it does not imply that the individual will be indulging in shady deals. He may even meddle with religious observances and rituals, but all these will be directed towards securing a better social status for the family members and a more secured position for himself. The lives of individuals who are influenced by Pisces is unique in many ways. They are blessed with children and socially desirable husband/wife. Their social status is high. Their official position is very respectful. Often one may find that their life or business partners are a little uncomfortable with them. But as long as the life of the person is secure, he does not care much for others. Such individuals can happily accept any situation provided his status and respectability are not compromised. They may like to seek their fulfillment through their children. But inspite of such seemingly contented and social attitudes, these individuals will be markedly differentiated; they can drop any one out of their company and group without any remorse.

The psychological traits emerging from zodiacal considerations are very much affected by the influence of various planets. Sun and Mars and greatly self-centred planets; Jupiter and Venus make a person interested and attracted to others; Mercury only desires to show off its own 'greatness' or uniqueness. The most important influence is generated by Saturn, Rahu, Ketu and Jupiter. When Saturn aspects the ascendant, the individual is bound to be extremely self-conscious. Depending upon the nature and other characteristics of the planet, the aspect or association of Saturn with ascendant will make the person selfish, inward-turned and concerned with his own achievements and what he can get from others. Inspite of much beneficence from other planets, such an individual will always feel that he has been badly treated in life. Rahu will put so much heavy responsibilities under this situation, that the individual will have no chance for active voluntary involvements in social and public welfare activities. Whether these influences will make the person actively related with shady deals or not, will depend upon other factors, but the impact of Saturn and Rahu will make the individual attracted towards socially disapproved activities and behaviour. Such persons will not have much respect for the views of the society and others. What matters to them is their personal satisfaction for which they may even resort to any mean act.

Jupiter has the best influence on the ascendant. Better by aspects than by its placement, Jupiter makes the individual more genuinely interested in impersonal behaviour, righteous dealings and respect for traditional values. Persons under its impact work for others. Philanthropy and altruism are evident in their character.

There is an inner contentment which cannot be disturbed by any external difficulty. Such persons are genuinely attracted towards religious activities. They wish to be a part and an active agent for the welfare of the society. The best enduring influence on an individual can be expected with Jovian aspect on the ascendant which not only make the individual outward turned, but also contented, concerned about his family and social welfare, and ethically oriented.

Astrological indications of the psychology of an individual as suggested above, are very elementary, but in actual practice, gets complicated as a result of diverse forces interacting on the individual's life. These suggestions are, however, useful in understanding oneself so that corrective forces and attitudes could be generated in order to attain long-lasting stability. These corrective measures which could be useful for the person concerned, are also indicated by the astrological delineation of the nativity.

6

SEVEN CHANNELS OF HUMAN DEVELOPMENT

In *Mundakopanishad,* there are two mantras which very clearly state the importance of seven channels in creation. Initially, while describing the flames of the cosmic fire, it states its seven names as *Kali, Karali, Manojava, Sudhumravarna,* etc., to describe the seven flames through which the various oblations to *agni,* fire, are consumed. Later, while narrating the splintering of the Akshara-Brahma into innumerable fireballs, it talks of Seven Life Currents (*Prana*), Seven Lustres (*Archisa*), Seven Sacrificial Woods (*Samidha*) and so on which are included in the Cosmic Man (*Purusha*) and from these everything else arises in the universe. Approaching this creative process astrologically, one feels the significance of seven principles pervading everywhere. To understand the deeper impulses working within every individual, we may postulate that there are seven main channels of human development. Those who have had clairvoyant sight, those who have attained higher levels of perfection (*Siddhis*), and those who are serious students of psychology confirm that there are seven basic human temperaments. The seven *rishis* (*Saptarishis*) who are represented by the Great Bear and who are constantly watching over the cosmic evolution, stand at the helm of these seven channels, beckoning us to those sublime heights. These may sound meaningless abracadabra to a large number of students, but we may soon find that there could be much more reality in this assumption of seven channels of human development than it appears on a superficial examination.

The importance of this subject increases greatly because a realisation of this truth solves many of our everyday problems. Even when the individual is not aware of its deeper purpose of life, and is ignorant of the final goal towards which its inner self is always guiding him, the specific star is always aware of its responsibilities. As each individual has a radically specific path to tread, though the final channels of development would be differentiated into seven streams before it is later on, again merged together prior to their mingling with the Cosmic Man, the *Paramatman,* having attained *Nirvana.* His experiences will be distinctly different from everyone else. In basic principles, the nature of the flame burning inside him would be similar to those who are on the same channel, but in details each event and every condition of his various relationships would be different from others. By understanding what is generally known as the Seven Rays of Human Temperament, the individual can succeed in unravelling many of his intricate problems of life.

This subject of self-discovery revealing the special flame of the cosmic fire irradiating the individual had been, in the ancient religious circles, an esoteric teaching imparted by the teacher to his specially prepared disciples. Even in Egypt, the knowledge of seven basic human channels of development was imparted at very late stages of several initiations before the Final Mystery was revealed to the student. The subject is very intimately linked with different forms of yogic practices meant for the novice to unfold his latent qualities. Naturally therefore, the subject has many dangerous possibilities. Due to this, it was kept very carefully concealed. But astrology could not do so. It reveals the relationship between the planets and the different channels through which the individuals attain their final destiny. In many of the general astrological principles, a discerning student can decipher the hidden message, though from them, he cannot work out the details, unless the subject is studied in relationship with Indian yogic literature, metaphysics and astrology.

In Vedic Astrology, there are only seven planets as Rahu and Ketu are not considered actual planets. They are mere shadow planets, *Chhaya Grahas.* In this scheme, the Sun and the Moon are not treated in the same way as other planets. In the various signs of the zodiac, Sun and Moon are assigned only one sign each for their rulership whereas other planets are assigned two signs each. While doing so, the ancient seers did not assign any rulership to Rahu and Ketu in a general way. As a result of these differences, one could postulate that the ancient seers who gave us the knowledge of Astrology had reasons to classify the so-called nine planets into three categories, namely, Sun and Moon in one group, Rahu and Ketu in another, while the rest of the five planets occupied the third group.

This assumption can be reinforced by another treatment of the planets. An important planetary combination of immense significance is categorised as *Pancha Mahapurusha Yogas*. As the very name of this combination suggests, this planetary combination is linked with *Maha* (Immensely Great) *Purusha* (Human), which is formed by auspicious and powerful placements of five planets placed in the third group (as indicated in the previous paragraph). If one goes into minute details of the essentials of the results indicated on the basis of such placements, one finds that these planets pour profusely on the individual those special qualities with which they are endowed. It does not necessarily make the person internationally or even widely renowned, or politically powerful. This should make the student a little sceptical about this planetary combination. He should find out the rationale of the combination. There should be some reason for differentiating these planets from others. As Vedic Astrology is not just a collection of rules which do not have valid rationale (as many pseudo-scientists are apt to believe) behind them, the reason for the ancient seers not making it explicit and available to every desirable or undesirable curious seeker does not make these rules less effective. In the present context, we may accept that these seers had some valid reason for not making the various interrelationship explicit.

Each individual, whether he knows it or not, is linked with his special star. During the course of his evolutionary journey from the time of his fragmentation from the Absolute All, the Cosmic Fire which splits itself in seven flames, his special planet stands behind him permitting him enough scope for action to gain experiences which would make him capable of understanding the Reality for which his splintering has taken place. At the same time these planets, in "consultation" with the Lords of Karma, manage to get the karmic conditions so arranged that the individual gradually becomes capable of unfolding his latent potential. In this process, though the Sun and the Moon are also related with certain special egos directly in certain special cases, yet they take over the individuals from other planets at a very late stage of their evolutionary growth and development. There is no arbitrariness in this decision. It is so because the Sun and the Moon have very specialised functions in this cosmogenesis which link them with certain principles. These cannot function on lower planes of concretisation. Without going into details of the esoteric significance of the *Pancha Mahapurusha Yogas* at present, it may be indicated that this planetary combination does throw some light on some esoteric relationships of the combination.

The diagram on page 52 attempts to indicate some of the essential features of the seven channels of human development. The basic framework in which all the planets function consists of triple manifestation of the Original Cause or the Unmanifest and the polarisation of the same in *Purusha* (Male or the Positive Creative Force/Impulse) and *Prakriti* (Nature or the essential foundation on which the Positive or the Male Impulse operates). An area of operation in the diagram is shaded which suggests that these forces are operating on objective planes of existence, which consist of concrete actions. The unshaded portion represents the realm of consciousness where thinking, feeling and subjective experiences and functions are more important. For example, a scientist works on matter, examines its constituents, uses instruments and scientific gadgets to understand the working of the matter under examination. These are some of the objective, concrete forms of activities. Similarly, an architect is concerned with building structural constructions. All these are objective aspects of life; they are concerned with the world of things and matter. As against these activities that with which a poet or a philosopher is concerned, are the subjective feelings. A great religious reformer is not concerned with temples and rituals, but is concerned with mental revolution. A person who meets another person and instantly understands the thoughts and feelings of the other, is working on the plane of consciousness. Some other person working on the plane of matter will under such a circumstance note the clothes the individual wore, the postures he assumed, the tone and the accent of the voice he was using and such other external details. In this way, there are two

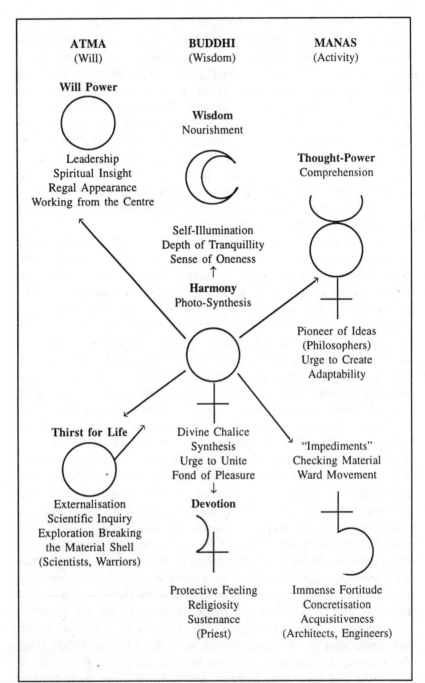

sides to everything; one group of people work primarily on planes of consciousness and the other, on matter. This is a primary consideration.

Another set of considerations is related with *Atma, Buddhi* and *Manas.* These are basic elements in creation and they have been dealt in great detail in Indian metaphysical literature. *Atma* is concerned with the Will aspect of life, *Buddhi* with Wisdom or Understanding while *Manas* is connected with Thought and is the essence or the foundation of all activities. These three operate on consciousness as well as on the planes of matter. Will is connected with personal initiative, functioning independently without seeking any support or assistance. It reflects the central inherent potential within the individual. Wisdom leads to understanding. It reveals the wisdom contained in the subject under consideration. For an individual on this ray, there may not be any great interest in expressing himself or in acting the way he does, but he may desire ardently to understand the various relationships in which he is involved and with such an understanding his personal actions and behaviour will change. But the important point is not the reactions or his behaviour, his personal understanding of the relationship is important for *buddhic* consciousness. *Manas* is related to the thinking principle of the individual. When a person has rightly comprehended a relationship or some truth, he cannot but act in the light of this comprehension. Action is there at all the levels, but the impulse for the action comes in different ways from different planets. *Atma, Buddhi* and *Manas* are those differentiations which indicate the three faces through which the original source supplies the basic motivating impulses to different individuals.

The various planets, excluding Rahu and Ketu, can be considered in this context. The Sun, Moon and Mercury are classified under subjective planets working on the planes of consciousness whereas Mars, Jupiter and Saturn are concerned with the objective realms of manifestation and are intimately linked with matter. Venus has a unique position. One portion of it is related to consciousness aspect of life and another with matter.

The painter, musician, dancer and such other artists who are governed by Venus have subjective as well as an objective world to work in. A classical Indian dancer endeavours to actualise certain subjective expressions, experiences and feelings in concrete, objective forms, by different postures, *mudras* and so on. Similarly, a painter attempts to concretise certain subjective ideas in his drawings and paintings through the medium of different lines, shapes and colours. The outstanding quality of Venus is harmonisation of subjective and objective worlds, a synthesis between the world of matter and consciousness. These ideas are represented in a diagram on page 52, which, it is hoped, would simplify and clarify the various ideas mentioned above.

As all the planets reflect the lustre of one of the seven flames of the Cosmic Fire, which is in essence the Life Giving Impulse of the Cosmic Man, we prefer to call these differentiated impulses of different planets as they impinge upon different individuals as the Seven Human Rays on which the different individuals evolve during the course of their various incarnations. The ray dominated by the Sun could be called the Solar Ray or we may even call it the First Ray. It represents the Positive Spark of the Divine Life, the Basic Impulse of the Cosmic Man. It works from within but expresses itself on the outer surface. It links all the aspects of life to the primary nature of the individual, his innermost purpose of existence which is to energies his latent potential and let it shine in its full glory. On the plane of everyday existence, it will appear that the individual has the quality of leadership, he is inspired, he is independent, not seeking favour from others, but functioning in his own light. He will appear always full of energy, engaged in activity and never attracted by anything mean or sectional in life. His mental attitude will be cosmopolitan.

The Moon is self-illuminating and since it understands, its main function is to reflect the central cosmic power electrifying everything. The Moon understands one's real nature and its relationship with the Cosmic Man. Its primary role is to shed tranquility and generative potential in every form of life coming under its influence. The Moon imparts nourishment because it has been given that quality from the central source of energy to shed to others. "I am Brahma" not because of "its identity which is established with the First Ray, but because Brahma has implanted in me the same essence, of which it is itself made of." The Moon is the Receptacle of the Life Spark and the understanding of its various relationships imparts a great unifying impulse to the Lunar Ray. All actions, motives, aspirations of the persons evolving under this impulse will have the basic foundation of understanding as the primary motivating and the centralising force in their life. This we call the Second Ray.

Mercury leads to comprehension which is different from understanding aroused under the impulse of the Moon. The difference between the Second Ray and the Ray of Mercury is very subtle. It is not without any significance that Mercury is said to be the son of Soma, the Moon. Comprehension arises when a situation, certain relationships, ideas, or facts are presented to the individual. Out of the given, Mercury recognises or discovers a new relationship which is not obvious. It leads to an understanding of the real significance of the situations and facts presented. This understanding arises as a result of mentation. Mentation is a subjective process but it has a nucleus. Wisdom does not have a cause, it does not have a seed, or a nucleus. Wisdom is at the back of comprehension which arises from the Second Ray radiated by the Moon.

If and when we consider the relationship between the two planets namely, the Sun and the Moon, and the remaining five planets namely, Mercury, Venus, Mars, Jupiter and Saturn, we shall see how all these have to merge in the former two, before merging in the Original Cause, but here we shall not go into these details. Under the Third Ray, one becomes pioneer of ideas, a philosopher. There is polarisation between the real essence of things and the situations presented as the nuclei, and there is also a difference between the real import or the significance of these situations and the phenomena. This polarisation could lead to conflicts, as well as the desire to unify the two – the ideas and the reality, which might be understood as the urge to create (which is different from the creative urges under the impulse of Venus and Mars). It also leads to adaptability which occurs when comprehension is tinged with understanding. The nature of the Third Ray is very enigmatic.

The earlier diagram also shows the significance of the other planetary impulses, but the individuals do not necessarily express the primeval qualities of the planets linked with them at each birth, because we generally meet individuals during the middle course of their evolutionary journey. The karmic forces which have enmeshed them in diverse situations often blur the clear ray of the specific planet. The horoscopic planetary conjuncture reveals the situation of the individual's journey. It indicates the stage of his soul's evolution.

When he receives clearer flashing of his specific ray, his personality is greatly differentiated and individualised. It is helpful for the individual to approach his chart with a view to understand his stage in his evolutionary pilgrimage. In this regard, the individual will have to examine the nature of different planets and the pattern emerging in his horoscope. These patterns reveal how karmic forces are inducing him through certain situations which could ultimately make the path clearer so that he could embark on his ultimate pilgrimage when the pure ray of the specific planet shines through his life.

It is important for an individual to know the nature of one's ray and the stage of one's evolutionary status. But the discovery and the understanding of these subjects on the basis of horoscopic indications will require much more deeper understanding of the method of 'reading' a horoscope. In classical works, only hints and suggestions are given. Direct teachings and clues are given only to special students while they are veiled from the ordinary prying individuals. Due to intuition and other occult teachings one may however pierce the veil but it has to be an arduous individual effort.

7

INDICATIONS OF THE MATURITY OF THE SOUL

In contemporary society almost all over the world, almost every practitioner is engaged in mundane predictions to satisfy the immediate superficial curiosities of his clients. There is even a tendency to approach to the media to publicise one's forecasts concerning persons and situations for which the concerned persons or the parties did not make any query. The primary purpose of such displays has been self-publicity. These practitioners are many a time very precise in their day-to-day predictions but they do overlook and ignore the basic spiritual objective of this occult knowledge. It is in this special area that Vedic Astrology has tremendous contribution to make.

The essence of Indian philosophy is that each individual has the primeval spark of Divinity in him which he gradually discovers and finally realises as his real self. The maturity of the evolving self, which in common parlance is often called soul, depends upon the stage of this realisation of one's inner essential nature. The natural process of this evolution or the usual course of this pilgrimage is guided by two basic considerations namely, the Law of Karma and the Law of Reincarnation. In Vedic Astrology, these two laws are assumed as facts in nature. Even the rationality of astrological predictions are explained and justified on the basis of these guiding principles. But if someone enquires about the causes of one's misfortune, some abstruse explanations are given. For example, if someone's offsprings are always dying early, or if one is not able to conceive, he is told that the same is due to *Naga Doshas* or something similar. A meaningful explanation of every event in one's daily life, auspicious as well as unfortunate, can only be given if an attempt is made to discover the lost bridge between the Indian metaphysics and astrology. Every event is a reflection of the eternal life. It reflects the individual's destiny as well as the series of his lives and acts done and not done.

In every individual's life the burden of past karmas, even those which had begun during the previous births, reappears in every birth. The very first human incarnation reflects the past and this according to some system is indicated by the planetary position at birth. In most individuals, the life during the animal period is colourless except the strong streak of affection felt for the master, and other relationships which enabled the animal to be incarnated as a human being. The individual karmas at the early stages of his growth are of general kind. He has to learn and develop the faculties which later make him a unique person. At this stage, inertia is the motivating factor. It activates the various principles or the primeval faculties essential for a human being. The individual has to develop physical strength, emotional faculties, life sustaining energy, social traits, intelligence, self-awareness and various other qualities inherent in men and women. Every planet gradually, instills its qualities in the individual. As there is no special differentiation among the individuals, the planetary situation in an individual's chart at this stage, does not reveal any marked trait. This is the initial stage when the individual soul is looking for and indulging in every possible experience.

The second stage of egoic development occurs when the law of inertia takes the individual to different activities during the course of his everyday existence. The basic impulses of human individuals are not identical for everybody. The final destiny of each individual begins to assert itself from the very beginning. The entire humanity, before it ultimately attains its final goal and merges in the Infinite, is channelised in seven streams. This differentiation begins by directing the forces of inertia in such a manner that the main characteristics of the ray on which the individual has to develop becomes prominent. Those planets which have to play a significant role in the individual's egoic long journey begin to acquire greater role. As a result of more active role of these planets, the individual acquires greater strength and differentiation during the course of his following births. The differences in the relative strength of different planets suggest that the individual is getting more immersed in the materialisation process and has advanced from his early (primitive) stage of development. He is no more pure impressionable ego. He has begun to acquire various experiences and he reacts to them in a manner that later on he could learn important lessons from them. This stage of egoic development could be considered the early second stage of human evolution.

The third stage shows the Law of Karma operating more intensively. The various indulgences along with the individual's likes, dislikes, attractions and repulsions change the proclivities of the individual. Some of them will be favourable for his growth, while others will be disadvantageous. The intensity of these proclivities will also gradually increase. The relative strength of different planets will alter according to differing intensities of actions and reactions to various conditions of life presented to the individual. The various reactions depending on emotional and mental attitudes of the person will affect the disposition of different planets. At this stage, therefore, the nature of the soul's evolutionary course and its maturity will be reflected in the planetary alignments. This is the stage when the planetary combinations given in astrological texts do not necessarily emerge, but some different kind of alignment among the planets takes place which can be discerned by a careful astrologer.

It is the fourth stage of egoic evolution, that important planetary combinations begin to reflect the karmic involvement of the individual, the experiences derived so far and the lines on which the soul wanted him to proceed further. At this stage, one finds many individuals with exalted planets in different situations (not forming *Pancha Mahapurusha Yogas*) which are intriguing as the individuals do not show any corresponding marked degree of eminence. Such individuals have gathered strength and different faculties but the direction for the use of these faculties is yet to be revealed. No efforts are yet made to regulate the individual's activities as he has to learn many more lessons before he moves pointedly to his final goal. When important planetary combinations are present in the chart, it shows that the ego is becoming ready and is being prepared for important experiences. His ability to absorb lessons from various experiences is increasing. His karmas are becoming more complex. His various principles have begun to mature.

At this phase, the Moon assumes charge of the ego. So far the importance of the Moon in the chart would be non-descript, not very significant. At this phase of the Soul's development, the Moon begins to play a crucial role. The main function of the Moon is to reflect the rays of the Sun. The Moon has to transmit to the ego the message that the Divine Primordial Spirit, the· Soul, has for the personality, the living entity. The Moon is primarily a passive planet. A strong placid Moon with ripples of water without any disturbance by the surface wind only can reflect the Sun's rays clearly and without any distortion. A mature soul is one which is able to have self-knowledge without any illusions; when the lower mind can clearly perceive the nature of his inner or real self, then only can it be considered matured. It does not mark the end of the spiritual journey, but certainly, it marks an important milestone in it.

The Moon at the beginning of this new phase has a two-fold goal—firstly, the reflective, perceptive, intuitive and meditative qualities of the higher mind, *Chitta,* must be strengthened, and secondly, the digressions to material indulgences must be gradually checked. These two functions of the Moon are evident from the several planetary combinations laid down relating to this planet. The most important positive combinations are *Adhi Yoga, Sunapha, Anapha, Durudhara Yogas,* the *Gajakesari Yoga* and the *Kemadruma Yoga.* During this phase of egoic development, *Kala Sarpa Yoga* also begins to assume its special role.

The positive set of *yogas* strengthen the quality of receptivity of Moon. Jupiter, Mercury and Venus are all auspicious planets. They are helpful in producing such conditions of life which would not disturb the placidity of the mind. When the higher mind, the Moon, is thus prepared, the individual gets into the habit of experiencing the creative forces in Nature. The planets flanking the Moon strengthen the reflective quality of its placidity; such proximity of planets also tests as well as activates the response of this luminary to various conditions, disturbing as well as elevating situations. The importance of the *Gajakesari Yoga* is in strengthening the placidity of the reflective mind. When there is smooth sailing in life, when troubles and difficulties are removed, and harmonious feelings and emotions abound in and around the life of the person, there is contentment in life, and under such a situation, a normal human being is expected to turn his gaze inward, to muse over the bounties of Nature and to the merciful nature of the Supreme Power. In that absolute faith in the Supreme, even if it is just a superstitious belief, the unruffled mind would get rid of innumerable everyday difficulties. This unruffled mind is the most important result of *Gajakesari Yoga*. The positive *yogas* at this stage of egoic development aim at strengthening the reflective quality of Moon, making the individual more concerned with his long-term destiny. The maturing ego takes a firmer hold of the personality, while the later, by nature, is more concerned with fleeting pleasures and sensations of life.

The negative *yogas* of Moon have the main purpose of disentangling the ego from material attachments. The periodic ups and downs in life which characterise *Sakata Yoga* make a deep imprint on the consciousness of the individual. He gets the first hand experience of the transitoriness of everything material and manifest in the universe. With this realisation, the attachment with the personality and its changing sensations and pleasures are loosened. This is the period when the personality is tested in various ways. The trials of the neophytes come at this stage. Their past karmas are arranged in such a manner that the loss and the various vicissitudes appear without any apparent cause and the neophytes are made to wail. It is not the stage of renunciation, *sanyasa*, but it is the beginning of the lessons leading to disillusionment. That is the main objective of *Sakata Yoga* as well as of *Kala Sarpa Yoga*. These *yogas* are not present in ordinary horoscopes. They indicate that the ego has invoked higher powers for the bestowal of illumination and self-knowledge and these *yogas* test him of his readiness for this gift of self-awareness.

With this invocation, while the ego is gradually gaining increasing degree of strength to bear his cross, leading to the final illumination, the past karmas of benefic nature are arranged in such a way that fruitful opportunities come in the life of the individuals. They evolve the individual in such a way that his personality is ultimately differentiated and he is able to express his destined ray more radiantly. He proceeds more confidently on his final journey towards emancipation. These arrangements of beneficial opportunities by the Lords of Karma are evident through various patterns of planetary alignments. These are different kind of patterns each suited to the individual ego and the stage of his egoic development. All of them however, aim at making all his activities very purposeful. These patterns are different from various planetary combinations given in different astrological texts. An example of such patterns is given in Chart I.

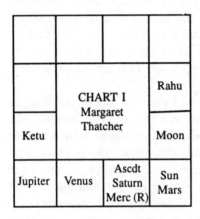 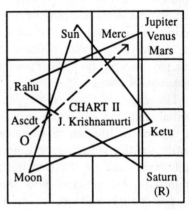

Chart I pertains to Margaret Thatcher and it is unique in many ways. The planetary configuration shows many specialities. From the standpoint of emerging patterns of planets, it shows the special task assigned to the ego based on the maturity of experiences gained in previous lives. We find in this chart that a large number of planets are placed second from their own signs. It shows much interest and efforts towards creativity which is the special feature of the second house. The Sun is in the second position from its sign Leo, the Moon is in second position from its sign Cancer, Mercury is in second from Virgo and Venus is in the second house from its sign Libra. Apart from these, Saturn in exaltation is situated in the tenth from its sign Capricorn, and Jupiter in its own sign, Sagittarius is tenth from its sign Pisces. Enlightened approach to the professional career and the performance of the task assigned to her in this life specially in the interest of larger population without any personal bias, are very well exemplified in everything that Lady Thatcher did. The fairly evolved nature of her ego (Soul) standing at a crucial stage of its further development is also shown by the presence of *Kala Sarpa Yoga* about which we have spoken earlier.

A large number of such patterns available in fairly evolved persons are given in *Predictive Techniques of Vedic Astrology* (Passage Press, USA). It gives many examples of evolved personalities with special missions working under special planetary configurations which are expected to prepare them for their onward evolutionary journey (Study Chapter 27 for greater details on this subject).

When the individuals are ready to shoulder greater responsibilities and work in harmony with Nature, at times they are assigned special tasks to perform. When the planetary configuration presents some mystifying patterns which appear unusual from the general astrological rules, one must look deeper in the nature of planets and their configuration. Sometimes even in seemingly ordinary persons, unusual traits are discovered which provide the key to the unusual quality of their personality. In this context one may refer to the horoscope of J. Krishnamurti (Chart II). From the very beginning there were spiritualists and clairvoyants who were hammering that the young boy loitering on the Adyar beach was destined to be great as he was going to be a messenger of the spiritual forces. His chart had several unfortunate combinations if we examine it from the standpoint of superficial common astrological principles. But a close examination shows that the planets situated fifth from certain other planets together formed a six-pointed star with Mercury standing separate from the rest. One triangle is formed by joining the Sun (in fourth house in Aries) and Ketu (in eighth in Leo) and Moon (in twelfth in Sagittarius); another triangle is formed by joining Rahu (in second house in Aquarius) and Jupiter, Venus and Mars (in sixth house in Gemini) and Saturn (in tenth house in Libra and in retrogression). The six-pointed star is an ancient symbol of Divine benediction in many esoteric religions. Wherever this star flashes, the Divine presence is assumed. In several religions such symbols are given and in tantric literature several such figures are mentioned. One has to look for such figures to find out whether any special kind of pattern has emerged in the chart. In this case, the influence of six-pointed star is amply demonstrated by the biographical details of J. Krishnamurti who was almost everytime shadowed by some Divine Presence. The singular star Mercury away from this six-pointed star represents the special mission for which he was born. He was engaged for the last several decades of his life in disseminating the Divine message. He was for the last several incarnations prepared for it, his soul was developed and various experiences were provided so that he could discharge this task effectively. He had to be a messenger, which is the special portfolio of Mercury.

Such missionary patterns are found even in seemingly ordinary persons but with evolved souls prepared for some special work essential for their own personal development as well as for Nature's evolutionary impulse. Once such evidence could be deciphered in one's chart, it would be justified to infer that the soul of the person is quite advanced and he has progressed far on the evolutionary path.

When the soul has attained such a level of growth as is evident from the above two charts, it is now ready for greater illumination and greater understanding of the Self. *Atma-Bodha* or Self-Awareness is a very special quality of one's consciousness in which the Divinity of man is reflected in his egoic consciousness and his entire behaviour and relationships significantly alter. It assumes that the ego is now able to establish with much clarity its relationship with its Inner Ruler Immortal or the Sun. At this stage, the Sun begins to take greater charge of the individual. The various mundane experiences gathered during the course of several incarnations are distilled and pure wisdom is taken out of them. The rational mind points to the presence of some universal energy sweetly guiding everything in the manifest universe. It often reaches the outer fringe of this energy and as a reflection of this contact the higher *Manas, Chitta,* gets purified, and the storms of passing events which disturbed the placid waters of tranquility completely subside. There

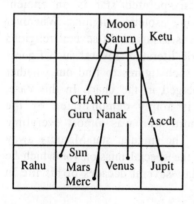

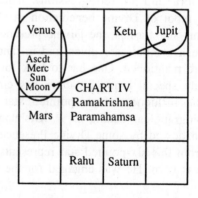

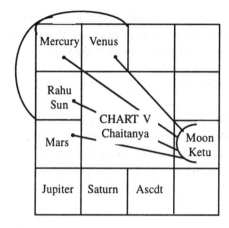

is a new beginning, a new realisation which opens the gates of higher spiritual downpour. It cleanses the heart and gives enormous flow of the life-force even to detached individuals. This is the stage often spoken as that of *Sthitaprajna*, of equable understanding. Astrologically this situation is deciphered by the relationship between the Sun and Mercury and their reflection on the Moon.

In horoscopes of such evolved persons, *Buddha-Aditya Yoga* is usually present, the Moon is usually in the seventh place from the Sun, and the Sun is fortified by *Vesi, Vasi* and *Ubhayachari Yogas*. One also finds the Moon under the benign influence of Jupiter and under the austere control of Saturn so that no trace of worldly attachments born out of *avidya* is present. Many saints and sages who have been widely known to have attained high status of self-illumination, have many of these planetary configurations in their natal charts. Chart III, IV and V show that the positions of the Sun and the Moon are such that Moon is either reflecting the message of the Sun or is associated with it. It is also having special relationship with Mercury and Venus as well as with Jupiter. These reveal the greatness of the incarnating soul. Sometimes one finds the Moon situated in the fifth from the Sun but that is usually a special case. From the horoscopes of Guru Nanak, Ramakrishna Paramahamsa and Sri Chaitanya, one would be fairly convinced that the relationship between the Sun and the Moon along with their special disposition in relationship with Mercury reveals the maturity of the incarnating soul.

The next phase of the journey takes us to the differentiation of the soul on its special ray on which it has to finally evolve. At that stage it also has the task of alignment of the Seven Principles in man which finally leads to the unity of the individual with the universal energy called God or the Absolute All. This phase requires special treatment.

The stages mentioned above are not as well demarcated from one another as it is described here; several of them occur simultaneously. The planetary configurations also require consideration with regard to the signs and the houses in which the relationships of different planets occur. These astrological considerations should enable an experienced (esoteric) astrologer to decipher the status of the soul.

8

FOUNDATION OF AN
INTEGRATED PERSONALITY

In *Brihat Parasara Hora Sastra,* the sage Parasara on his own volition revealed to Lord Maitreya the secret of *Sudarshan Chakra* which was originally revealed to him by Brahma himself, for the welfare of the mankind. Often the *Sudarshan Chakra* is not directly applied by the astrologers in everyday mundane progonstications, though many discerning astrologers do take into consideration the placement of Sun and Moon in making general predictions. In fact, in revealing the psychological complexities of modern life, the *Sudarshan Chakra* can be of immense value. This technique is very useful in unravelling the deeper layers of one's personality.

In Hindu metaphysics, the individual is often described as a unity between *Atman* or the Universal Spirit, and the personality or the individualised physical self. The Universal Spirit, the impersonal life-essence, is the one which is popularly called the *Atman,* which is beyond the limitations and restrictions of evolutionary impetus. In everyday life, the eternal or the permanent essence in man often strikes the note of conscience and gives to some individuals the special majesty and grace flowing from this basic nature of the human beings which inspite of being universal in nature, expresses in individualised life-particles as well. *Atman* is one extreme of a human with all its subtlety and universal nature: it does not accumulate any experience, but always radiates beneficence. The direction in one's life, in its basic impulse, comes from this central spark in the individual.

The other extreme in man is his personality or the physical self which is made of various chemical elements. The portion of one's personality which consists of face, hands, legs, body, etc., which can be touched, seen and photographed constitutes the physical portion of one's constitution. This physical body has its own volition and is a vehicle of the other constituents of the human being. This physical component of the being is often described as the mansion in which the *Atman* dwells. In between these two extremes, there is a vast realm of psycho-spiritual-divine forces which connect the two to give an integrated wholeness to the individual.

Once this integration is achieved, much of the life's battle is won and the clarity of vision attained. Unless this unity or the integration is realised, the individual will be in sorrow. In everyday life, one finds that his everyday circumstances, psychological motivations and the voice of the inner conscience are not harmoniously blended together; it indicates that the three components of the being need careful synchronisation. With this awareness, the individual may have an understanding of the task before him in any one particular incarnation. This knowledge could produce much satisfaction and enlightenment to the individual. *Sudarshan Chakra* provides this knowledge.

In order to prepare the *Sudarshan Chakra,* it is necessary to draw three concentric circles (actually one will be required to draw four concentric circumferences) each of these divided into twelve parts. Each subdivision will represent one house-division or a *bhava* of the horoscope. Thus there will be three house-divisions, one each in every concentric circle, which would represent the specific *bhava* of the person. These three house divisions will be delineated in such a way that the Ascendant in the original chart represents the Ascendant noted on the inner-most circle. The sign posited by the Moon will represent the Ascendant on the middle circle, and in that circle all the planets will be described in their respective zodiacal signs. Similarly, the sing posited by the Sun will represent the Ascendant on the outermost circle and other planets located as in the case of the Moon, that is, they will be described in their respective zodiacal signs. In this way, the entire planetary positions of Lord Buddha, (as given by Dr. B. V. Raman) will appear as follows:

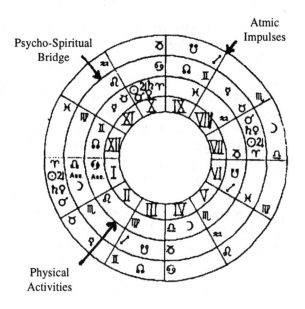

Planetary Positions: Sun 29" 3'; Moon 200" 45'; Mars 26" 54'; Mercury 53" 6';
Jupiter 11"; Venus 6" 12'; Saturn 24" 36'; Rahu 86" 54' and
Ascendant 116" 45'; Ayanamsa +14" 16'

Before venturing any astrological predictions on the basis of this
kind of triple representation of planetary positions, it is important to
keep in mind a few basic astrological principles. As it has been
mentioned earlier, the innermost circle will represent the physical
conditions of the individual. If, say, the fifth house in this
delineation is afflicted, that will indicate the physical aspect of the
problem. Affliction existing even in the second or the middle circle
in which case the Moon is in the Ascendant position, it would
signify the psychological repercussions of the physical affliction. The
condition in the outermost circle as it existed in relation to the fifth
house would indicate the creative impulses flowing to the individual
from higher realms. Thus the middle circle could be viewed as the
battleground of the forces flowing downward from the central
Divine Impulse which in short could be called the *atmic* impulses
and the psychological factors aroused by physical conditions of life.
The creative forces flowing from the *atmic* impulses downwards
towards the physical life of the individual represented by the inner

circle, meets it at the middle circle represented as the Psycho-Spiritual Bridge. Unless the three forces are blended harmoniously, there will be a churning operation at the psychological level causing much stress and strain to the individual. The psychological-spiritual repercussions of the denial of the creative opportunities or its fructification (the fifth *bhava*) as evident from the innermost circle, will meet the creative impulses coming from the outermost circle at the middle circle. The practising astrologer will have to use his understanding and ingenuity in interpreting the various forces as evident from the triplicity of each *bhava* evident from this method of horoscopic delineation.

In dealing with the triplicity of the various house-divisions, there are certain basic principles which could be kept in view. The first consideration relates to the nature of different signs of the zodiac which occupy these house-divisions. The astrological texts have already attributed the various elements to different zodiacs. Aries, Leo and Sagittarius are considered fiery signs; Taurus, Virgo and Capricorn are earthly signs; Gemini, Libra and Aquarius are airy while Cancer, Scorpio and Pisces are watery signs. When the same house-division at different levels is occupied by disharmonious signs, the result will inevitably be disturbing. Earthly Capricorn at the physical level, watery cancer at the psycho-spiritual middle level, and airy Gemini at the *atmic* level will not produce a well-integrated expression of the particular *bhava*. There could be turmoil at the physical level, unperturbed and cool-headed reaction at the middle emotional or psycho-mental bridge while deep down in the individual's heart there could be a great upsurge for intense activity. The forces operating at the three different levels of the being in relation to the specific *bhava* would be so much conflicting that peace would be denied in that respect. On the same principle, when the three zodiacal signs are well blended, the result pertaining to that specific *bhava* could be heartening.

Furthermore, the three attributes namely, *rajas* (activity), *tamas* (inertia or sloth), and *sattwa* (harmony or pristine nature), basic in Hindu metaphysics which underlie almost every activity and every operation in this world, also influence the different zodiacs. The first four zodiacs namely, Aries, Taurus, Gemini and Cancer, are under the sway of *rajas* or activity principle, while the next four namely, Leo, Virgo, Libra and Scorpio are governed by *tamas* or sloth;

Sagittarius, Capricorn, Aquarius and Pisces are related to *sattwa,* the essential or the pristine nature of the being. At this stage of consideration, it would be helpful to incorporate the relationship between different *nakshatras* or the lunar mansions. Each set of four zodiacs under the major influence of the basic impulses or the *gunas* consists of nine *nakshatras,* the first three of these are under the secondary influence of *rajas,* the next three under *tamas* and the last three under *sattwa.* Again, at the tertiary level, these three *nakshatras* will be under the sway of *rajas, tamas,* and *sattwa* respectively. All the different zodiacs throughout their expansion therefore will not have the same basic impulse or *guna* operating at the secondary and tertiary levels. At these levels, it will be necessary to take the degrees of the ascendant, the Moon and the Sun into account for assessing the impact of various impulses. While dealing with different house-divisions, this study becomes a little complicated, but with a little familiarisation of extension of different *bhavas* occupied by different zodiacs, the predictive methodology could be easily grasped.

While on the topic of the nature of harmony existing at different house-divisions, it will perhaps be important to take note of primary motivations of the different zodiacs in these *bhavas.* In this connection, one needs to recapitulate that *artha* (purposeful motivation), *kama* (passionate involvement), *dharma* (religion or the righteous behaviour) and *moksha* (liberation) are given much importance in Indian metaphysics and they motivate all actions. The table below shows the sway of these basic motivations of different *nakshatras.*

Categorisation of Asterisms into Four Primary Motivational Impulses

Dharma	Artha	Kama	Moksha
Aswini	Bharani	Krittika	Rohini
Pushya	Punarvasu	Aridra	Mrigasira
Aslesha	Makha	P. Phalguni	U. Phalguni
Visakha	Swati	Chitra	Hasta
Anuradha	Jyeshta	Moola	P. Ashadha
Dhanishta	Sravana	(Abhijit)	U. Ashadha
Satabhisha	P. Bhadra	U. Bhadra	Revati

For a clearer understanding of the nature of different *bhavas* at the three levels mentioned above, it will be necessary to synchronise the different lunar mansions and the different signs of the zodiac and then evaluate the impact of different elements, basic impulses *(gunas)* and the primary motivational forces influencing the various *bhavas,* specially the Ascendant at the three levels and assess their harmonious blending in order to find out the integration of the life-force operating at these three levels.

The next stage involves the assessment of the quality of the Moon and the Sun along with the Ascendant at the innermost circle. The results of different zodiacal signs in the Ascendant are well known. It is very important to consider the Ascendant sign very carefully. If the reader wishes to have an extensive knowledge of the life of the individual in its considerable depth, he could find several books presenting the theme very expertly. On this knowledge, he will be required to superimpose the knowledge about the radiation of the Moon described in the middle circle and affecting the psycho-spiritual bridge of the individual. The Moon in Aries will make the psyche of the individual disturbed, always wanting change, never satisfied and never accepting the advice of others. Unless the individual experiences the repercussions himself, his life cannot be moulded on the advice of others coming from the physical level or even from his own *atmic* mentor at the outer circle. In Taurus, the individual becomes extremely receptive to others; he wants to remain in whatever situation he is placed. He is always careful about the feelings and reactions of others which accentuates the sensitivity.

In Gemini, the Moon activates the psyche towards finding a base for its own foundation. In ideas and opinions of others which agree with its own experiences, or in association with those thought currents which make the individual a little parochial, the individual psyche will feel restful and harmonised. When the Moon is in Cancer, the psychic bridge of the individual is oriented towards the impulses coming through it from the higher sources. Many a time, the individual may not understand what messages are flowing through his mind, but he will be receptive to those messages and will like to express them at the physical levels of existence. In Leo, the Moon at the middle level will pine for the understanding of the premonitions, urges and messages and when received, it will endeavour to mould itself accordingly. At this level, the psyche under the influence of the Moon will like to be influenced more by the higher forces than by the attractions and influences of the lower planes of existence. In Virgo, the Moon makes the psyche susceptible to influences of earthly life and involvements in pleasures derived from sensual gratifications. It will be almost shut against the admonitions coming from the higher plane. Even in Libra, the Moon will induce greater movement towards pleasures of life. At this stage, the psyche will struggle to have increasingly more and more intense experience of worldly pleasures. It becomes incapable of learning spiritualising lessons from the earthly experiences. The *'tamasic'* proclivities will be greatly accentuated.

The desire to move in the realm of psychic experiences, delving in psychic phenomena, and craving for such forbidden pleasures which destroy the susceptibilities of the individual to higher realm impulses, will be heightened under the lunar situation in Scorpio. With the Moon's placement in Sagittarius, the attraction towards pristine existence, the desire for closer association with higher influences will be greatly pronounced. In Capricorn, the Moon could restructure the psyche in such a way that the individual could without much remorse, sacrifice his worldly pleasures for gaining higher experiences. In Aquarius, the Moon will impart an unusual understanding and will restructure the psyche in such a manner that the individual may seem listless, lost to the ideas and visions of an imaginary character. At this stage, the psychic bridge is open more to the influences of the higher impulses. When the Moon is situated in Pisces at the middle circle, it enables the psyche of the person to acquire great tranquillity where every single ripple or vibration at the higher realm could be clearly registered. Given the favorable physical level conditions, the bridge between the highest level of one's existence and the physical level of activities could be effectively established. In considering the various influences of the Moon in different zodiacal signs in the middle circle, the centre of attention for prognostic purposes should be at the fluid condition of human consciousness which is perennially affected by numerous physical and non-physical influences. The Moon's position in different signs will indicate how this stream of consciousness in its immense depth and extension is structured so as to guide the course of human behaviour.

The Sun is the most powerful planet in a horoscope. On its disposition depends much of the progress and welfare of the individual. In the present approach to prognostication, the importance of the Sun is special in the sense that it always attempts to direct the individual to his destiny. Sometimes the middle principle or the bridge whose main function is to transmit this message, completely distorts it. It also happens that the central planet guiding the destiny of the individual takes him to such a course of action that the seeming retrograde situations ultimately enable him to proceed faster towards the goal. It is therefore very necessary that the role of the Sun in an individual's life is properly comprehended in order to rightly assess the significance of different aspects of his life-events. If the Sun in the first house in the outer circle is posited in Aries, it will always radiate powerful impulses impelling the individual towards his goal of self-knowledge. If the lower levels of existence is unharmoniously situated, there could be violent storms but the solar impulse must reach the individual and his life significantly reorganised accordingly. The zodiacal-mix of the three circles will only indicate the difficulties or helpfulness of the intervening forces.

The Sun in Taurus indicates that the powerful voice indicating the fruitlessness of sensual involvements will impress the middle circle, and in case the Moon is not well attuned to this message, the individual will have to be prepared for some stress and strain. In Gemini, the Sun will send its message in intelligent language so that the mid-principle of the individual is activated and he begins to see the wisdom and reasonableness of what the soul of the individual wants him to follow. In Cancer, the Sun's message will be to understand one's worldly obligations but not to get immersed in it. Destroy your personal affiliations without the world realising that you are neglecting your social obligations. In Leo, the Sun will make the individual extremely self-centred: the message is that— "You are the God." In case the individual could rightly, in all his humility, which can happen if he is spiritually evolved, comprehend the message, it will lead him to glory. Otherwise, the strain of the impulse may be unbearable, often leading to nervous breakdown.

When the Sun is in Virgo and it synchronises with the Ascendant, the individual will be capable of getting mysterious knowledge of the universal spirit pervading every event of life. It will demand that the individual gives up all his sense of personal attachments. In Libra, the Sun will send a very disturbing message. The individual will be surrounded by undesirable situations and the individual will feel that he is missing something precious in life which he is unable to comprehend. A kind of veil of ignorance, a shadow of illusion will intensify around him and his soul will weep from the core of his being and he will not know whereform that sorrowful voice is coming. In Scorpio, the Sun will send the message of universal truths which will vaguely impel him to search for these, but his physical and psychic bridge may determine whether he could understand and follow it. When Sagittarius is the zodiacal sign in which the Sun is placed, it will enable the individual to draw upon the experiences of his past which would easily enable him to listen to the voice of his conscience. There will be an innate understanding of the fact that the voice of the conscience has strength and its own rationale which must be listened to and respected. In Capricorn, the Sun will have difficulties in making his message heard and appreciated by the individual. The voice will demand very high level of morality and sacrifice which may seem difficult to follow unless the individual has been prepared for it for the last few lives. When the personal vanity of the individual is not permitted to blossom, the individual at the physical level may feel his life disintegrating, but in this dissolution, there will be the seed for fresh realignments of a permanent character. In Aquarius, the demand of the Sun will require the individual to give up everything that belongs to his personal self, thus completely identifying himself with the universal spirit. Whether he could fulfil the challenge and meet the demand or not would depend upon the disposition of the conditions and the forces generated at the middle level and the physical level of his being. When the Sun is in Pisces and it occupies the Ascendant in the outer circle, there will be the inner urge for complete dedication to the Supreme and full surrender of all personal considerations at the altar of the Universal Spirit. In case the individual is able to adjust and arrange his personal life to obey this inner compulsion, there could be peace and harmony in his life. He will feel his destiny fulfilled.

On the lines suggested above, it could be helpful if the disposition of all planets at all the three levels is properly delineated, but even in the absence of such detailed evaluation, it may be possible to get a glimpse of one's wider life's perspective. Hence sage Parasara emphasised the importance of the *Sudarshan Chakra*. The method of drawing conclusions can very briefly be indicated on the basis of Chart 1 given earlier. This chart as indicated above, pertains to Gautam Buddha which illustrates some of the suggestions made above. In this case, the Ascendant in the innermost circle representing the physical life conditions pertains to the zodiacal sign Cancer. The life-force operating at his physical level symbolised by Cancer shows immense possibilities of extension and development of sympathetic sensibilities. Cancer-born persons play the role of the vehicle and as such will surrender themselves to the circumstances and let the events mould them. Further, Cancer is capable of reflecting the highest glory of God, of achieving and assuming the noblest form of divine manifestation, and of sacrificing every form of personal egotism at the altar of the higher triad, yet it is a fully individualised sign with full awareness of what it does. In this way, on the physical plane Gautam Buddha was well equipped to undertake serious penance for fulfilling his mission if such a need arose. The Moon was in Libra which created much trial. At the middle or the *kama-manasic* level he was confronted with every kind of psychological obstacles. Even during the last hours of his final trial before he could attain final enlightenment of *Nirvana,* he had to wage a war against *Mara* which represented the past physical proclivities, including attachment in the form of his wife Yashodhara. But the inner voice represented by the outer circle was invincible. The exalted Sun itself could not be resisted by any other force but in the present case it was supported by Mars in its own sign providing enormous courage and strength to the voice of the higher principle. Jupiter in a friendly house gave much spiritual support and purity of intention. Venus providing sensibility and sensitivity and rulership of the Moon-sign at the middle level contributed its own might to the Sun. Saturn, the planet of *Nirvana,* is not less significant in this position. Thus the highest principle in the case of Gautam Buddha was very powerful, becoming almost irresistible. The difficulties raised by the middle principle or the middle psychic bridge were overcome and made to operate as a bridge between the highest impulse and the physical level of existence; thanks to the placement of Venus. The tenth house is also very significant in the present case. His purpose of birth was the very fulfillment of his higher principle as the Sun was in his tenth house. The tenth sign from his Ascendant in the outer circle was Capricorn, signifying the universalisation of his life-essence. The three zodiacal signs in the Ascendant – trinity represented by Cancer, Libra and Aries are all placed at a particular angle from one another. Libra moreover was the fourth sign from Cancer and seventh from the higher principle (Aries), thus enabling it (Moon) to reflect the impulse generated at that level very effectively and adequately. There are many other significant relationships in this chart which we would not discuss presently. Here we merely wish to emphasise that there is much in the application of *Sudarshan Chakra* approach in prognosticating conditions of inner life of a person. On the basis of this knowledge one could possibly effectively integrate various principles of one's life.

PART-III
Planetary Impulses

9

COMBINATIONS FOR POPULARITY

In one's life many things happen which cannot ordinarily be explained. Belief in karma, which in fact is the foundation of astrological prognostications, emphasises that every event in life has a cause. This causal relationship is visible in every single, whether important or seemingly minor, incident. We often find that there are certain persons who receive approbation sometimes resulting from seemingly unmerited action. Finding that there are individuals who have been toiling for years, have been living an ethical life, have been religious but without any recognition while others with quite contrary to these character traits enjoy much public approbation. Often the glaring evidence of someone's gross misdemeanour is disbelieved, while in another case, even when one has not committed any criminal act, he is believed to have done so. Such everyday common experiences create much psychological frustration. A careful understanding of one's astrological chart may give an insight in one's karmic influences to indicate whether the individual is entitled to such merited or unmerited popular esteem. This problem is difficult to categorise and explain, nonetheless, it is important in order to unravel one's psychological intricacies, or to provide the clue to one's psychological frustration.

What we are going to explore in the present context is not whether the result or the fruits of one's efforts commensurate or otherwise with the toil one has made. In the present case, we are also not delving into the degree of eminence one will attain in life. What we are trying to study can to some extent, (though it may not be very correct to say so) be considered as the chances of one's getting or receiving 'unmerited' praise. It will not exactly be the 'luck' factor because it will be different from what we are going to discuss. For example, let us assume that someone has written an article which has been published in an ordinary journal. In an ordinary situation, the writer may be justified in receiving some consideration (recognition or monetary compensation) for the fact that his article has been published but if people go on talking that so and so is an important writer whose articles are published in eminent journals and so praise him or her, it is undue or unmerited approbation. Take another case. Someone has given a paltry donation to a poor person without undergoing any hardship on his own, but his renown as a great philanthropic person spreads far and wide. This would be another case of unmerited renown. Another case could be slightly different. Supposing a person attracted by the physical charm of a woman, goes to her house for satisfying his personal psychological craving, but the family relations attribute this visit to the person's great concern for the welfare of the other family members. Such a reaction is based on unmerited popularity of the person.

Such events occur in everyday life. Some persons are accorded unmerited regard, placed charitable interpretation at their conduct, and awarded praise and respect out of proportion with what they have been reasonably entitled. This factor is very important in cases of those who wish to take up political activities or even employment in popular movies, though in every walk of life it forms an important factor in formulating one's social relationships and understanding other's reaction to him. If one is not gifted with such possibilities of popular esteem, one should behave stoically, act with belief in karma expecting that the proper fruit of one's efforts must accrue to him. Unmerited recognition or reward is in fact not unmerited but that is the consequence of the individual's past actions whose results he or she is reaping in the present life. The action which has given him recognition, though popularly attributed as a cause for the fructification of it, is merely a channel for the same.

Such recognition though not directly (and apparently) the result of one's efforts or at least not commensurate with and proportionate to the quantum of toil put in, yet is a reflection of 'Divine Spark' inherent in the individual whose some aspect has been ignited due to past efforts which presently has become ripe. This Divine Spark in astrological context can be deciphered by the disposition of the Sun. Moon being a reflection of the Sun, its planetary position as an indicator of the reflective potential of this Divine Spark would also to a great extent be important in the present context. There would however be some differences between the two. Moon being an agent of the Sun's glory would be more active in carrying the glory than the Sun itself, for the latter does not have to beat its own drum, so to say. When the Sun is active, the recognition would have an element of awe in it, but with Moon it would be all glory and the element of popularity *par excellence*. The individual ego, which is greatly represented by the Ascendant and its lord is also important. When the individual strives, he strives to express his individuality, or the essence of Divine Spark latent in him. Ordinarily when the Ascendant or its lord is concerned, the element of one's toil is important but the popularity is not necessarily only due to it. In the present context, Sun, Moon and the Ascendant and/ or its lord must come in contact with that power which enables them to draw from the world at large, or from the society the necessary response to applaud the shining glory in the individual. That factor comes from Jupiter.

Jupiter has special contribution to make in everyone's life. It radiates the influence which is like the spring wind enabling each individual to express and develop powers latent in him. The Supreme Essence of God has decreed special line of unfoldment for each entity. Even when he receives adulation, it aims at directing the individual to proceed on his special line of unfoldment. God always shines through the special line of individual's growth and development. Thus even in those cases where the praise or the approbation is based on not so sound ground, that should be considered as God's incentive for the person to grow on that line of unfoldment. When Jupiter adds its strength and influence to the individual, it enables the individual to blossom into luxuriance on his special ray.

When an individual is born under Aries, the influence of Jupiter on the Ascendant, Sun or the Moon will make it possible for him to be considered as a person who has original thoughts and special inspiration to impart to the world. Under such an influence, people may feel that the individual is very intelligent, often more intelligent than what he is. People will consider him an original thinker and very well connected. These impressions will create a special aura around the person.

With Taurus as the Ascendant, the individual will generally be considered as an important philanthropist, who is always willing to help others. In fact, this may not be the actual trait of the person, but he will be considered so. The person will be considered very rich, capable of enjoying life. He may be considered a social elite.

When Gemini is the Ascendant, the individual will have great repute as a very efficient person with a sharp intellect and trying to help his relations and friends. Such a person will often be skilful in concealing his real intentions and actual situations. To his admirers, he will appear as a person of correct behaviour and very understanding temperament.

With Cancer as the Ascendant, the specific condition that has been indicated above, will make the individual appear as a person of great integrity of character, well meaning in his actions and behaviour and having much concern for his family relations. Such persons are even considered parochial and narrow-minded to some extent, but his pious nature, docile temperament, and intuitive faculties are well spoken of.

When Leo becomes the Ascendant, the public approbation of the person centres around three characteristics − he is considered an individual of great principles in life, a person who is open fisted and whose sympathy extends much beyond his personal circle of friends and relatives. He may be considered as a person who is very intellectual, learned and spiritually developed, but these will be less important than the former three characteristics.

With Virgo as the Ascendant, the individual will have a large number of sympathisers who would be willing to consider him as a martyr; a person who has suffered much in his life; a person who has had such adverse conditions in life that he has not been able to develop his own personality. There will always appear an aroma of helpfulness in his activities and responses.

With Libra as the Ascendant, there is a danger that the approbation may take the form of slander. There is every likelihood of his being considered a selfish person. His seeming quietitude may be misconstrued as a facade to hide his motives.

Those persons who have Scorpio as the Ascendant have the special quality of concealing their vile nature and selfish proclivities. These persons will be considered as very righteous, ethical, benevolent and of high-class society. In fact, there is a possibility that they would in their daily life be quite the contrary. Nonetheless, the public and the society will flock around such a person and will like to do his biddings expecting much favour from him though the hope for consideration may never come forth.

When Sagittarius is the Ascendant, the individual under the above combination will be renowned for his religious and occult attainments. He may even be considered gifted with sixth-sense and many persons would come to him for personal guidance. He will be esteemed as a very venerable person.

In the case of person with Capricorn as the Ascendant with Sun, Moon and Ascendant Lord in favourable aspect of Jupiter, his respectability will extol him as a very helpful person, always willing to sacrifice his personal convenience for the sake of others. People will not mind unfolding and revealing their personal and confidential problems to him in order to seek his guidance.

An Aquarius born person under the above combination will be considered more a mystic than a man of the world. His occult attainments and development of psychic faculties may be exaggerated. Under this main line of adulation, there could however be the general feeling of his being much attached to his close family circle.

When Pisces becomes the Ascendant, the individual's 'unmerited' quality would be that he has suffered much in life. He would be considered very capable, very moral, very religious but his intelligence has not found enough nurture. Such a person will be more pitied than what he deserved.

In the above cases, some indications are given of the possible type of 'respectability' the individual will enjoy but these are of very general nature. In each individual horoscope one will have to apply the general rule in order to find out what are its special features which his ego wishes to cultivate. Sometimes it is the quality which has been exaggerated so that the individual is encouraged to imbibe them, while on another occasion it is the accentuation of a very minor fault so that he feels sorry for such public remarks and tries to overcome his shortcomings. In the above combination, one may note that Jupiter's aspect is preferred than its association with the planets suggested.

In order to illustrate how this combination operates, it may not be possible to take the example for each ascendant to show how the combination operates, but one may illustrate some points on the basis of following two horoscopes. For obvious reasons, we shall not give full details of the charts. The basic characteristics which suffice to illustrate the operation of astrological influences could be considered sufficient for the present purpose.

Chart I belongs to a reputed cine-personality. Neither the education of the person has been very exceptional, nor the personal qualities have been so much important as to deserve much lofty status. But the Ascendant and the Ascendant Lord both are aspected by Jupiter from the ninth house. Exalted Moon in the fifth house is also fully aspected by Jupiter. These aspects have made the person greatly renowned, attracting persons of all walks of life to him and many persons have been seeking personal help from the person concerned.

		Moon	
Rahu			Sun Mer.
Asc. Sat. (R)		CHART I	Venus Ketu
			Jup. Mars

Chart II belongs to a person who is not much affluent and the level of his education is also not very high. In this case Jupiter from the tenth house aspects Moon in the sixth house. Without commenting upon other aspects of the chart, simply because the aspect of Jupiter on Moon is effective, the individual is considered a great authority on astrology. It is always interesting to see a large number of persons who may not like to associate with the astrologer

Ascdt / Mars			Rahu
	CHART II		Sun Venus Mer.
Jup (R)			
Ketu		Sat.	Moon

publicly and socially yet desirous of getting his 'readings' on their horoscopes, meet him frequently because his interpretations always made them satisfied. It is however another matter whether he has an indepth knowledge of astrology.

From these two illustrations, it may be emphasised that the aspect of Jupiter on Moon, Sun, the Ascendant and its lord, or of Moon on Sun or the Ascendant Lord will always make the individual enjoy a kind of respectability for which there may not be enough justification (It does not imply that in all cases, the laudation is unfounded). What is emphasised is that their popularity with whatever personality defects, will be extraordinary.

10

PLANNED PARENTHOOD

Astrological savants have developed elaborate methods by which the future of the forthcoming baby can be predicted in great detail. Ancient scriptures carry many instances when copulation was arranged for begetting specific type of offspring. Working on the same principles, it is possible even in modern times to plan the type of children one would like to have. This would be an application of astrological science for applied objectives. Conscious efforts in this direction can indeed be a contribution towards building a better society. If we want to have efficient administrators, scientists and research workers, or enterprising industrialists, we have to consciously begin working towards this goal.

There is a popular adage in some parts of India which says that the offspring thrive in life as a result of the meritorious deeds of parents. Those who are unaware of the occult background of family relationships in determining the type of egos born in any specific case, may be amused at this adage. It was not merely a chance occurrence that Prince Siddhartha was born only to such parents as Suddhodhana and Maya, or Rama was born to ethical Dasaratha and Kaushalya; Jesus Christ was born in a pious carpenter's family. In nature, there is no favouritism and astrology proves that the minutest events in everyday life are intricately linked with cosmic evolution. The relationship between parents and the child is not relegated to fortuitous circumstances.

Astrologically, the ninth house, the tenth house as well as the Sun in many ways indicate the main features of one's father. The fourth house and the Moon have links with mother. These houses are significators of many other aspects of one's life. The ninth house determines the past meritorious deeds of the native. It determines the general approach to life, one's association with sages and saints; the tenth house reflects the profession, the way the individual would go about in this world, his eminence or otherwise. The Sun represents the soul of the person. There has to be some relationship between the father of the child and his profession, otherwise these predictions would be faulty.

Let us illustrate the point with a few examples. Chart I pertains to a boy born on 10 September 1954. The father belonged to an ordinary landed family from Punjab and was very well-off financially. The educational level of the father was not very high. He served the government in subordinate positions. He, however, devoted much of his spare time in social service. The mother was psychologically extrovert and physically very healthy. Soon after their marriage, the parents became very desirous of an issue. The father was very ambitious and he wanted to provide for his child all that he felt he was denied by way of education, social position, and the means of day-to-day conveniences. He wanted that the child should not suffer any psychological inferiority or neglect. The wife also was eager to have a baby as quickly as possible so that she could have social recognition and the prestige of motherhood prevalent in her social circle. Within less than a year of their marriage she began visiting temples and offering prayers for begetting a child. Neither the father, nor the mother had any definite idea of the type of baby they wanted to have except the fact that they wanted a 'good' son for whom they could take best care. The child was born with important stars as it would be seen from Chart I.

The Ascendant Lord powerful Sun is in its own sign. Mercury was exalted and placed as lords of eleventh and second houses in second. Venus, the lord of the tenth house posited in its own house is in the third. Saturn, the lord of the seventh in exaltation occupies the third house. Jupiter the lord of the fifth house is in the twelfth house in exaltation. Mars, a *Yoga Karaka* for the native is in a trine house, i.e. the fifth house. Evidently, this is a powerful horoscope. The child was god's gift, a reward of sincere prayers offered to the gods. The ego born was confident of suitable opportunity for its karmic unfoldment.

			Ketu
	CHART I (10 Sept. 1954)		Jupiter
Moon			Ascdt Sun
Mars Rahu		Venus Sat	Mercury

When the child grew up, the parents provided him the best affectionate and protective care. The child did not feel neglected but education was his weakest point. He could not, inspite of best provision of schooling facilities, secure for himself any worthwhile grade. Extracurricular activities were his forte. His personal character was flawless; his social contacts were so remarkable that even late Sanjay Gandhi, the son of late Indira Gandhi, used to come to his house. The native finally turned out to be earning much money by hard work, caring for his parents and family members, and having the most affectionate regard for any one who cared for him but he was deadly dangerous for those who tried to ill-treat him. He did not enter politics but in his personal life, he was gem of a person, evolving and reaping karmic lessons of his life in a cheerful manner.

In this case, the parents' openness to have a baby for which they had tried to provide the best that was possible for them, suffering the denial of their personal comforts for the satisfaction of the child, earned them the right to have some ego over a son who was very powerful and cared for them.

Chart II is another horoscope of a child whose parents were also very remarkable in many ways. The father was educated though not much, and the mother was also of the same type. Both, the father and the mother were very practical in their life and were well balanced in their relationships. There was no psychological imbalance in them. They were realistic, dutiful, and sincere in their job. They wanted to be good well-caring parents, and important members of the community. They did not neglect any human relationship. They were married in their thirties, not early as was the case with the previous example (Chart I). Soon after their marriage, they did not consider sex as the primary concern in a husband-wife relationship. They took the marriage as a social obligation in which the birth of a healthy baby played an important part. The resulting child born within a couple of years of their married life, was eagerly expected not only by the parents, but also by the grandparents as well as by their friends. The child was born with the stars as given in Chart II.

Rahu Moon			
Jupiter	CHART II (19 Sept. 1986)		Ascdt
Mars	Saturn	Venus	Sun Ketu Merc.

The Ascendant Lord Moon is placed in the ninth house; the tenth lord and a *Yoga Karaka;* Mars is in sixth house. These features gave special strength to the Chart. The Sun in third house, a house where it gets special power is associated with exalted Mercury, while Venus the lord of the eleventh house is in the fourth house which pertains to itself. The chart revolves around the Sun-Moon axis. There is no affliction of *Kala Sarpa Yoga.* During the very first few months of the birth, the child began attracting attention of the family relations and others. Not being a problem child, already the parents and the relations were quite proud of him and they showered much affection. The child established a greater and firmer bond between the various constituents of the family tree. It is expected that the child on becoming older would be an efficient executive, unhesitatingly taking bold decisions which could be effective. Not specially committed to any 'ism' either in religion or

in life, he would forge ahead like a very efficient and useful
member of the community in which he would live. The association
of nodes with the luminaries also showed that the present was an
important karmic birth of the child.

Another example of a child whose chart is exceptional in many
ways would show the requirements for the birth of unusual babies.
The Chart III pertains to a boy who was born almost decade after
the first child. He had an elder sister who was also very much a
darling baby of her parents. The parents belonged to higher class of
the society. Both sides of the parents were connected with legal
profession – one grandfather was a reputed advocate while another,
the father of the mother was a judge in the High Court. Both the
parents were loved children of their parents. There was no financial
strain on any of the families, they had all that could be desired.

Rahu Jupiter Venus	Sun Mercury	Mars	
	CHART III (5 May 1987)		Moon
	Sat (R)	Ascdt	Ketu

The personal life of the father of the child was scrupulously
pure. When the father of the child was conceived, his parents were
already vegetarians; the father of the boy never wanted to embellish
his body with foul food. He had been highly educated, possessed a
doctorate degree and was a professor of science at a college. His
house was a kind of science laboratory itself, but inspite of his so
much concern for his own subject, he never neglected his wife, his
daughter, or his parents. He served his parents with so much
devotion that his five brothers could not find anything to do for the
old parents. He had acquired managerial skill to such perfection that
the entire city where he resided was willing to follow him and

accept his command. The students community, the police, the public, the rotarians, all had tremendous regard for him. His wife was not ambitious, but wanted to be a good partner to him and an ideal mother to her child. When they had a baby girl, they did not show any frustration and bestowed all their love and affection to her. The daughter in turn responded lovingly to all the family relations. She became very smart and turned out to be a bright student in her class. At this stage was born the prodigy son whose future will (and should) be watched with care and attention.

The child (Chart III) is born under Libra Ascendant where involutionary impulse of materialistic penetration ends and evolutionary course begins. There has to be a unique equipoise in the person born under this sign. The Ascendant Lord Venus in exaltation is placed with Jupiter which occupies its own sign. The togetherness of the lords of sixth and eighth houses gives a kind of *Viparitha Raja Yoga.* The lord of the ninth house; Mercury, is placed with exalted Sun both of which are aspecting the Ascendant. Moon in its own sign is in the tenth house aspected only by Jupiter from its own house. Six planets are clustered around his exalted Sun. Saturn in retrogression tends to proceed to its exaltation sign though for some special reasons it does not want to afflict the Ascendant and is aspected in a special way by Mars placed in the eighth house.

It is likely that the child would follow the footsteps of his father and turn out to be a noted life-science experimentalist. All the planets are connected with life-giving energy. Moon is the planet which receives life-energy from Sun and directs the same for the growth and development of plants and animals on this Earth and this planet in the tenth house must involve the child in such a pursuit when he grows up. Being aspected by Jupiter in a powerful way, specially with its association with Rahu (which gets special strength in the sixth house, and has drunk the nectar which was special prerogative only of the devas, while Moon itself is placed in tenth house), must make the child, when he grows up, intimately connected with this aspect of life. Sun around which most of the planets are clustered would make him some kind of provider of energy in many different areas of life. Saturn and Mars, both enjoying special portfolios and being intimately connected with life-energy again, may involve the child in his actual life as a discoverer of certain important laws relating to life and how it works in the world around him.

But, the point we are making is not about the future of the child or that of the parents. What we are endeavouring to show is that the parents, by regulating their own personal life can make the birth of specially gifted children became a reality. They moulded their personal life in a pattern that the prospective prodigies could find such a 'den' helpful for their own karmic unfoldment. The last couple was not looking forward for any more issues. Their contentment itself was a great attraction for the evolved egos. This kind of contentment, with their utter indifference as to their having or not having another child, assured the unborn ego that if it condescended to take its birth in the womb of this mother, it could have a better possibility for pursuing its mission in life.

One would have noted another warning signal in all these cases. Even Lord Buddha as well as Rama were not unmitigated bliss for their parents. The paternal sadness related with their universal glory which pervaded far and wide is universally known. The same rule applies from the highest to the lowest. Sometimes, among the parents there is also a tendency to seek their own fulfillment through their children. The parents of Chart I suffered a pang that their child did not become much educated and 'respected' in the worldly social sense. The parents of Chart II had to take note of Rahu with Moon and Ketu with Sun. The combination is bound to affect the parents' happiness on account of the child sometime in their own life. In Chart III, the child may have to stand on his own because very few persons could ever help him. His Ascendant is flanked by two malefic elements, and his seventh house with Sun in it would also give a hard lesson to his close associates. There is a natural law with regard to these evolved egos that they look for fertile soil to grow, and very efficient gardeners to tend them with utter indifference to their own personal likes and dislikes. This rule makes it imperative that the parents desirous of evolved egos as their progeny, must prepare themselves to undergo many hardships on their account.

The above examples show that the parents when they orient their own life in such a way that it has affinity with evolved egos, then such egos could take their births in such families. This needs careful preparations for years. Both physical and psychological preparations are necessary. Social life of the person as well as material affluence do not have any special importance in this regard. One has to think of the special requirements of the future baby and begin adapting a way of life which could be sympathetic to the ninth and tenth houses of the expected child, and to the disposition of Sun and Moon. A father whose own mind is polluted cannot ordinarily beget a child who is calm and satisfied; a father who is basically mean and dishonest cannot hope to beget a child of exalted disposition. We need happy, contended and sympathetic family life for promising progeny to take birth in them.

11

PROFESSION AND MARRIAGE

An important principle of Parashari Astrology* is to examine the characteristics of a *bhava* by examining the nature of the house situated from it at the same distance as it is from the Ascendant. It implies that the nature of the fifth house will be considerably influenced by the nature of the ninth house which is the fifth house from the fifth house itself. While considering the effect of the tenth house, in the same way, one may do well to examine the relationship of the seventh house with it. But this principle of astrological examination is often overlooked particularly as far as the tenth house is concerned. Most of the aspects of one's profession are determined by studying the nature of the tenth house itself.

The influence of the seventh house on one's profession is considerable. The nature of the tenth house is difficult to decipher. The karma of an individual is not necessarily the channel through which he earns his livelihood. Karma comprises the whole gamut of activities which bring the individual in contact with the world outside him. Professional success or failure is not decided merely by assessing the results of his actual efforts. A person may have musical talents while he may also have a sharp brain for scientific investigations. One of these, or both, or may be there is an entirely

---

*Classical principles of Vedic Astrology based on the treatise attributed to Sage Parashar.

different source of income. In some cases, it is also possible that an individual is a better musician, but his renown as a scientist is greater. Another aspect of professional activity is the extent of one's renown or discredit. An individual may be more cruel than Hitler, he may commit murders more cold bloodedly, without any ideal (whether laudable or ignoble) with much less organising capacity and nationalistic spirit, yet Hitler is denounced by a much larger number of persons over a larger number of years. The expertise in any line of activity does not necessarily ensure that the individual will be considered by the people at large as important in that field. These are some of the considerations with which Astrology is as much concerned as the mere prediction of the line of pursuit which could provide him his daily bread. For such an examination, the astrologer has to cast his vision extensively. The nature and characteristics of the seventh house have much interesting light to shed on any comprehensive study of one's profession.

There is a popular saying that behind every successful man there is a woman. This is true even astrologically. There is however a snag in this statement, because the influence of the woman is not always very glorifying. Often the meaning of the word 'woman' itself has to be understood in the sense in which the seventh house in an astrological chart represents her. Leaving aside much of the abstruse significance of the seventh house, one can assume that this house represents the female counterpart of the individual– *Ardhangini**. The English word 'the better half' signifying the wife has something which needs serious consideration for the welfare and growth of the man. The seventh house stands for one's wife but wife, astrologically speaking, stands for the other part of one's own self. In the present context it stands for the external conditions presented to the individual for his expression of the self, that which is latent in him. How far the world provides adequate opportunities for the expression of those attributes represented by the tenth house is indicated by the seventh house. Restrictions or the possibilities for the expression of the inherent qualities are signified by the seventh house. In a way it is the significator of the possible path, the

---

*Ardhangini—meaning the half-female body, the full composite man being symbolised in its completeness as the pictorial image of Lord Shiva comprising the half as male figure and the other half as the female form together known as *Ardhanarishwara*.

channels through which the various proclivities of the individual can find expression. All these are abstract and difficult to describe. Therefore, the relationship between the tenth and the seventh house may be first attempted through some examples before enunciating the general principle.

The first horoscope (Chart I) pertains to Sri Aurobindo. The tenth house contains the Moon in Sagittarius along with Saturn. No planet aspects this house. The seventh house has Virgo sign whose lord Mercury is posited in the sixth house along with the Sun and Venus. Saturn aspects the seventh house; no other planet aspects the seventh house and the sixth house is also not aspected by any planet. The life of Sri Aurobindo is well known. In the external world, he is known as a spiritual guide who has helped a large number of people. His organisation, the Aurobindo Ashram, is internationally acclaimed to be of a very high order. Personally, Sri Aurobindo began his life as a very special child in a very highly cultured British-type Anglicised Indian family with brilliant scholarship. His literary fame spread at a very early stage. As an administrator, even when he was at Baroda serving the native ruler, his dignity and respectability was acclaimed as regal and exceptional. As a revolutionary, he was more feared by his adversary—the British government, than looked down upon for specific charges framed against him. He was a nationalist and a moralist. His fame as a literary writer, even without considering his eminence as a revolutionary or as an occultist, mystic and a yogi was of extraordinary order. His relationship with 'Mother,' a French lady, is universally acclaimed as of untainted relationship; his

Ascdt		Rahu	
	CHART I Sri Aurobindo		Mars Jupiter
			Sun Venus Mercury
Saturn Moon	Ketu		

chastity and morality had ever been seer-like, at par with ancient *rishis*. His whole approach to yogic philosophy had been 'supramental' without decrying traditional rituals. Even Astrology was held in very high esteem by him. These are some of the reactions of the world to him based on what he was known for, by the public.

By considering merely the nature and disposition of the tenth house, it is difficult to relate his 'profession' with what he is known as. One does not have to stretch this point very far, because there must have been some ingredient in the tenth house for these; otherwise, he would not have succeeded in achieving them. But what we intend to indicate here is, that the world as it understands and feels about his profession, or his work—the reaction of the world to his activities—could probably be better appreciated by relating his profession with his seventh house as well. Saturn and the Moon posited in the tenth house can provide enough justification for his occult attainments, very disciplined mind but what gave him the flight of his imagination, or his superb administrative and organising capacity, or his ability to guide others? What gave stability to the establishment of his Ashram?

Virgo the sign of his seventh house is primarily a psychological sign. It is also linked with latent faculties of the Cosmic Man suggesting subordination of the physical plane activities to the influence of supramental influences. Virgo is said to represent *Shakti* (Power) personified by *Mahamaya* who represented the six primary forces in Nature. The primary impulse of occult attainments aroused by Saturn-Moon combination in Sagittarius could fructify well under the favourable channellising efforts of Virgo. The planetary ruler of Virgo namely Mercury is placed twelfth from it (Virgo) which implies the decay of earthliness of its impulses and the arousal of other-worldliness which was admirably well applicable in the present case. The association of Mercury with Venus, the planet of harmony and sensitivity, has not only enabled him to express his sublime experiences in poetic language (*Savitri,* for example) but also to bring complete synthesis between this *Anandamaya Kosa, Vijnanamaya Kosa,* and *Manomaya Kosa* thus enabling him to establish an immediate contact with others on higher planes of existence and to vividly stabilise the images on lower vehicles of his own. This is what his immediate disciples thought him capable of.

The world considered him a very strict disciplinarian. His disciples thought him very understanding (a result of Mercury-Venus association) though a very hard task master (Mercury-Sun association). As an administrator, both at the Ashram and at Baroda, the Sun's impact was reflected clearly in his administrative efficiency, organising capacity and nearness to the seat of power. An important aspect of Aurobindo's life was his defiance of authority which is not clearly expressed by a mere examination of his tenth house, but his debilitated Mars with exalted Jupiter, has given righteous indignation which resulted in the present case as dauntless pursuit of nationalist activities, later on turned into spiritual conquest. The relationship with Mother with a mystic aroma around the relationship untainted by any sexual relationship either overt or covert was exceptional. It can be explained by going deeper in the impact of the sixth lord associated with the seventh and eighth lords in the sixth house and functioning at the supramental level. This mystic bond is revealed by the position of Saturn and its association with Moon, the life-giving planet energising mind. What one wishes to convey in the present case is that the inherent impulse indicated by the disposition of the tenth house has been reflected to the people at large only through the filter of the seventh house disposition.

Let us take another example. Pandit Jawaharlal Nehru was a multifaced personality. His profession or avocation has throughout his life remained very vague and undefined, specially when we wish to discover and establish his means of livelihood. Chart II belongs to Pandit Nehru. His Ascendant lord Moon posited in the Ascendant

			Rahu
			Ascdt Moon
	CHART II Pt. J.L. Nehru		Sat (R)
Jupiter Ketu	Sun	Venus Mercury	Mars

itself, directly aspects the seventh house which is untenanted by any planet; it is also unaspected by any other planet except Moon, the Ascendant lord. His tenth house is aspected by its lord Mars located in the third house Virgo, by Venus from the fourth house, Libra with Mercury, having been posited in its own sign, and by Jupiter from the sixth house, Sagittarius posited there with Ketu. Venus and Mercury, which are directly aspecting the tenth house, their enemy's house, themselves are aspected by retrograde Saturn posited in its enemy's house. But Saturn happens to be the lord of Pandit Nehru's seventh house.

In a way, this chart is an example of many adverse combinations, ordinarily persuading the astrologer to predict a very miserable life and unhappy experiences. The Ascendant lord suffers from *Sakat Yoga*, an unhappy combination; the Ascendant and its lord are afflicted by *Papakartari Yoga*, by being flanked by two malefic elements; the fourth house indicating the comfort of mother, house, peace and quietitude of heart and emotion, also suffers from *Papakartari Yoga;* and Jupiter has been afflicted by the association of Ketu and the aspect of Mars, a malefic planet posited in an enemy's house. In spite of such adverse combinations, Pandit Nehru rose to dizzy heights and was proficient in many ways.

The world knows Pandit Nehru as a person with a very broad heart who believed in freedom in the widest sense. He was a nationalist not because the British were bad, but because political liberty for every country was preferred. He appreciated personal freedom and freedom of one's thought and action because only such an impulse could lead to fuller expansion of one's personality. Whatever he did was irrespective of his own status, position or office, and it was for the cause of freedom. He is known to the world as a person who was politically oriented. His whole life was dedicated for national and international political activities. But in literary field also, he made contribution which in its own right could make him outstanding. The profession of Pandit Nehru till he became the Prime Minister of India had been unstable; he did not have any firm basis of personal income except some royalty that he received fairly late in his life. As a barrister-at-law, he was not of any consequence. Inspite of these uncertain and adverse factors, he was always affluent. His behaviour and actions were non-traditional; personally he was not very happy; he was imprisoned and bereft of personal conforts of family life, yet he was a person whose spirit could not be curbed and he was a very difficult person to live with.

The tenth house of Pandit Nehru could to a limited extent explain all the various traits of his personality. If we consider this house as the store-house of the possibilities to be developed further, we may accept that the potential is the tenth house while the seventh house is the channel for its expression. The inherent qualities do not flower in life unless the seventh house provides adequate support for the same. The seventh house has Capricorn as the sign owned by Saturn retrograde in the sign of Sun. The primary influence of Saturn is to restrict the physical in order to arouse the philosophical, abstract, humanitarian impulses. The lord of the ninth house, Jupiter, posited in its Mooltrikona sign Sagittarius aspects Saturn, the lord of seventh house. The dreary family life and his non-traditional approach to family relations and the people at large which was the central core of his life, and the urge towards freedom of spirit which seemed to him restricted in several kind of bondages, arose from the special disposition of Saturn under the influence of Jupiter. It is the Jupiterian influence on Saturn which did not tarnish the image of Pandit Nehru inspite of his non-traditional approach to sex and family life. It is also responsible for making him a popular hero. The lord of the seventh in the second made him intimately dependent on his relations. His family relations received much reward and help from him so much so that there were hushed tones of nepotism under his government, and his growth in politics was also greatly dependent upon different kinds of assistance rendered to him by his family members. The lord of the seventh in the Sun-sign (Leo) made him a difficult person to live with. There have been stories about his colleagues and relations who had complained that Nehru was a good person for the public but those who had to come in daily intercourse with him could not and did not feel well-at-ease with him. His father, mother, wife, could not feel happy in their relationships with Nehru as they could have been with any other person (in similar situations). The Moon's aspect on the seventh house would wash out all his misbehaviours, specially because of its placement in Cancer, its own house. One of the greatest assets of Pandit Nehru was the response to him of the people at large, the masses, which made his 'avocation' fruitful. This could happen because of the Moon's aspect on the seventh house. His fame depended to a great extent on this situation. The best influence of Mercury and Venus fully aspecting the tenth house from a position of strength (specially when Venus produced *Malavya Yoga*) did not give Pandit Nehru a steady job either of a writer or of law though these potentials could express themselves only within the parameter sanctified b the seventh house disposition (especially due to the relationship between the lord of the seventh house Saturn in retrogression fully aspected by the ninth lord Jupiter). He made use of his law-degree sometime for national and social purpose.

Chart III is another instance of a horoscope whose tenth house could reveal the potential of the avocation or the way of functioning in the world whereas the seventh house conditions suggested the extent of its fructification; the tenth showed the possibility whereas the seventh house showed its actualitisation. The chart pertains to Dr. Rajendra Prasad[1], the first President of the Indian Republic. The tenth house has Venus in Libra unaspected by any planet whereas the seventh house has Cancer. The Moon, the lord of the seventh house, is posited with retrograde Saturn in the fifth house; the seventh house is fully aspected by Mars, the lord of the fourth and the eleventh posited along with Mercury, the lord of sixth (and ninth houses). The Ascendant lord Saturn which happens to be the lord of the second house also aspects the seventh house.

Ketu		Moon Sat (R)	
	CHART III Dr. Rajendra Prasad		
Ascdt			Jupiter
Mars Mercury	Sun	Venus	Rahu

---

[1]Dr. B.V. Raman and Devakinandan Sinha give the Ascendant sign as Sagittarius, but V.A.K. Iyer has assigned Capricorn as true Ascendant sign to Dr. Prasad.

Dr. Rajendra Prasad had been a very promising advocate having a brilliant academic career. Joining the educational line as a professor, he subsequently joined the political movement and always worked with dedication, never wanting to come to the limelight though always willing to share any work of responsibility. Whatever the accomplishment of Dr. Rajendra Prasad, the world knew him as a pious and saintly man. He could perform thoroughly and meticulously whatever was entrusted to him. He could converse fluently in eight or nine languages, but the people at large did not recognise him as a linguist. He wrote several treatises on political issues. *India Divided* is one of his monumental works arguing out the follies of the division of India and upholding the cause of undivided country. The world did not even seem to have taken cognizance of his arguments on the issue. He was more Gandhian than many others who received kudos for their political achievements. He was very careful in taking initiatives even on crucial controversial matters, always careful as not to arouse public passion for the sides or for his views. The famous instance of his calling for studying in depth the Presidential powers as well as the study of the basic problems—traditional, social, economical and human with regard to Hindu Code Bill, can be remembered in the present context. Inspite of *Malavya Yoga,* his life had been a life of sacrifice, and this kind of sacrifice had put great strain on him, inhibited his personal emotions and desires, and restrictions on his family members.

Much of the enigma of his life can be clarified when we take the tenth from the tenth house as suggested above into consideration. The lord of the seventh house is Moon and Cancer is the sign of the zodiac of the seventh house. Cancer would give the quality of being at ease with diverse types of people and with widely differing spectrum of intellectual rays. The Ascendant lord in retrogression posited in Taurus is located with the seventh lord in a *trikona* house *viz.,* the fifth suggesting great harmony between him and the world at large; between him and his wife. Both were not of the same nature: his way of life was entirely different from that of the world in which he functioned. The people recognised the chasm existing between him and them but always held him in great respect. The seventh house was fully aspected by Mars, the lord of the eleventh and fourth posited along with Mercury, the lord of ninth (and sixth) showing great courage and initiative in working for the people. Whatever he did was much more influenced by his thought and past proclivities (*Poorvajanma Karma*) rather than by a sense of personal aggrandisement. The Ascendant lord Saturn also aspected the seventh house indicating great restrictions and sacrifice in his pursuit for the public activities. One may recall that all his professional and personal qualities and talents were offered at the service of the nation and the people at large. He never felt that his own accomplishments, his past legal or other academic qualifications should be given any recognition in assigning responsibilities to him. The tenth house with Libra sign gave him great equanimity, balance and poise for taking decisions. Venus therein provided the quality of sensitivity to the needs of the people; the seventh house disposition was indicative of what the world would consider his contribution to the world to be. Inspite of *Malavya Yoga* occurring in his tenth house signifying a well-developed physique, strong mind, wealth, happiness with children and wife, command over vehicles, clean sense-organs, renown and learned, he was almost a *sanyasi*. Undoubtedly much of the auspicious effects were correct in a theoretical sense but actually, inspite of these, Dr. Rajendra Prasad was personally a sad person: the seventh lord Moon in association with Saturn, the planet of constriction, could not but make him so.

Applying the principle to common people, the guidelines inferred from the above works out well. For example, let us examine Chart IV pertaining to a senior central government officer. The gentleman had a very difficult childhood. He obtained an ordinary postgraduate degree, entered government service in a subordinate

Sun Jupiter Venus	Ascdt	Rahu	
Mars Mercury	CHART IV		
	Saturn Ketu		Moon

position, was not well spoken of by his colleagues, but by sheer fortuitous circumstances rose to a senior position in the central government. From his chart, it could be seen that the lord of the tenth house, *viz.,* Saturn is posited in the eighth house along with Ketu which cannot be considered very auspicious. There is an exchange between the lords of the eleventh and the eighth which also is not very auspicious. The lord of the tenth has the full aspect of Jupiter located in its own house but from the twelfth house. These factors do not suggest a very happy future and a very high administrative or advisory status in the central government. But the enigma is resolved by examining the tenth from the tenth house. The lord of the seventh house *viz.,* Venus is exalted with Jupiter who is the lord of the ninth house and is posited in its own house. Both of these are with the Sun, the lord of an angular or trine house. There is a *Raja Yoga* also resulting from the association of a *kendra* lord with the lord of a trine house. In fact, this *yoga* is very strong because the planets concerned are quite strong, and the *yoga* is doubly reinforced. There is also *Gajakesari Yoga.* These combinations show that the administrative and advisory status are well within his reach because the aspect of Jupiter on the tenth lord has given the native the talents for the same while its association with the exalted seventh lord enabled him to rise high in this sphere. The association of the Sun with these planets strengthened these possibilities.

Chart V belongs to a person whose father died very early. Education of the native was neglected. He could somehow complete graduation. He did not have a job but was married, had several very

	Ascdt Mars		Rahu
	CHART V		Sun Venus Mercury
Jup (R)			
Ketu		Saturn	Moon

promising children. At one stage he got a job of teaching school children which was more in name than in actual practice. This however gave him a stable income. His respect in the society he lives was not of a very high order. He even suffered from many physical handicaps.

The lord of the tenth house is exalted in this case. The Ascendant lord is strong; Jupiter is posited in the tenth house and is strong specially when it is the lord of the ninth and is in retrogression. Rahu in the third is also considered favourable. Though Mercury and Venus are together with the Sun, yet they are not combust. Jupiter aspects the Moon. These are very favourable combinations to bestow good material position, but these inherent possibilities were greatly denied to the native. Apart from the meagre salary that he drew, he eked out his income by making astrological predictions and suggesting mantras and *tantras*. The position of Saturn in the seventh though exalted, restricted the fuller utilisation of his inherent talents. The aspect of Mars, the Ascendant lord but bereft of any benefic aspect reinforced the restrictive qualities of Saturn. Mars being the lord of his eighth house and having some influence on the lord of the tenth house and that also placed in the seventh though, it created many problems in his own marriage, also influenced his counselling on matters pertaining to occultism, *mantras* and *tantras*.

Chart VI, has great resemblance with the previous chart but the result is greatly different because of the change in the house positions. In this case the lord of the tenth house, Moon is exalted in the eighth house and is fully aspected by Jupiter though in

	Mars	Moon	Rahu
Jup (R)	CHART VI		Sun Venus
Ketu		Ascdt Saturn	Mercury

debilitation (which in some way may be argued to bestow *Neecha Bhanga Raja Yoga*). The Ascendant lord in the eleventh house cannot be considered adverse. It is a combination for financial prosperity. But its impact on the chart in reality has been very different. The person retired from the central government but not from any senior position. He was a very stable worker; his officers and superiors always felt that he was a capable person but the conditions had never been helpful for making him better placed.

He remained throughout his life unmarried. His personal character was above board. He had *Sasa Yoga* and *Ruchaka Yoga* but nothing has been perceptible which can be considered the result of these auspicious *yogas*. The placement of Mars has been very significant. The individual had been full of initiative; very loyal to his family members, to his friends, and to his office. The aspect of Saturn on Mars specially from an exaltation position gave him idealism but the seventh house not having any benefic aspect and only malefic aspects were related to this house, and made the native bereft of a wife, bereft of good official position and bereft of any opportunity to express the various literary, creative, advisory and administrative talents he possessed.

The above illustrations show that the problems in the tenth house require very intensive examination before meaningful conclusions for helpful counselling can be drawn. The nature of the tenth house does not restrict it merely to the prediction of one's avocation in the ordinary sense of the term. It signifies how the individual would like to express his abilities. It shows the talents which can be expressed as the individual begins to play his role in life. It shows the store house of capabilities in different areas of life in which the individual would have the possibility of developing. This shows the latent capabilities through which the individual could establish his rapport with the world outside him, the world external to himself. The tenth from the tenth house shows the extent of actualisation of the inherent potentialities. By examining the seventh house, the individual's chances for the success of the activities, the chances for the expression of his inherent faculties can be predicted. These however do not show the renown or otherwise which the individual may get during the process of actualisation of his inherent qualities, aptitudes and capabilities. For instance, whether the individual will have any musical talent will be studied in relation to the tenth house but whether he would have the possibility of developing his talents, whether the world at large will consider him fit enough to be a musician or not, would depend upon the disposition of the seventh house. Whether he will become famous as a musician or not will depend on other factors. The fame or otherwise of a person is more difficult to predict than the possibilities of expressing one's inherent qualities. Here, we merely wish to emphasise that the marriage of a person and the role of wife in one's development of inherent faculties are strongly linked together.

12

AVOCATION AND INCOME

The decision regarding anyone's profession is very complicated. The growing sophistication, technological and specialisation factors are very important in this regard. They have increased the number and type of business possibilities available at present which cannot be classified in a few limited categories. Presently there is also an interest in one's social and official status. The desire to know one's status, renown, income and wealth is becoming increasingly more and more pressing. The astrological texts have provided several clues to these aspects. Generally speaking, there is a growing tendency to bundle together the tenth and the eleventh houses in determining the profession, status and income of a person. This approach needs caution: the tenth house should be distinguished from the eleventh house. The tenth house is primarily concerned with popularity, renown and general relationship with the people and the society while the eleventh house is concerned with the income of the person. The manner in which the person functions, behaves, comes in contact with others is the area dealt with by the tenth house and what he gains by way of income, sociability and sensual gratifications are known by the eleventh house.

The classical texts have given many different items as signified by the tenth house. If one could recognise that these are mere symptoms of the central impulse generated by this house, much of the confusion in this regard could be eliminated. Such words as commerce *(vyapara),* action *(karma)* and livelihood *(jivanam)* are frequently used in the present context, but these words have such wide connotations and they cannot be restricted to merely everyday physical level of existence. *Vyapara,* which is roughly translated as commerce, and *jivanam* as livelihood do not very well indicate the depth of meaning attached to these terms. Similarly the word *karma* cannot be restricted only to the English word action. To understand the essential features of the tenth house, it would be useful to go to the root of such words used in the present context.

For example, let us take *Jataka Parijata* where Vaidyanath Dikshit advises the astrologers to ascertain a person's authority, his honourable rank, ornaments, retirement from the world, means of livelihood, fame, knowledge of the special arts and learning, beneficent acts sanctioned in scriptures and such other activities from the tenth house, as well as from the Sun, Mercury, Jupiter and Saturn. These attributes of one's life are so extensive that the identification of this house only with one's avocation, or the means of livelihood does not seem very valid. *Uttara Kalamrita,* ascribed to Kalidasa, makes the tenth house more abstruse and deeper. According to Kalidasa, from the tenth house one can predict the honour from the sovereign, riding on a horse, fame, sacrifice, pre-eminence, magnitude of moral merits, honour, honourable living, renown, etc. The determination of one's avocation takes into account almost every aspect of one's personality but these different indicators to the tenth house do not suggest merely such an integrated approach, rather they are indicative of something subtler. The way one earns one's livelihood does not always take into account all the talents one possesses.

Albert Einstein was a great scientist, a great physicist who could be considered an abstract philosopher of stellar relationships, but his understanding and expertise as a violin player was of no ordinary significance. Winston Churchill was a supreme politician but as a painter as well he had a high level of proficiency. In such cases, however, if the astrologer predicted that Einstein would earn his livelihood as a violinist or Winston Churchill as a painter, he would not be correct in actuality, though he could justify his prediction on a superficial basis. The eleventh house is said to indicate the income of a person, in which case we must distinguish the role of the tenth and eleventh houses very clearly. The tenth house represents occupation, respect, means of livelihood, self-respect, rank, temporal honours, religious knowledge and dignity. From these, one can notice that means of livelihood and temporal honours are the two main indications of the tenth house. In fact, once we go behind these two aspects of one's life, we would find that there is a great common ground between these two aspects of one's life which we must understand in order to grasp the significance of the tenth house. Through these two key words and the unity between the two, one may be able to see not only the various forces working underneath numerous vague and ornate classical references which often confuse the readers, but may even get at the root of the basic impulse flowing through the tenth house. Therefore, in order to make these two key-words, means of livelihood and temporal honours effective, one would do well to understand the basic motivation for them so that the significance of the tenth house could be understood realistically.

The tenth house of the *Kalapurusha* represents the main purpose for which the very manifestation has taken place. Esoterically, it is this house which enables the individual to merge in the universal. In terms of occultism, under its impulse the individual aspirant is linked with occult hierarchy and thereby he becomes an important limb of the divine agent. Hardships and struggles in this transformation becomes a function of the house. The various organs of action and knowledge under the impulse of the tenth house are activated and they are made to serve the divine purpose thus annihilating everything personal and making the individual life a channel of divine outpouring. In this process, that which is latent in the individual becomes patent and this externalisation of energy is the prime goal of *Kalapurusha* which is considered his avocation. In the case of humans also, one may recognise that the entire life of a person is a process through which this externalisation takes place. The tenth house shows the manner in which this externalisation of the energy contained within the person is activated to make it patent.

When the individual begins to live his life on this earth, there is reaction to his actions leading to an interaction between the individual and the world. This interaction arouses various situations which are described by various terms used in astrological textbooks. The attributes indicated as the features of the tenth house are merely the external symptoms or the conditions which arise as a result of the externalisation process which occurs as a result of the life lived by the individual. The tenth house in a nutshell, stands for the manner in which an individual involves himself in his environment. When it occurs, there is a kind of action and reaction. The talents, the knowledge of special arts, sacrifice (*yajna* – meritorious moral deeds), commerce (*vyapara* – social intercourse), means of livelihood as well as everyday conduct of the individuals are all expressions and indications of the manner in which they function in their external environment. In such an interaction, the proclivities, imagination, ambition and supra-mental faculties (all symbolised by *gagana* meaning the open sky) and travel (*gamana* = departure) come into operation. These are the impulses which induce the individual to pull down the barriers between his individual personal self and the universal existence.

Such an impulse going from the individual to the universal or from the subjective psyche to the objective physical existence has a response from the latter. These responses are the compliments or the considerations that the world gives to the individual actors who act their part of the specified life/incarnation on the stage and are heard no more (i.e. are merged in the cosmic reservoir of energy). This kind of complementary relationship between the action of the individual and the response of the society to him, is expressed in various ways depending upon the society, time and the status of the parties concerned. For a kingly act, the success is adorned as victory and great royal festivities accompanied by religious observances (*yajna*), for a noble man riding on a horse symbolises the glory and recognition of his merit, for others, it is renown, respect, bestowal of power to command (may be appointment to administrative service or to a ministerial position). The social action and reaction to such activities are included in the two keywords namely, avocation and honour, but behind these two characteristics several other intricate and finer aspects of life are involved which must also be taken into account.

While the action of the individual is induced by self-centred personal considerations, thereby often eliciting unfavorable response from the world, but there could also be personal aura of the individual and his adjoining atmosphere surcharged with unfriendly and unhappy feeling. If the action is induced by sympathetic and helpful considerations, there would be satisfying response and helpful aura around him. It is an occult law. As the tenth is the house of social interaction, the inevitable occult law operates in this area of human conduct. The personal as well as social happiness of the individual can be gauged by the nature and disposition of the tenth house. As most average persons, or individuals with very few interests and capabilities have their profession or the means of earning livelihood as their most important means of getting involved in their society, the tenth house for such persons would indeed be the most important basis for predicting their profession. Otherwise, for a person with diversely developed personality having many talents and interests in life, his relationships and activities which relate him to his society, and also the responses from the society to his actions would be much varied. Often one finds that a person may receive bouquets and bricks simultaneously. For example, a professor may get hooted in his class by his students for very poor delivery of his classroom lecture, but on the same day he may receive a letter from the government seeking his advice and help, appointing him on some committee with much financial gain. Such experiences are not rare, but they can happen only when someone has varied talents and relationships. Such persons may experience success and failure simultaneously, depending on the impulses generated by him in different areas of his activities and relationships.

Considered this way, income of the person may arise from some of his activities, but there may be certain areas of his activities which may not be carried out for livelihood. Whether the person earns income from any of his activities or not, whatever he does has some basis in his proclivities, tendencies, talents and capabilities which induce him to act in a certain manner. A man may be a financial wizard, a great administrator, a deep student of history and diplomacy, a lover of art and an art critic, and an expert flute player, but he may not use all these for earning his livelihood. Nonetheless, whatever he does arises from his inherent talents. This is the basic relationship between the tenth and the eleventh houses. Even if the cause of the flow of one's income, or the basis of his employment depended upon the nature and influences of the tenth house, the income as such of the person would be indicated by the eleventh house. The fine relationship between the tenth and the eleventh houses arises from this sort of linkage and as such, in astrological counselling, this fine distinction ought to be taken into account.

It is not necessary that the tenth and the eleventh houses of a person are equally good or bad. The two houses may show their own disposition which at times may be contradictory. Someone may have a very afflicted tenth house, whereas his eleventh house is very powerful. On another occasion, one may find a chart with very significant tenth house, but his eleventh house may not be so promising. This creates much confusion. We have examples of many famous persons, both for their good deeds as well as for bad who had unspecified sources of income, not commensurate with their merit. We also have examples of persons who have had negative interaction with the society and the group in which they lived, yet they had a very coveted level of income. It may be useful to examine few such horoscopes to understand the difference that is necessary between the tenth and the eleventh houses.

Chart I pertains to Dr. Rajendra Prasad, the first President of the Indian Republic. In this chart one finds the tenth house superbly placed with the lord of the fifth house and the tenth house; the lord of the tenth house Venus is in his own house forming one of the *Pancha Mahapurusha Yogas (Malavya)*. The house does not receive any other benefic or malefic ray. The tenth house however is hemmed by two malefic rays namely Rahu in the ninth and the Sun in the eleventh. In this connection, one may point out that the *Papakartri Yoga* thus formed is fizzled out as the Sun has the forward motion towards the twelfth and Rahu with retrograde

Ketu		Moon Sat (R)	
	CHART I Dr. Rajendra Prasad		
Ascdt			Jupiter
Mars Mercury	Sun	Venus	Rahu

motion towards the eighth, thus clearing the cloud formed by their
flanking the tenth house. These combinations show that the person
though may be handicapped and at times restricted in his activities,
will have the most positive response from the people. Venus would
make him the most respectful and affectionately regarded person.
Venus is the planet of superb sensitivity and deep-acting social
relationships. As a result of the disposition of this planet, the
interaction between the individual and his society would be very
natural, free from every kind of affliction. The relationship
established between the person and his society or the group
associated with him, is induced by the downpour of influences from
supraphysical levels of existence. Venus has attained the *navamsa* of
Pisces while Jupiter the lord of this *navamsa* is in the eighth house
which is the secret recess of one's being. Eighth house has Leo
sign, and its lord Sun is in Scorpio which represents the eighth
house of the Cosmic Man – *Kalapurusha* (which happens to be the
eleventh house in the present case). These conditions indicated that
the sociability of Rajendra Prasad arose from deep equanimity and
universality of his central core. These provided unexpected and deep
impulses from the secret and hidden parts of his real being, the soul.
It is, therefore, not surprising that everyone who ever came in
contact with him felt deeply attracted to the mysterious and
magnetic personality he possessed. While fighting the British
government, he did not have a single European adversely
commenting on his personal conduct and behaviour. Venus in the
present chart is in *Visakha Nakshatra* which is symbolised by the
potter's wheel. The impact of this *nakshatra* is to enable the
individual to completely surrender himself to the will of God. In Dr.
Rajendra Prasad's life, one finds that he never calculated any of his
actions in the light of his personal gains. The letter that he wrote to
his elder brother on the eve of his joining active politics is a
glowing example of selfless dedication to the call of duty
representing the will of God. Even as the Food Minister or as the
President of the Indian Republic, he worked with the same surrender
of his personal will to the will of God. Rajendra Prasad always
aimed at impersonality, and fashioned his life and action
idealistically. Everyone appreciated his personal character, integrity,
helpfulness and charity, but his income and avocation were not
directly reflected from this house.

Dr. Rajendra Prasad was born in a very rich landed aristocratic family. As a legal practitioner he had shown much promise; as a professor he was extremely respected; as a writer and author he showed rare scholarship and maturity. But even when he was the President of India, inspite of his frugal habits and care in his household management, every member of his family did not have even enough clothes. Evidently, Dr. Rajendra Prasad's avocation by way of earning his livelihood, or his income was not well reflected by his tenth house. One will have to seek other houses of the horoscope to examine those details. But as a guide to his social relationship, the springboard of his life's impulse and the response of the people who came in his contact or of those who heard and knew him, the tenth house of his horoscope seems to give a realistic picture.

	Jupiter		
Ketu	CHART II		
Saturn	Lal Bahadur Shastri		Mars Rahu
Ascdt		Venus	Moon Sun Mercury

In the horoscope of Lal Bahadur Shastri (Chart II), the tenth house with exalted Mercury itself leading to *Bhadra Yoga*, placed with the lord of the ninth house yields of *Raja Yoga;* besides the association of Mercury with Sun leading to *Budha-Aditya Yoga.* Thus the tenth house becomes exceptionally powerful. The most important point to note is the togetherness of Sun, Moon, and Mercury which indicated well-integrated *Atma*(Sun) *Buddhi*(Moon) *Manas*(Mercury) making him absolutely honest, self-reliant, single-minded and able to do what his higher consciousness bid him to perform. His higher consciousness was pure enough to receive the *atmic* message clearly. There is no malefic influence on this house.

Furthermore, the three planets situated in the tenth house are powerfully placed in favourable asterisms. These asterisms are strong enough to support his involvement in public activities. The Sun in *Hasta* symbolised by a palm is an asterism which induces the individual to be extremely occupied with physical activities. Lal Bahadur Shastri, from his very childhood, had been renowned for his ingenuity, pragmatic approach and effective implementation of the programmes. He was a successful trouble shooter. His imaginative approach much induced by the Moon which ruled over the fourth quarter of *Hasta* where the Sun finds itself placed, gave him fertile and imaginative approach in mobilising popular support for his action-programmes. His *'Jai Jawan, Jai Kisan'* slogan became the most popular and encouraging morale building message for the country at a time when it was greatly needed. Mercury in *Uttara Phalguni* having Aryamanam, the powerful Vedic deity presiding over it and the asterism itself symbolised by a leg of a bed, made Lal Bahadur Shastri not an intellectual soaring in cloudy theoretical imaginations but a planner down to the earth. It was this planning ability which made him an unbeaten planner (as the Chairman of the Planning Commission, he made such down to earth suggestions that other members often shuddered in confronting him). The victorious Commander-in-Chief of the Indo-Pakistan war paid glowing tributes to his understanding and acumen. The Moon in *chitta* presided over by *Twastra,* the celestial architect *Viswakarman,* made Shastri's contribution to the nation (as well as to his family members and friends) pearl-like pure, which symbolised this asterism. The main point that needs to be emphasised in the present context is, that despite all these and his attainment to the highest position in the country, he was not a rich man, and his status in life did not show much wealth or income. In his social relationships, he was what the influences flowing from the tenth house made him, but the high status that he had acquired among his social circle (which later on became his political circle) did not commensurate with his income and wealth.

The same distinction has to be made in the case of another notable personality whose horoscope (Chart III) has already been examined by many eminent astrologers. Dr. B.V. Raman's eminence, his social achievements, popularity and universally acclaimed authority over the ancient science of astrology are well known. But

Rahu		Moon Saturn	
Ascdt	CHART III Dr. B.V. Raman		Sun
			Mars Merc Venus
	Jupiter		Ketu

his wealth and income do show that the two, *viz.*, his fame and income, bear no comparison. Looking at his horoscope, one finds that the lord of the tenth house which in his case happens to be the highly occult sign of the zodiac namely Scorpio, is placed in tenth from the tenth house (discussed in Chapter 11). Here we may mention that Mars, the most positive (some may call it aggressive) of all the planets owns the tenth house. Jupiter the lord of the eleventh and second houses (which contains one of the bases of the Grand Material Triangle) is importantly placed in its friendly house owned by the Sun. Jupiter is fully aspected by Moon forming *Gaja Kesari Yoga* and by Saturn, the lord of the Ascendant and the twelfth (the house connected with life-beyond, the supraphysical, etc.); Jupiter is also aspected by Mars, which aspects its own sign which also happens to be the tenth house. It may be emphasised that Mars also happens to be the lord of the third house signifying courage. Jupiter itself is aspecting its own sign which happens to be the second house, the house linked with the unfathomable depth of the cosmos from which all manifestation begins at the primeval stage. Jupiter also aspects the sixth house, the house signifying latent powers of the individual, his *siddhis* which also happens to be tenanted by the Sun, the most important planet of occultism, the central or from which all energy sources and occult sciences originate. Jupiter also aspects the fourth house, the house of emotions and personal feelings and sympathies and it also aspects Saturn thereby completely altering the malefic character of this *tamasic* planet. Jupiter is placed in the third quarter (*pada*) of

Anuradha Nakshatra symbolised by an umbrella or a lotus signifying spiritual growth.

Dr. Raman's involvement in the physical world is primarily guided by Jupiter in *Anuradha,* supported by Moon which aspects it from Taurus from the first quarter of *Mrigasira Nakshatra* symbolised by a deer's head, and by Saturn's aspect on it which is in *Rohini* symbolising a chariot and by Mars from Leo placed in Poorva Phalguni. These features indicated the depth and serenity or Raman's psychic being. It also indicated his tremendous courage, fearless initiative and persistence in his deep and extensive exposition of the ancient occult ideas. Politicians, professors (signified by Jupiter), scientists, doctors and philosophers (as a result of Moon and Saturn) and the men of the world (indicated by Mars, Mercury and Venus) would also be related in one way or the other with Dr. Raman. All of them would approach him with a kind of awe, fear, admiration, jealousy, greed, and a desire to get something from him, but his reactions to all of them would be a kind of detached benevolent protection. An important point to note is that Jupiter in Anuradha symbolised by a lotus would enable Dr. Raman, in all his involvements and interactions, to receive a sort of divine benediction which is a special characteristic of this asterism, and the flowering of his inner qualities and capabilities as revealed by the symbol of this *nakshatra.* In his life and social relationships, from the early childhood there would always be a gradual unfoldment and progress representing the growth from mud, muddy water, water and flowering of the inner energy into the open expansive sky receiving the solar radiation and finally getting nearer to the supreme power. But the financial status of Dr. Raman is not influenced by these planets which have almost raised him to sky heights as far as astrological and occult learning and understanding and the people's appreciation of and regard for him are concerned. The planets in the tenth house have influenced his social relationships, his interaction to the environment in which he is placed, the unfoldment of his latent capabilities and the everyday involvement in the areas of his activities destined for him. But his financial status is to be explained from other conditions. One of the reasons for not so commensurate financial status is the placement of eleventh lord Jupiter in twelfth position from its own house. The very house which made Raman so eminent, also produced financial hardships on him to a great extent.

Thus, one can find that the level of one's income may not have much direct relationship with the tenth house which, in fact, shows the manner in which the person would interact with his social situations which being an indication of his involvement in the physical world around him would in some indirect way be linked with his profession. What work he does and the various interests in life he developed and the talents and capacities he has acquired, need not all be linked with his means of livelihood or the channels for earning income. The tenth house may be considered specifically to indicate the manner in which the individual is associated with the world around him therein including his activities, his general philosophy and motivation in approaching different social relationships as well as the reaction of the people to him, his popularity and otherwise, while the eleventh house should be primarily considered as an indicator of the financial status of the individual.

13

MARRIAGE COUNSELLING

Marriage counselling is a complicated affair. On the one hand, it is the most popular and constructive aspect of astrology, on the other, it raises the question of thwarting any possible planetary impact. It also involves the question of the significance of marriage itself. What is the meaning of harmony in marital life? What is the purpose of marriage as an institution? The modern trend in unconventional marriages also needs to be taken into account. Above all, the astrologer has to be very clear in his mind as to what he is striving for? Is he trying to warn his clients of the impending danger, or is he going to indicate the possible consequences and adjustment problems likely to be faced in a marriage? What are the possible difficulties and how can the contracting parties face them? And above all, what is the meaning of marriage itself from a deeper standpoint? These are some of the questions which the astrologers and the enquirers both ought to be aware of, before venturing into the realm of marriage counselling.

A recent trend among some of the earnest astrologers is to produce a large number of natal charts of married partners or of such couples, revealing their personal weaknesses and justifying their inevitability on the basis of planetary combinations. If some one has been indulging in extramarital sexual relationships, there must have been some planetary combination which led the person to that situation. But could there be any other implication of such a combination which if known by the person concerned, could have led him to overcome those difficulties? If extramarital relationship or any deviation from the socially approved norm is wrong, then planetary forces (which in fact are benevolent impulses of the Divine for the evolution of the individual ego) could not induce him to get trapped in those unfortunate events. It is indeed a moral duty of the astrologers capable of comprehending the impact of planetary impulses on an individual's intimate life, to find out the deeper implications of those forces and indicate how the individual could transmute those physical conditions (or sex-arousing impulses) towards higher end. In this way, the task of marriage counselling is indeed a very onerous responsibility which the astrologers must discharge with conscience.

Strijataka or Female Horoscopy gave many valuable hints about marriage and the problems related to special features of women which need special considerations and which distinguishes a male horoscope from that of a female. Widowhood by itself does not determine the misfortune or otherwise of a female. Extramarital lapses have planetary causes as well as social consequences. The first appearance of menses which is beyond the control of human individuals has far-reaching impact on the psychological and physiological state of the female. In marriages, it is not merely the longevity of the married partners, but many other factors are important. For personal appearance, character, general health, position and happiness, the Ascendant as well as Moon should be consulted in a female chart; for the husband, his appearance, position and behaviour, the seventh from the Ascendant should be consulted. For conception, pregnancy, delivery, married life, prosperity, jewels, ornaments, prosperity and adversity of children, the fifth from Moon or Ascendant or from both should be examined. For the longevity of the husband, for the married state and widowhood, the eighth house should be consulted. Obviously, in the matching of the horoscopes between two persons likely to enter into wedlock, one will have to be very careful as to what one is looking for. Usually the guardians, or even the prospective partners put the questions whether the partners would be happy together, or sometimes they put the question as to the compatibility of the horoscopes. Do the horoscopes match? Before answering such questions, it is imperative to know what one is enquirying.

Generally speaking, many astrologers take into consideration what is known as the *Kuja Dosha* and on the basis of this criterion they check the compatibility or otherwise of the horoscopes. In brief, it implies the presence of Mars in first, second, fourth, seventh, eighth or twelfth houses. From this it could be seen that the presence or aspect of Mars on seventh or eighth house is not considered auspicious. If it is present in the case of a male, it implies the death of the wife, and if present in the case of a wife, it implies the death of her husband. In the same way, any association of Saturn with the eighth house, specially when it is weak or afflicted, is considered inauspicious. In the case of a male, if there is any malefic planet in the second or seventh, it is considered harmful. But, it is said that the presence of similar combinations in both, the male and the female, nullifies the impact. This is the general rule by which many astrologers decide the compatibility of horoscopes. But this is a very weak ground for matching horoscopes. Another set of rules pointing to the widowhood of the girl is also taken into account. Some of the rules link the malefics with the seventh and eighth houses. For example, it is said that Moon in Ascendant while Mars in seventh house will cause widowhood within eight years of marriage. Saturn or the Sun in his own sign identical with the eighth house, denotes a barren female. On the other hand, relationship between the Ascendant lord and the seventh lord is also said to be important. Some texts have mentioned that the Ascendant lord individually disposed in any manner in the first or the seventh or joining one of these houses portends that the couple will be exceedingly amicable to each other.

The following eight rules are considered important for deciding the compatibility of the partners:

1. If the girl has her Moon in the same sign as that in which the lord of the seventh house in the boy's horoscope is placed.

2. If the Moon in the girl's horoscope is the exaltation sign of the lord of seventh house in the boy's horoscope.

3. Even if the Moon in the girl's horoscope happens to be the depression sign of the lord of the seventh house in the boy's chart.

4. If the Moon-sign of the girl is the same as that in which Venus in a boy's chart is placed.

5. Even if the seventh house has the same sign in a boy's chart as the Moon-sign in the girl's chart.
6. The sign in which the Ascendant lord of the boy is placed happens to be the Moon-sign of the girl.
7. If the Ascendant of the girl happens to be the same as the seventh sign from the boy's Moon-sign.
8. If the girl has her Moon-sign as one of those in which the planets aspecting the Moon-sign in a boy's chart are placed.

The above eight rules are quite common among some astrologers in deciding whether a girl and a boy should be married to each other. But a more prevalent method for matching the horoscopes of a boy and a girl is to ascertain the *nakshatra* in which the Moon in a boy's chart is placed and on that basis consider the *nakshatra* in which the Moon in the girl's chart is placed and on this consideration ascertain the compatibility of these two *nakshatras*. On this basis various points are given for different kinds of harmonious relationships between the two individuals. The highest point accorded is thirty-six which obtains when the boy is born in first half of *Mrigasira* and the girl is born in *Rohini Nakshatra*. If the total of such points comes to eighteen, then also the marriage obtains the passing mark, below which the compatibility factor is less than average and such marriages are not advisable.

This method of tallying horoscopes is very comprehensive and goes to the root of the compatibility and harmony principle in Nature. The total of the points is an aggregate of eight kinds of relationships. These are: castes such as Brahmin, Kshatriya, Vaisya and Sudra; species such as quadruped, human, aquatic, forest-dweller and insects; *Yonis* classified into fourteen kinds such as horse, elephant, ram, serpent, dog, cat, mouse, cow, bull, tiger, deer, monkey, mongoose and lion; *Ganas* such as god, human and demon; *Nadis* which classified the twenty-seven *nakshatras* into beginning, middle and terminal sections; *Tara* takes into account the number of *nakshatras* that elapsed from that of the boy to that of the girl and vice versa and this number is divided by nine and the remainder taken into account in order to determine the auspicious relationship between the two or otherwise; and *Bhakut* takes into account the relationship between the Moon signs of the partners; and the planetary relationships. The aggregate points of these eight bases of compatibility are known as the total *gunas*.

These are the traditional methods of matching the horoscopes. They are important in order to comprehend the inherent harmonious affinity existing between the partners. But presently, the concept of marriage itself has changed. In different parts of the world, heterosexual marriages are not the only prevalent modes of sexual companionship. Lesbian relationships and homosexual marriages are also being solemnised. What is more pertinent in the present context is that these 'marriages' are even legalised. Astrologers in some countries are approached to indicate whether such partners could be happy with each other. This upsets the traditional technique of matching charts. Any astrological pointer to such horoscopes will not depend upon the traditional marital compatibility rules in ancient Hindu texts but one will have to approach the problem differently. There are various methods of matching horoscopes. The determination of widowhood or otherwise or the examination with regard to extramarital sexual relationship only relate the examination to limited aspects of the problem. The relationship between the *nakshatras* of the natal Moon attempts to reveal the basic inherent impulses underlying the two egos likely to get united in the bond of marriage. A scientific matching would depend upon at first on determining what we are looking for, whether our intention is to find out harmony and external happiness of the partnership or the union which fosters the growth and development of the inner ego. The best result is possible when the impact of one on the other in the context of the whole personality is taken into account.

Marriage is primarily a relationship for sexual compatibility. This takes into account physical health, blood circulation, sexual virility and mutual physical attraction as well as commonness of the attitude to sex. For this purpose, the state of the Ascendants, Mars and Venus are important. Secondly, after the sexual relationship merges in emotional blending, the happiness in marriage will assume emotional fusion of the one into another; mutual respect, sympathy and empathy, desire to feel life together would become more significant at this stage. For this purpose, the relationship between the position of the Moon and the fourth sign will be important. All marriages must end in creativity between the partners. This is the domain of the fifth house. And then there is the question of dependence of one on the other for furthering their dharma or their purpose of life. The importance of the ninth house should be considered in this connection. The relationship between the egos can be decided on the basis of the disposition of the Sun. Thus the compatibility of the entire horoscope in their external and internal aspects is very significant and this does not depend merely on one or the other factors. The results of the planetary disposition in totality are important for harmony and spiritual togetherness in marriage.

Another aspect which is equally important, but very often overlooked, is the periodisation of the planetary impact. The *Dasa-Bhukti* of the planets should be such as to cancel adverse periods in one another's life. The different periods of various planetary dispositions should be such that there is always harmony in the conditions and cancellation of adverse periods. Indeed, matching of horoscopes is a challenge to astrologers, but it is the most helpful chapter in astrological prognostications.

14

FOREIGN TRAVEL

The third house represents short journeys, ninth house represents long journeys and travels, whereas the seventh house indicates honour in foreign land. The eighth house signifies the place and surrounding of death. As a large number of people are migrating from one country to another for change of permanent residence, the disposition of the eighth house requires to be emphasised in this context. In practical experience however many other considerations also intervene to provide the pointers to foreign travels. *Uttara Kalamrita* refers to fourth, ninth and twelfth houses in connection with travels.

The three Sanskrit words used in this connection are *prayana, yatra* and *anya-desha-gamana. Prayana,* in relations to the fourth house means a journey as well as the commencement of a journey. In relation to the ninth house the word *yatra* is used which could mean a journey but more precisely a pilgrimage, while in connection with twelfth house *anya-desha-gamana* which refers to travel to a foreign country, has been used. In the modern age of rapid locomotion and close proximity of various countries with changing national boundaries, the precise delineation of 'foreign' and 'national' travels is meaningless. However, the special character of ninth house journeys cannot be overlooked. It refers not so much to the act of travel as much to the purpose for which it is undertaken.

While predicting foreign travel in modern times, one has to keep the basic principles of astrology in mind but on this knowledge, one has to superimpose modern changing conditions in order to provide any purposeful and valid guidelines.

We can begin our study in this regard with the famous travel of Swami Vivekananda to the United States. He left India for America on May 1893 just before the end of his Jupiter sub period in Jupiter main period and addressed the Parliament of Religions in Chicago in September 1893 in the sub period of Saturn. In this case (Chart I) Jupiter is the Ascendant lord and owns the fourth house. It is not otherwise linked with fourth or the ninth house; it is aspecting the third and seventh houses. Only on this basis should we predict significant overseas travel for Swami Vivekananda. Learned astrologers have tried to explain this event in the following way: "In Vivekananda's horoscope, Saturn, Rahu and Jupiter are the tripod of spiritual life. Jupiter the major lord is in the constellation of *Chitta* ruled by Mars, while Saturn is in *Hasta* ruled by the Moon. Both Mars and the Moon are in water signs and as the Moon is with Saturn, he was obliged to cross the ocean." Here, a new criterion for judging the possibility of foreign travel, namely, the element of different signs has been introduced. In case, the individual takes the aeroplane for his travel, the water element may probably require to be modified to air signs. What is significant is that Mars in the present case also happened to be the lord of the twelfth sign from the Ascendant and is placed in its own sign and is the ruler of the seventh house from Jupiter under whose main planetary rulership Swami Vivekananda left the country. From this example, one is apt to conclude that the house consideration is a minor consideration whereas the planets related to certain important susceptible houses play a major role. Another hint from the above, which is very significant, is the purpose for which the journey is undertaken. As

	Mars	Ketu	
	CHART I Swami Vivekananda 12 January, 1863 6.33 a.m. (LMT)		
Mercury Sun Venus			
Ascdt	Rahu	Jupiter	Moon Saturn

Vivekananda had predominantly a spiritual foundation to his chart resulting from Saturn, Rahu and Jupiter, these planets somehow became the prime movers in his case.

Presently, one can decipher more than half a dozen objects of foreign travels. Holidaying, studies and permanent settlement abroad may form one set of conditions, whereas those who go abroad on some mission, such as overseas assignment, government posting, business trip, teaching mission, religious discourse and philosophical discussion could fall under a separate category. Those individuals who travel abroad on diplomatic assignments, smuggling and drug trafficking or on military expeditions can be classified differently. Even those who go on exploratory missions such as to the Antarctica and other inaccessible regions, they will require a different set of rules. Readings of the horoscope as a whole should be the first and foremost consideration before considering the possibility of foreign travels and the nature of the same. One has to bear in mind that those foreign travels which create a significant imprint on the psyche of the person or on his life-pattern and life's mission, must be present in the horoscope in a pronounced manner.

Let us examine Chart II. It is an important horoscope in many ways, but we are not concerned with the general nature of it. It pertains to S. Ramanujan who went abroad in Ketu period, created a spectacular impression there, attained many laurels, lost his health by contracting tuberculosis, returned home and died at the very young age of thirty-two years which, more or less, coincided with the end of Ketu main period. In this horoscope, Jupiter, Saturn and the Nodes play a very important role.

Moon			Ascdt
	CHART II S. Ramanujan		Saturn Rahu
Ketu			
Sun	Jup (R) Mercury	Venus	Mars

When in the Ketu main period, Rahu began to influence the course of his life, overseas travel began to loom large on Ramanujan's life. Under the impact of Rahu, Jupiter, Saturn and Mercury, Ramanujan fulfilled his mission in life by crossing the seas, concretising his highly incomprehensible abstract theories (thoughts-Ketu) in a foreign country (Saturn and Rahu), and suffered physically (Mercury in sixth). Capricorn was an earthy sign, but Cancer in which Saturn and Rahu are placed, is a watery sign, and so is Scorpio in which Jupiter is placed which aspects the tenth house, twelfth house and the sign in which Saturn and Rahu are placed. This horoscope is an important example for taking an integral view before predicting overseas travel. In a weaker horoscope such a combination may perhaps lead to mental derangement.

Let us consider another example. Chart III belongs to a housewife whose life was very changeable. She had travelled extensively in India. In 1972, she went for a holiday-cum-religious seminar to Europe and spent several weeks touring other European countries. At that time she was running Mercury-Saturn. Her horoscope is very special in the present context. All her quadrant houses were occupied by movable signs. Four of her planets were located in these houses which included her Ascendant lord Moon as well. Mercury which is a planet specially connected with travels, which happens to be the lord of twelfth as well as third houses, both of which are connected with travels, is placed in seventh house which is also connected with travel. Saturn which is the lord of seventh (as well as eighth) house aspects twelfth as well as the third

	Venus Jupiter	Rahu	Mars
Sun			Ascdt
Merc	CHART III		
Saturn	Ketu	Moon	

house. None of these houses were occupied by watery signs. Even Moon, the Ascendant lord, famous for quick movement is only in an airy sign. Her travel was therefore by air; Saturn is posited in the twelfth from Mercury implying expenditure but as it is aspected by Jupiter from the tenth house, this expenditure could be for some kind of religious-educational trip.

Towards the middle of her Venus-Venus, she changed her residence and went to live in a European country where all the comforts of life were available to her. She was provided with a respectable status She travelled extensively during this period and returned to India only towards the end of Venus-Sun. This travel was definitely influenced by a different set of planetary combinations. Venus is the ruler of eleventh (sociability and money) and fourth (concerned with living conditions and travels) which at the very outset began to show its effect. Jupiter, the lord of ninth (travel and *poorva punya**) gave her travels, comforts and respectability. Venus is placed in Aries whose lord is placed in twelfth, the house of travel. It also happens to be very auspicious for Cancer Ascendants and aspected by Saturn which is also the ruler of the seventh house. In this case, the occupancy of Venus, the lord of the fourth house in Aries whose lord Mars is posited in the twelfth house, the sign ruled by Mercury which also is occupying seventh house, has been the cause of her foreign residence.

A very unusual factor entered in the case of Chart IV where the usual rules of foreign travels do not operate. It is an example of

	Moon	Rahu	Jupiter
Sat			
	CHART IV		
Venus			
Mars	Sun Merc Ketu		Ascdt

---

*Good deeds done in past lives whose results are indicated by the ninth house in the natal chart.

foreign trip for educational purpose. The horoscope belongs to a person who has been a good student and the son of a rich father. Towards the end of his graduation in India, he began to toy with the idea of having some exposure to foreign universities. While he was running Mars-Venus and when Jupiter began transiting over the Moon-sign, he left the country and went to the United Kingdom. Having completed a short diploma course for a year, even when he was being offered some higher scholarship for the continuance of the studies in that country, he left and returned to India. In this case, Mars' occupancy of the fourth house, in the sign of Jupiter occupying Mercury's sign in the tenth house while Mercury itself was in the third house, made Mars capable of taking a resident away from home and when Jupiter in transit over the sign where Moon is placed which happened to be Aries, the sign owned by Mars, aspected Mars in the fourth house, the result fructified. Venus, the sub-lord placed in fifth house which also happened to own the ninth house reinforced the trip specially for some educational purpose.

Chart V illustrates a situation when the individual was suddenly made to go on a very short training course to Indonesia on government account under an international agency programme. The quadrant houses are occupied by movable signs of the zodiac and Mars in Aries in fourth house bestows *Ruchaka Yoga.* The several planets in the third house, the house of short travels, in a common sign, are not combust. Jupiter is debilitated but it has exchanged places with Saturn in the third house. No planet, malefic or benefic, aspects Jupiter enabling it to influence the individual by its own force. From the Moon-sign, Mars is in the ninth house. Mars is therefore capable

Sun Mercury Venus Saturn	Mars	Ketu	
	CHART V		
Ascdt Jupiter			Moon
	Rahu		

of making the individual stay away from his house. During Mars-Saturn period, Saturn becomes twelfth from Mars, occupies third house being the Ascendant lord, aspects fifth or the house of learning, ninth the house of long travels, and twelfth, the house representing foreign countries. While transiting the Moon-sign, Mars aspected Saturn which was in twelfth house from its (Mars') own natal position while the latter (Saturn) occupied the third house. So as soon as Mars occupied this position while Mars-Saturn period was in currency, the combination made the person suddenly leave for a foreign country where he stayed as long as the transiting Mars permitted him to do so.

Now, a very unusual type of horoscope is presented to show that there are other considerations when an individual is destined to work on a different plane of existence. Chart VI pertains to the famous and controversial philosopher, J. Krishnamurti, who had been in his later years always on the move.

	Sun	Mercury	Venus Jupiter Mars
Rahu	CHART VI J. Krishnamurti		
Ascdt			Ketu
Moon		Sat (R)	

In a way it could be said that he did not have a home in later years and like an ascetic he always wandered from place to place. To pinpoint the specific planet which made him leave one place to go to another country in his later years will not be very enlightening. But here we propose to indicate the planetary impulses which began the journey. In May 1908, he began his Venus-Rahu period which marked a very important beginning for him. He left India for educational purpose in which he did not succeed. He could not pass the entrance examination to London University, or get the desired admission to Oxford University, as his capacity to learn the various required subjects inspite of very strenuous coaching was very limited. But this trip began to expose him to the western civilisation and the European lifestyle which became very important for him. Venus is the lord of his fifth house as well as of the tenth house. It is associated with Mars the lord of fourth house as well as with Jupiter which rules over twelfth house and the third house, both connected with travels. Venus is seventh from the Moon-sign which itself is placed in the twelfth house. Rahu was placed ninth from the *Dasha* lord and was aspected by Jupiter. Rahu is related to foreign (western) countries. So when Venus-Rahu period started, J. Krishnamurti began to be exposed to western countries which finally became the major plank of his life-work.

Another example of Venus making the individual leave one's homeland to travel abroad in such a way that such trips became ultimately the way of life for the person is obtained from the horoscope of Smt. Rukmini Devi Arundale. Chart VII pertains to her. Soon after the stormy opposition to her marriage with a foreigner, the domestic and personal life of Mrs. Arundale became so disturbed that she had to leave the country. It all began with Venus main period. Soon after this period began in 1923, Rukmini Devi Arundale, till the end of her life, made world tours several times. But the beginning of this in fact began with Venus main period. Venus is the lord of the Ascendant and that of the sixth house and as such it may not be considered important for world tour, but its other influences led her to be constantly on tour abroad. Being the Ascendant lord, Venus had to bestow something which was important

Ketu Mars Jupiter		Ascdt	
Sun	CHART VII Smt. Rukmini Devi		Moon
Venus Saturn Mercury			
			Rahu

for her. Her mission in life was the propagation of dance-drama abroad and to make it popular. It could happen only when she toured in different countries. In this regard the association of Venus with Saturn which is *Yoga Karaka* being the ruler of the ninth and tenth houses, its placement in ninth along with Mercury which is a planet connected with travels, and all the three planets namely Venus, Saturn, and Mercury being seventh from the Moon-sign led to making Venus an important contributory planet in this direction.

Chart VIII pertains to Morarji Desai, who had a very austere life and in his thought-frame travels to foreign countries had very limited importance. But, being a politician when he was an important cabinet minister in the Central Government, it was considered beneficial that he received exposure from the world abroad and met foreign financial administrators and others connected with this subject. It was important for him to meet such people and familiarise himself with their thought. This world tour took place during the Saturn-Mercury period. He had several other world tours but this is important in a special manner. It could be seen from his chart that Mercury has been his Ascendant lord and it is connected with tours, accounting and growth of intellect. Besides being placed with exalted Mars while the sign in which it is placed is ruled by Saturn which occupies third house which is linked with travels. Mercury is also associated with Venus which is a ruler of the twelfth house connected with foreign travels. All these planets are aspected by exalted Jupiter which also happened to be the ruler of the seventh house connected with travels.

			Ascdt
Sun Rahu	CHART VIII Morarji Desai		Jup (R)
Mars Venus Mercury			Moon Saturn Ketu

From the above examples, it can be seen that foreign travels do not have any single rule for prediction. Firstly, one should decide which type of travel the person is looking for. If it is for assignment or permanent residence, special set of combinations should be considered. They are guided by different set of rules depending upon the type of the assignment, the job to be performed, the duration of stay, all such points will have to be considered. Generally speaking, the third, fourth, seventh, ninth and twelfth houses are important which come into operation in deciding one's trips abroad. If the travel is for study and training purposes, there should be some relationship with the planet connected with fifth house as well, which includes the relationship with its lord. If the travel is going to make an important effect in the overall lifestyle of the person or his life's mission, the planet leading to the travel must be connected with this impact. It is also seen, though examples of such charts have not been given above, where malefic elements like the Nodes or the Saturn's transit around Moon (as in the case of 7½ year period when it transits over twelfth, first and second signs from Moon) lead to troubles through travels abroad. Mars also leads to foreign travels while Jupiter, Venus and Mercury are in many cases importantly connected with this event. If the chart has the basic potential leading to foreign travel, the planetary periodicity and planetary transits activating those basic factors actualise the result. But in fact, these days foreign travels are becoming so common, that unless this is going to make an important impact on the life of the person, foreign travels in many cases may not be evident in any significant manner.

15

DESTINY OF MAN

The ninth is an auspicious house. Everyone looks to it for the auspicious features of the horoscope. If the ninth house is good and beneficial, happy events are foretold. Even when there are several disquieting features in a natal chart, if the ninth house is well fortified, the life of the person is expected to be smooth sailing. The understanding of the significance of this house, however, depends on astrologers' own intuition and insight. While discussing the ninth house, *Brihat Parasara Hora* has been very concise and terse; often it describes this house as the *Dharmasthana* (the house of righteousness) and on other occasions mentions it as *Bhagyasthana* (the house of fortune). While giving the results of various planets in the *Bhagyasthana* and mentioning the effect of *Bhagyesha* (the lord of the ninth house), it talked more of the benefic results flowing from father (*pitrisukha*). These allusions sometimes baffle the student. Even *Uttara Kalamrita,* while indicating the various matters related to the ninth house begins by stating *Danam* (offering), *Dharma* (righteousness), *Tirtha-sevanam* (serving pilgrimage), and *Tapas* (penance) connected with the ninth house and continues mentioning such items as purity of mind, exertion for wisdom, dignity, travels, wealth, elephants, horses, buffaloes and so on as the main subject matter of the house. In short, all that matters in life can be linked with the ninth house. *Jataka Parijatam* has been more specific by stating that the ninth house will indicate fortune, power, father or such elderly person, good works, strict observance of duty and general welfare. In *Brihat Jataka,* Varaha Mihira calls the ninth house as *subha* meaning auspicious and stops at that.

From these, one can infer that there are many ethereal qualities connected with the ninth house which relates the present life of the individual with beneficial and uplifting forces flowing to him from the unknown dimensions. Any expression of these forces in concrete terms whether by way of travels, charity, deeper studies of Nature's secrets or acquisition of elephants, buffaloes and horses are merely peripheral expressions of the inner forces working on the individual. In fact, every house in a horoscope to some extent reveals the inner forces working on the individual but the ninth house more specifically shows the relationship between the forces from the non-physical side of existence impinging on the individual and on everyday activities and opportunities met by him. In this way, Varaha Mihira's attribute of *subha* (auspicious) as the nature of the house is much more directly relevant than various other descriptions of the house. The several attributes of the ninth house may be considered mere elaboration of this basic feature. Astrologers have put these elaborations as godliness, righteousness, preceptor, grandchildren, metaphysical studies, imagination and intuition, religion, devotion, law, sympathy, philosophy, science and literature, lasting fame, leadership, charities, communication with spirits, ghosts and the like, long journeys, father and travels primarily as practical guidelines for the house.

Among the various attributes mentioned above, the two references that intrigue very much are travel and father. Their association in relation with benefic influences from the other side of life is indeed baffling. But this relationship reveals the importance of this house vis-a-vis *Bhagya* and *Dharma* which have been emphasised in the present context.

It is not irrelevant to consider the ninth house as the past accumulated karmas. The accumulated karmas of the individual are many and to suggest that all these are revealed by the ninth house is too much to expect. Only a portion of the past is allocated in the present or in any one incarnation of the individual. How has this allocation been made so as to provide adequate opportunities to the person concerned so that he evolves rapidly and effectively towards his goal of Liberation, towards his deeper understanding of the beneficent forces working around the world, is what is importantly shown by the ninth house. In this arrangement, if the individual has earned favourable opportunities and conditions from the Invisible

Guide so as to be rightly guided towards the distant goal, that should be considered the auspicious condition for the individual. In this way, the ninth house reveals a portion of the past accumulated karmas, the special interest taken by the Invisible Guides of the world in general and for the concerned individual in particular, the expected distant goal towards his future and the line or the course through which this passage for the individual will be pursued. Such an approach will, to some extent, indicate the assumptions on which Parasara based his conclusion regarding the ninth house when he related it to travel and father, implying spiritual journey as the travel (though it has reference also to the mundane movement from one place to another) and the Father in Heaven (though it also indicates conditions of one's worldly father).

The term travel in relation to the ninth house is used either as a pilgrimage or long travels which are important for the concerned individual. The soul evolves through various experiences which open out to it the various expressions of the One Reality. Ordinarily travel implies change of place, more experience, greater awakening to different aspects of human behaviour. In short, the individual is exposed to different lifestyle as a result of which his mind expands and his behaviour changes. Such changes bring in certain enduring changes. Travel stands as a symbol for all movements either in the physical realm in which one moves from one place to another or it may even imply the movement of the psyche from the physical to super-physical and spiritual planes of existence where the ego learns new things, acquires new wisdom and comes out more refined, more mature and so on. Approached this way, travel is a means of evolution for the human psyche, it is an opportunity which everybody does not get and even among those who get such opportunities there are only a few who utilise them in the right way. One gets the opportunity to travel and to meet people and see places only when the individual deep down has acquired the desire to see, to know and to gain wider experiences of life. Over a number of years, and even over a number of lives when such desires accumulate and the aspiration matures, that an individual gets such opportunities which show the benediction of the Lords of Karma and their willingness to arrange things for the incarnating ego in such a way that its consciousness expands and it gains true knowledge of its surroundings before it transcends the bondage of births and deaths.

The ninth house is also related to father in a special sense. There is unity between Sun, Soul and Father but from purely astrological—karmic view point. It is quite easy for a student to establish the relationship between a loving father and a psychologically well-developed son on the basis of this house. Only those parents who have good karmas and who have had a good life of their own, beget good (and evolved souls as) sons and daughters. A good father-son relationship does not only reveal a closer integration between the lower and the higher self of the individual, it also reveals that both are quite advanced on the path of evolution. When Parasara talked of father-son relationship in the context of *bhagya* or lucky house in the horoscope, he was indirectly talking about the good karmic forces working on the individual.

Very strange rules and relationships exist between wisdom, karma and *bhagya* which are all contained in the ninth house. All of these are also personified by *Brihaspati* represented by Jupiter which has the unique impact on this house. Strange humility emanating from the understanding of the universal energy represented by the Sun incarnating in individual-forms as soul and father takes its devotees not to the isolation of a forest but makes him a warrior in life, playing the diverse role as destiny bestows on him. Changing from one condition to another, immersing oneself in deep action as demanded by destiny, believing in the wisdom, father and righteousness, the Sun demands action in the light of one's wisdom. This is a very complex situation which cannot be clearly portrayed by any single aspect of life: many factors impinge on the development of this kind of attitude. Only in humility, not sticking to any specific condition of the situation with complete humility and obedience to one's father which also implies one's father in heaven or one's own soul represented by the Sun, the individual moves with righteousness. Only then the individual receives the benediction of fate, *bhagya*. In this context, the association of Jupiter as the most important planet is not the end of the story, though Jupiter representing wisdom aspect of life is certainly very important; the contribution of other planets cannot be minimised. The judgement on the strength and quality of the ninth house, or the destiny of the individual will require a comprehensive knowledge of all planets and how they express the wisdom aspect of life. The benefic planets are certainly important in bestowing their boons, but even the malefic planets like Saturn and

Mars cannot be overlooked. This is the important aspect of the ninth house prognostication that must be emphasised. Among the planetary hierarchy and even in several zodiacal signs, Saturn and Mars are not considered very helpful for a righteous living and for bestowing auspicious result. To some limited extent they should be studied in relation with the ninth house. There is a verse in *Jataka Parijata* which states that the malefic planets occupying the ninth *bhava* or if they be hostile, depressed or eclipsed, will make the person devoid of good name, wealth or moral worth. But in the same breath it states that even a malefic planet in the ninth *bhava*, if in exaltation, in *swakshetra* or in a friendly house, invariably does good to the individual concerned. It suggests that it is not the malefic planets which destroy the good reputation of the person, or make him unhappy as far as wealth and moral fevour is concerned, but the maleficence of the planet that causes such deprivations to make the individual miserable. In the case of Lord Krishna, Ascendant being Taurus, his ninth house fell in the zodiacal sign of Capricorn ruled by Saturn. Ordinarily one considers Capricorn as a bad sign and its lordship to Saturn is not considered auspicious. To add to the difficulty of Saturn, we find it in Scorpio which is by no means an auspicious sign. Over and above this, the ninth house in this case is aspected by Saturn as well as debilitated Mars is situated along with Venus and Rahu, thus making the ninth house tenanted by inauspicious Ketu. But, should we consider that Lord Krishna had a miserable *bhagya?* Eyebrows will be raised on posing such a question and many kinds of astrological and metaphysical explanations will be put forward to explain the situation. But, if we stick to the basics of Astrology, we shall realise that even if this were the horoscope of any ordinary person, Capricorn will tend to make him universalise his consciousness. Saturn's position from enemy's house, notwithstanding its aspect from another occult sign, will enable the person to have his past karmas work out in such a way that occult wisdom will give him humility. Mars and Venus aspecting the ninth house in company with Rahu will externalise the karmic responsibilities. In this case, the most important points for consideration are twofold, namely, the occult nature of the planets concerned and the full aspect of exalted Moon on Saturn and aspect of Mars on ninth house having obtained *Neecha Bhanga Raja Yoga* and association of benefic Venus which happened to be the

Ascendant lord also. Obviously therefore it is not the malefic planet as such, but the very nature of the ninth house which discloses the destiny (*bhagya*) of the person.

Let us examine another interesting example of Shivaji who had been one of those Indians on whose destiny fell the task of reviving Indianism and to maintain the country's identity. His personal life might be considered full of risks and dangers, but his righteousness and the sense of duty were of the highest order. Inspite of personal sufferings and deprivations, very few persons will like to classify him as unfortunate. In his case, he had Leo as his Ascendant and Aries as the sign constituting the ninth house. The lord of the ninth house, Mars, is in Gemini along with Rahu, a karmic planet. Saturn from the sign of exaltation placed in the third house aspects the ninth house. The lord of the ninth house is aspected by Jupiter placed in Aquarius, another highly esoteric sign, and is associated with Sun which is Shivaji's Ascendant lord. Evidently, the ninth house inspite of being aspected by a malefic planet whose maleficence is completely eliminated by its exaltation and aspect of Jupiter which is uniquely placed in Aquarius along with Sun, is very effective. Saturn has certainly under the situation made Shivaji one of the few righteous and lucky persons that India has seen.

Let us study another example (Chart II) of Chengiz Khan. Almost everyone who knows his history well would not like to consider Chengiz Khan a saint, but no one will deny that he had a destiny closely linked with the destiny of several nations. He had turned the course of history in several parts of the world. *Bhagya* is a very difficult word to explain which however becomes very clear

Mercury	Venus		Mars Rahu
Sun Jupiter	CHART I Shivaji the Great 19 Feb., 1630		
			Ascdt
Ketu		Saturn	Moon

	Rahu		
	CHART II Chengiz Khan 16/15th Sept., 1186	Ascdt
		Moon Ketu	Sun Mars Merc Jupiter Venus Saturn

from this case. Chengiz Khan was not a pious man, he was not well spoken of either, but he was definitely a person with very strong destiny. He was born in Cancer sign and he had six planets (excepting the Moon and Nodes) in his third house. All of them aspected Pisces, his ninth house. Among the planets which aspected the ninth house, we find the lord of the ninth itself that is, Jupiter, Mercury which is in exaltation, and Sun which practically made Jupiter combust, and so on. The special aspects and relationships enjoyed by the ninth house made Chengiz Khan important (and even the personal life of the individual cannot be considered bereft of any material comfort or indulgences).

The horoscope of Sri Ramakrishna Paramhamsa (Chart III) is very exceptional with regard to his ninth house. He was born with Aquarius as Ascendant and his ninth house was in Libra, the exaltation sign of Saturn, where this planet is placed. The lord of ninth house Venus is also exalted in Pisces. Jupiter aspects the ninth house. *Jataka Parijata* lays down that when the ninth house is occupied or aspected by its lord or a benefic planet, the person born does assuredly become possessed of good fortune. Here the first rate benefic planet intimately associated with the *bhagya* of a person, is aspecting the ninth house. The Ascendant is in the highly occult sign whose lord has attained exaltation and is aspected by Jupiter. These factors made Ramakrishna a great seer; his ninth lord is a benefic planet in exaltation and a planet friendly to the Ascendant lord while the ninth house itself is posited by Saturn and is aspected by the benefic Jupiter. These made his ninth house highly *subha—* auspicious.

Venus		Ketu	Jupiter
Ascdt Merc Moon Sun	CHART III Ramkrishna Paramahansa 18 Feb., 1836		
Mars			
	Rahu	Saturn	

From the various examples cited above, we may infer that the ninth house signifying *bhagya,* points to the destiny of the person. It can be in the field of social organisation, scientific achievements, conquests changing the course of history, spiritual development or in any other way by which the individual makes an impact on the society and carries forth his destiny towards his own goal of life. It need not bring material affluence and a comfortable life. The nature of destiny the individual will have, would depend upon the type of planets involved and combinations produced. The malefic planets do not necessarily make the person unlucky; if they are powerful, such a person will make his mark on society definitely. The malefic planets make the individual pay the price for his destiny in a hard way, he may have to suffer personal deprivations and hardships but depending upon the strength of the planets he must make his contribution felt on the society in which he lives. That is his destiny, his *bhagya,* the result of his past accumulated karmas and the destiny decreed by the Lords of Karma which he cannot escape. That is what the ninth house reveals.

PART-IV

Special Characteristics of Planets and Signs

16

PLANETARY CHARACTERISTICS

SUN

The Sun is the most important planet[1] of the orb. Its symbol is a circle with a central point. The point expresses the swelling of the divine essence in manifestation, its spreading over the area circumscribed within the circumference, and again returning back to the original source.

Wherever the Sun exists in the natal chart, that aspect of life must be of supreme importance to the person. It is there that the divine is concentrating its attention. The expression of personality in the present incarnation will be most important in that aspect of the person concerned.

The symbol consists of two parts, namely, the circumference and the point. The circumference represents the energy and the life-force sustaining and nourishing the demarcated area in which the divine impulse flows. In order to understand the quantum and the area of the energy-spread, it would be necessary to link the Sun-sign, that is, the sign of the zodiac in which the natal Sun is located with the house division in which the Sun is located as well as the Ascendant. This will indicate the quality of the divine inflow with the basic nature of the person concerned, on the basis of which the various problems confronting him in life could be resolved. The smoothness

---

[1](In old astronomy) a heavenly body whose place among the fixed stars is not fixed (including sun and moon).

with which some individuals live their day-to-day life and come to their final end depends on this relationship. If the two signs are harmonious, the relationship between the inner urge of the individual and the divine energy energising his activities would be in sync.

The area of the divine downpour would show that specific aspect of the individual which has the greatest possibility of expansion. If the Sun is placed in the fifth house showing the relationship of the person with his offspring and his intelligence, one can infer that the individual would have important experiences with regard to these conditions. His intelligence would be of special importance and so would be his children. The person may not even have any child but may have a very bright intelligence in himself. The circumference of the symbol signifies frustration and limitations as well. Only with the acceptance of limitations in life, there can be any hope for success for him. When the individual accepts his limitations with regard to his creative potential, whether on the physical plane or on the mental, then there could be effective utilisation of the divine potential bestowed on him. The circumference considered as a cycle suggests that in this aspect of the individual's life, there could be pronounced evidence of fluctuations; there could be occasions of unexpected happiness, recognition and public approbation while on other occasions the opposite of the same could also be possible.

As the circle is the symbol of the Absolute, the Sun should be linked with the Absolute in the manifest world, that is, the royalty, the monarchy, the head of the state or the administrative head of the region. The Cosmic Absolute is ever radiating light and energy. The influence of the Sun is also permanent in relating the individual with the central seat of power and administrative organisations which is connected with the everyday life of the individual. The linkage with the head of the State or the administrative head would be so intimately connected that the individual would be in some important way the channel of the supreme authority in the State. It could mean the state administrative services or even in other intimate manner by being included in the publicised or the unpublicised central advisory group.

The circle (along with the central point) though includes everything manifest within its ambit, is not such as to lose its independent identity because the central point does not merge with others. For this reason, though the influence of the Sun could instil a sense of oneness, identity with the masses and others, it cannot be established on the basis of equality. There would be a great sense of aristrocracy and exclusiveness, though there may not be any negative psychological reaction under this planet. Under some adverse conjuncture, it may, however, lead to dictatorial, autocratic or despotic temperament.

A special feature of this sign is its being the representative of the Supreme within the circumscribed region (within the circumference). This suggests that Sun would induce the individual to be the monarch even in a very small locality than a much influential or affluent person in a wider area with many other persons to share his glory. The feeling of being exclusive is very much implanted on such a temperament; the desire to shine even for a minor act is much more important than the performance of much beneficial and lasting work. Such a temperament would show its best result when it is assigned an independent charge rather than work in a team of talented persons. He would be capable of great initiative, would be invincible, unmindful of troubles and tribulations provided he is the leader and in full command of power.

The point in the symbol makes the sign unique. No other astrological symbol contains such a central point which stands for direct communion with the Supreme source of Energy. It links the outer with the innermost source of energy. The activity of the Sun whom it represents, therefore can always be expected to be the centre around which other activities would revolve. The influence of the Sun on the physical life of the individual as well as on his psychic life would be such that all others will have to be dependent and controlled by it. If the solar energy is not forthcoming, other activities would be very mediocre. There is also another condition (specially because of the nature of the central point in the symbol), namely that the utilisation of the solar impulse in right direction is an imperative condition for fresh swelling of the same from the innermost source. The solar energy would be forthcoming in direct relationship with the degree of its utilisation. So the individuals under the solar influence must engage themselves in the suggested line of activities without any sloth, half-heartedness, or with a defeatist feeling and lack of confidence. Unless the individual engages himself in activities suggested by the Sun, there is every likelihood of his feeling weak, fatigued and lacking inspiration. In such activities which are in harmony with the influence of the Sun, there would always be a beautiful symmetry and rhythmical movement. The point also suggests that there should always be intensity and profundity in all such endeavours, and the person working on its impulse would always look to the basic source of energy and motivating power for his inspiration and encouragement rather than on other human resources. The Sun is a primary symbol of universal activity and profundity giving guidance and energy to all other planets and impulses for the growth of the individual.

MOON

The symbol of the Moon, if carefully considered, is the most enigmatic one and the planet is also not less so. The symbol has many blinds and if one begins to question the nature of the symbol, he would find that it is not the apparent resemblance with Moon which is the basis of this symbol. The symbol is not just a representation of the visual appearance of the Moon. Had it been so, there could have been the representation of the Moon in many other ways, but it is in fact not so. Always one finds double concave lines to represent it; whether it is a lunar symbol or the Moon shining among the locks of the Lord Mahadeva, the representation is alike. Such an appearance can be possible under three conditions.

First, the Moon at the beginning of its bright phase; second, the Moon under partial eclipse when the solar rays are being obscured by the intervening appearance of the Earth; third, when the lower arc of the cycle (the circumference in the symbol of the Sun) is gradually ascending up like the two waves one above the other.

The first of these explanations is a simplistic approach to the most mystic planet which is intimately linked with the psychic development of man and with the acquisition and perfection of Black Magic. By popularising the symbol of the visual appearance of the Moon, the ancient seers have succeeded well in deflecting the public attention which became highly agitated under the following two conditions. The inherent characteristics of the Moon are so deeply interiorised in order to reflect the light and radiance it receives from the Sun that its real nature is almost incognisable and imperceptible. All that we get from the Moon, or all that we see of it, is due to the radiance of the Sun. When the material manifestation, the Earth, intervenes and obscures the solar rays, the Moon becomes completely invisible. In absence of spiritual beneficence, the psyche of the individual, howsoever powerful and effective it might otherwise appear, would be greatly restrained. Insanity in a man arises when the shadow of the Earth—the selfishness, self-centredness, and the acquisitive proclivities of the individual—obscures the personal psyche of the person concerned. Under this condition he is completely dissociated from the vital source of his life-giving energy—the Sun, the Atman. In order to exhume the primeval spark of the human being, the first task is to identify the relationship between the Sun and the Moon and next, to examine the nature of its obscuration and to assess the degree of the same by several materialistic influences. In this task of self-exploration, which every intelligent person would like to do, the knowledge regarding intellectual obscurantism is the prime necessity. This knowledge, unless protected well against psychological immaturity, could have devastating consequences making astrological knowledge a tool of Black Magic of the worst kind. Depressive temperament, and suicidal tendencies are highly pronounced under such planetary combinations. The centre for such psychic dangers can be found in the disposition of the Moon. One should remember that the New Moon, for such reasons, is astrologically considered baneful.

The symbol of ever-rising arcs signifying the surge in the psyche resulting from the downward pressure towards materialisation and upward attraction to the divine unity may reveal much more dangerous and vulnerable influences flowing from the Moon. The stability and growth of a human being largely depends upon his psycho-mental nourishment and well being. Even in Nature, the seasonal fluctuations, and the impact of wind, air, and water as well as of earthly nourishment, vitally control their cyclical growth. In case the sensitivity and vulnerability of the man's psyche to different influences aroused by planetary combinations and dispositions are identified, the individual may succeed in eradicating his emotional and mental impediments and smoothen his egoic journey. But in case this knowledge is utilised for damaging the personality of oneself or of others, the knowledge thus obtained could be very calamitous. Naturally, the symbol of the Moon is couched in very abstruse lines concealed within deeply veiled blinds. The Moon in a very simple manner shows the mystic nature of the planet and its relationship with the Sun. It exists to transmute solar radiance for the periodic growth-impulse to life on earth.

MARS

 The symbol of Mars is a circle with an arrow jutting from it. The circle refers to the bounded potential, a portion of the Divine Absolute in its primordial essence contained in the personality of the incarnating ego. The arrow projecting from the store house of divine energy represents human efforts containing that spiritual essence directed to some spiritual purpose (as the arrow in this case points upwards). This upward direction of the arrow is an expression of the externalisation impulse flowing from the planet. The urge to break up the shell, the outer crust of the spirit represented by the circumference, is the chief characteristic of Mars. The outer crust restricts the inner potential, the latent powers of the man while Mars directs the wholehearted attention to the utilisation of latent powers for non-personal goals. Impulsiveness of the behaviour under its influence results from the impediments to the smooth flow of this divine energy contained within the self. Presence of any clog in the pipeline, depending upon the blockage in it, would arouse the feeling of self-centredness understood in general parlance as selfishness, stubbornness, resistance, and obstinacy. The symbol has no reference to any specific goal in view. The only consideration is that the same must be non-personal, and the individual under its influence wholeheartedly and in right earnest considers the same as ethical. From the point of view of the individual, there is nothing 'mean' in his behaviour.

The symbol in its essential nature relates the attempted utilisation of the divine energy to some non-personal and ethical (as thought by the individual) purpose. Under the impact of Mars one may therefore become a dictator, not for his personal aggrandisement, but for some social, political, religious, or other impersonal objectives. Any negative trait of the planet arises not due to the nature of the flow of the planetary impulse but due to impediments confronting the arrow in the symbol. In such case, the milieu of the individual or the conjuncture of the planets is very important. Mars, as the symbol suggests, is pure divine energy, within some limitations, available for divine objectives which has always some good influence on the person concerned. That is why in Hindu astrology, the planet is known as *Mangal,* which means auspicious. The successful discharge of one's mundane responsibilities to a great extent depends upon the nature and power of Mars in one's chart.

VENUS

Venus is the very antithesis of Mars. Its symbol is a cross hanging down from the circle. Divine potential used for material objectives can manifest in many diverse ways: much noble usages can be made of it while the possibilities for its undesirable use are not few. The cross is the union between the positive and the negative or the male and the female energy channels. If the container of the divine downpour is lined with *Karma-Manasic* desire sheaths, the impact of the energy received therein would be to arouse sensuous feeling and indulgence in sense enjoyments, to enhance the perceptive faculties, and to highly sensitise the feelings and thoughts of others. The perceptive faculties of the individual could be limitless—wherever there is matter, whatever is ·the level of manifestation, the Venusian impact would enable the individual consciousness to establish rapport there. The emergence of artistic talents, music, painting, dancing, sculpturing, poetry, architecture, as a matter of fact, wherever fine sensitivity is required, the Venusiar. impact can be observed. The divine in the artist would arouse the inner depths of perception to the highest levels of manifestation. Such a person would have innate capabilities for establishing symbiotic relationship with every form of manifestation at all levels of existence. The Matter-Spirit combination is highly propitious for every social relationship where sensitivity, perceptivity, symbiosis and feeling for other persons are required. Under such an impact, unless there are strong inhibiting factors, the person may become great debauchee, sensualist, and indulgent. With strong spiritualising influence, the individual could be a seer who could intuitively comprehend the complexities of the manifestation. Such persons would instinctively establish sympathetic and emotional relationship with the greatest as well as with the lowliest. They can always or whenever they so wish, be at ease with all kinds of situations and persons. They could be the benediction of the divine at every situation.

The difference between Venus and Mars is marked by cross under the circle in the case of Venus while an arrow is jutting from the circle in the case of Mars. These differences represent the basic variation in the nature of impulsions of these two planets. As a result of these impulsions, the impact of Venus is primarily on sensuous experiences and establishment of emotional and symbiotic rapport. Mars vigorously endeavours to work for the downpour of the Divine energy and its direction to impersonal goals. The basic qualities of both the planets are similar to each other but in the case of Mars, it is the arrow which leads the individual heavenward while the hanging cross in the case of Venus shows its involvement with manifestation, the world, the union of polarised energies. The combination of Mars and Venus in any horoscope could lead the individual to sublime heights of spiritual quest undauntedly or to the intense sexual orgies. The difference between the arrow and the cross is that when the cross is superimposed on the arrow, the matter supremely predominates while the prominence of arrow over the circle transmutes the libido into martyrdom for social and spiritual goals.

MERCURY

Mercury is different from Venus by way of addition of a crest on that of the symbol of the latter. This crest which is a portion of the ascending arc of the Divine Cycle, makes the tremendous difference between the two. Mercury has all the qualities and characteristics of Venus within it, but it has something more represented by the upward moving arc. This arc represents the movement of involutionary impulses after it has crossed the stage of bestowing life. Within its scope it now includes death and the period slightly before reaching the stage of Immortality. This arc which in its 180° extension encompasses within its scope the phenomena of manifestation from life to immortality while traversing to birth through death. This is a very wide sweep. It provides an extensive area for the operation. The additionality in Mercury in this manner expresses its ability to mobilise and transmute all the Venusian potentiality and qualities into great creative activity almost touching agelessness. The Venusian perceptivity is well embedded in Mercury but it is not heavily weighed down by material propensities, rather the spiritual aspirations specially in order to reflect the immortal or the divine aspect of manifestation in its transitory nature radically alters the nature of Mercury.

Mercury and Venus are both, physically, nearer to the Sun, than other planets. Symbolically, the solar radiance in manifestation is expressed through consciousness by way of sensitivity and perceptivity which are the qualities of Venus and through creativity, thought, and speech which are the qualities of Mercury. The Mercurial crest has some features common with Moon which we have discussed earlier but here we may indicate that the single arc at the top of Mercury's symbol suggests the planet to be a receptacle. It is the chalice through which the divine potential contained in the circle is received. It is the chalice for receiving the Divine essence which after its reception is conveyed to the world of manifestation for its nurture and growth. It is this arc which represents Mercury as the link, a messenger between God and Man. In *Alchemy and Psychology,* Professor Jung has stated that Mercury as the divine winged Hermes manifests in matter, and he called it the god of revelation and the lord of thought. Further, he mentioned that his shadow falls upon the Earth, but his image is reflected in water. This kindles the love of the elements, and Hermes himself is so charmed with the reflected image of Divine beauty that he would fain take up his abode within it, but scarcely has he set foot upon the earth that Psyche locks him in a passionate embrace. From this embrace are born the first seven hermaphrodite beings. According to Jung, the seven beings are an obvious allusion to the seven planets. Whatever may be the other interpretations of the planets, Mercury has tremendous influence on human beings. According to Puranic stories, both Moon and Jupiter claimed his paternity. The planet has certainly a very expansive area of operation extending from the gods to human beings. Mercury does not get assimilated in any other force in Nature but maintains its own speciality. These are well indicated by the fact that the spiritual arc on the top of the circle with cross links the second and the fourth comers (*kendras* in a natal chart) representing the past and the future of the Divine cycle of manifestation.

The immortality aspect of Mercury and its being of the nature of thought principle, suggest its being in close relationship with superior planets like the Sun and the Moon. The three diverse figures included in the symbol suggest its quality of adaptability with all kinds of people and circumstances. The three components of the symbol are so arranged that one should be able to recognise its special role in representing man's ascension to spiritual, nominal heights. Mercury has the quality of being more pleasing and diplomatic than Venus as far as its multifarious interests, adaptability, intellect and sociability are concerned, but it does not have that amount of desire for self-gratification as Venus.

SATURN

Saturn's enigmatic characteristics are well explained and its deeper impulses revealed by the symbol assigned to it. This deep acting planet affecting the highest and the lowest in man is represented by a cross to which is attached the cycle whose upper end seemed unhooked so as to make the circle hang like two semi-circles. The mysterious nature of the son of the Sun, as this planet is known in Hindu mythology, lies in his special characteristic symbol. The cross represented the manifestative process by which the Divine energy is immersed in the material casement. This feature is certainly very prominent in this symbol. The relationship between Matter and Spirit is represented by a cross at the top linked with two semi-circles. The linkage points to the evolutionary purpose to enable the individual realise the purpose of his life and of the manifestation.

The special shape of the curve linked with the third corner of the cross representing death is of great significance. Death is an end of one series of event. The openness of the cycle can mean either the cessation of one cycle of events (leading to *Moksha* or *Nirvana*), or it may mean complete upsetting of one's life pattern and style of living. As the circular arc at the lower end is outward turned, it symbolises that the Saturnian experience of the person should end in spiritualising the person. It should be recognised that the impulses flowing through the planet are for infusing deeper understanding of the materialistic nature of human existence and thereby providing to the individual wisdom so that the veil of ignorance could be pierced to some extent.

JUPITER

The planets which have their foundation on a cross are Jupiter and Saturn besides Mercury and Venus. The first two are intrinsically planets of regenerations. There is, however, a fundamental difference between the two—Jupiter has a rightward convexing arc attached to the left end of the horizontal line, whereas Saturn has its arcs differently placed at its lower end of the vertical line. These characteristics show the essential difference between the two planets.

Two most important attributes of Jupiter are its intimate connection with the welfare of humanity and with imparting of religious impulses to the people. The welfare resulting from Jupiter is for both the physical well-being represented by the horizontal line of the cross and for material comforts represented by the left side of the line. The consciousness side, on which depends the more positive approach to life, is relegated to a subordinate position. This situation is hinted by the linkage of the creative active arc to the horizontal line. Every portion of the circle is symbolic of some active manifestative principle of the Absolute. The arc extending from the lowest point of the circle to the apex, represents that situation under which the *Purusha*-aspect of the Absolute, or his positive creative principle begins to liberate itself from the trammels of matter, *Prakriti,* the accumulated karma. Whatever way this can be achieved would be the domain of Jupiter. In accomplishing this result, the operation would be on the outer aspects of life. When a person gets engrossed in rituals, religious sacrifices, or suffers a physical illness directing him to look heavenward, the Jovian influence can be perceived therein.

Jupiter arouses spirituality as represented by the rightward convexing arc, but by restricting or exaggerating the physical and material component of existence as expressed by the horizontal line of the cross, it renews the life force in man and provides to him a new and fresh impetus towards spiritual understanding and efforts. Jovian influence is exerted from the form side and in a pleasant sort of way, while the Saturnian impact is by way of consciousness; the psychology of the affected person is altered and in doing so the method of restriction and thus inflicting pain is resorted to.

THE NODES OF THE MOON

RAHU   KETU

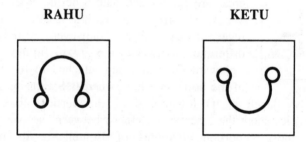

The nodes of the Moon are intimately connected with karmic retribution, but one has materialising influence while the other influences by way of spiritualising the consciousness. The two symbols used for Rahu and Ketu are very similar because they are both represented by two small circles linked by curved lines. The circles are symbols of Divine power apportioned in a particular incarnation to the individual. In the case of the Nodes, the two circles are connected with the past, *Sanchita Karma* and the future archetype, the individuality. The upper connection, as in the case of Rahu, is expressed like the upper arc of the circle which convexes upward. It links the second corner of the cross representing life to the fourth one representing immortality. Because of these two poles being joined, which occurs in Ketu as well, the domain of the

Nodes is the life beyond. They create long term lasting influences. But the upper arc is downward looking which implies materiality, though there is a spiritual bulge. Therefore one finds that Rahu afflicts in a peculiar way. The man suffers physically but while experiencing the pain, he also realises his helplessness and often remembers the Divine, for the redressal of the trouble. In the case of Ketu, the convexity is downwards so the gaze is heavenward though the individual does not look so much for release from the trouble or the karmic suffering rather he strives to seek the rationale of the affliction. He meditates over the problems of life to discover its mystic depth. The latter often makes the person philosophic, and sometimes even gives the individual name and fame (though ignomy also may not be ruled out). In all these cases, deep contemplation on the problems of existence is the final outcome.

17

FEATURES OF
ZODIACAL SIGNS

ARIES

 The geometrical symbol for Aries is a vertical line bifurcated at the top with forks looping downwards like two arcs of a circle resembling two horns of a ram or like two blades of the grass shooting from the central stem. Otherwise, the ram is the universal symbol of this sign. The vertical line represents the positive creative power represented by *Purusha* of the Sankhya philosophy. It is the consciousness aspect of manifestative process and has tremendous importance in representing the pre-manifestative creative intelligence. The outward turned forks of the vertical line add special importance to the sign. The fork is compared even with the bifurcated tongue of a serpent, or the two blades of the grass shooting from its stem; it is even compared with the Buddhist Tau. These symbols lead one to think that this sign represents the initial impulse of the Divine, like the new leaves of the grass struggling to sprout but not yet having seen the light of the day. It is a symbol which points to the polarisation of the creative energy in two opposite directions, the differentiation of the primeval manifestative potential into the male and the female which under suitable combinations would procreate the new vehicles of the Divine energy.

Astrologers often find that the Aries ascendants have great fascination for the opposite sex. It is often aroused without any regard to mundane sagacity but always with some supra-physical considerations, with some kind of idealistic or altruistic objectives. The emphasis in such a relationship is on some purpose transcending merely the satisfaction of animal passion. The forked tongue of the serpent, resembling the division of the vertical line into two at its top, is meaningful in the sense that the creative energy in Aries has the possibility of lowering itself to the grossest levels of materialistic considerations or the selfishness of the most ugly kind, or it can be elevated to altruism of the most sublime type. Like the venom of the serpent, the energy, expressed through Aries can destroy as well as protect and reconstruct (heal like the venom) depending upon its doses and the methods of application. The first sign of the zodiac can provide the necessary impetus to any action where initiative and intensity of efforts is needed, irrespective of the purpose. The sprouting of a young plant and the breaking of the seed-shell need tremendous creative energy.

On a higher plane of consideration, the two downward sloping curves attached to the vertical line assume deeper significance. Ascending from the plane of materialisation represented by the left hand arc, the life-force meets the central shaft of life and light, merges in it, and again, emerges as the right hand arc to portend its re-immersion in matter. Aries is the stage in one's evolutionary chain when one cycle of experiences ends and a new chain of experiences begins. This is evident from the fact that the persons born under this sign are generally confronted with many situations in life which are entirely new to them. Once they have gained experience and control over them, such situations do not occur again, rather these individuals are placed in an entirely new set of circumstances. There is always a novelty in the approach of such persons; they are always non-conventional. This sign does not signify liberation but the spirit eagerly struggles for Liberation. Such persons are explorers, and adventurers in new realms of knowledge, science, and philosophy. The important point to recognise in them is the novelty of their enterprise, rather than the object of their search. The similarity between Tau and this symbol is explained by the fact that Aries signifies a new beginning, a new way of life, a new approach to problems. All of these necessarily require courage, initiative, valour and determination to face life alone, unaided even without any clear-cut guidance.

The ram which also stands for this sign, is a symbol of freshness, innocence, purity, agility, and beauty. The ram is associated with almost all the great religions of world. It is thought to reflect the Divine glory, the Unmanifest reflecting itself in the Primordial Root Matter signifying it to contain all its potential in latency. The ram is almost divine-like, an atom of life which is pure, full of joy in its innocency, frolicsome, always eager to play and jump, an idol of pure spirit, enjoying the expression of its latent energy. From the standpoint of the Supreme Unmanifest all of us, the human and other forms of energy capsules are sporting entities, like a ram. Only at a later stage, the innocence is gone and the agile disposition gets immersed in material clothings. Whether we consider the first sign of the zodiac as a ram, or in its geometrical form of a bifurcated line, it represents the initial impulse of the Divine manifestation in all its freshness.

TAURUS

Taurus is the bull of the zodiac, geometrically represented by a circle with an ascending arc or a chalice at its top. In Hindu mythology, the Lord Mahadeva, the Supreme God of creation, has a bull called Nandi as his vehicle which is much worshipped by married ladies desirous of progeny and prosperity. This allegory is very suggestive. The second sign of the zodiac is the seat of this manifestative impulse of cosmic ideation; it succeeds the first sign representing the dynamic struggling energy eager to express itself. The second sign itself is the procreative energy in action, the energy eager to procreate and enable the manifestation to proceed on its natural course. At this stage, the divine energy has impelled an object which has to proceed to its desired goal. It is not an undirected passion; it is not the emotional upsurge without any purpose, without any expectation of the result. Under this impulse, the male and the female desire to unite in sexual congress for begetting children. The second zodiac represents the urge for procreation rather than the act of procreation. The impulse is pointed, it assigns the purpose to the Divine Energy emanating from the first zodiacal impulse. At some level of evolution and in some type of human constitution, it results in sexual urge for mating. When the first impulse of manifestation is made possible, there is no direction, but without any direction the manifestation itself cannot proceed further. In human constitution, undifferentiated energy is expressed by the phrase "a bull in the China-shop", generally seen like muscle-men who are hefty, strong, muscular, but they may not know how their energy can be utilised. But in the case of Taurus, the persons are well aware of their objectives. Unless they have any aim in view, such persons may seem very reserved as if they have no capacity for attention or any interest in life but once their desire is aroused, they would pounce upon their prey with irresistible puissance. These qualities are very much prominent in a bull which symbolises this sign. The worship of Shiva's Bull is important for the special benediction of the Lord in influencing the process of immaterialisation. Nothing happens without the will of the Lord, but at the stage when impulses of manifestation become well articulated, the Divine Energy has to be specially powerful. The second sign of the zodiac represents that stage when the Divine Energy is not merely overflowing in all directions without any purpose, but it is the stage when the programme of creation has already been formulated in the Divine Mind. In human beings, it represents the stage when the individual begins to have urges to mate and to possess others. In order to invoke the benediction of the Lord for successful procreation, the assistance and cooperation of the Lord's vehicle, the Bull, is worshipped and prayed for.

Geometrical symbol of this sign is a circle with an ascending arc of the circle at the top of it. The circle without the central point is the delimitation of the energy content of the Divine manifestation which is to be employed for any specific purpose. The ascending arc at the top of the circle indicates that the utilisation of this amount of energy would be for the expression of the Divine purpose of manifestation, the dynamic aspect of immaterialisation. The energy begins to unfold its potential under the second sign of the zodiac so that its latent faculties could be realised. The Divine Energy is for creative purpose, for enabling the encased (encircle) attributes to open and fructify. The circle without the central point is always delimitation of the material content, but perfectly related, always well poised, rhythmical, and every point at the circumstance being invisibly linked with its central core. The upward curving arc, which, in fact, represents the lower half of the circle, covers a wide sweep of the manifesting process, beginning with the first impulse of concretising the abstract intelligence and extending it upto the point represented by the tenth sign of the zodiac, where the concretised identity is once again reabsorbed in the universal impulse. The circular line at the top of the circle in the symbol of Taurus representing two horns of a bull indicates the identification of the energy earmarked for the evolutionary process. The second sign of the zodiac thus stands for the procreative energy specified for the manifestation in an identified manner. It represents the dynamic divine energy engaged in the identified object of procreation, either of the individual entities or the universe. In this way, the symbol suggests the involvement of the specified Divine Energy indicated by the enclosed circle with concretisation of the manifestation as shown by the ascending arc at the top of the circle.

GEMINI

The third stage of manifestation as shown by the third sign of the zodiac represents the stage o. anthropogenesis when androgynous birth of human beings ceased and the man produced out of himself the woman as a separate entity for the creation of the species. At this stage, the universal creative impulse differentiated itself into subjective and objective manifestation; the polarisation occurred between positive and negative aspects of Universal Intelligence. This stage of duality in abstraction within the delimited realm of cosmic manifestation created tremendous motion resulting from mutual attraction and repulsion between the two polarised pressures. It produced the triplication of Divine Energy, *trigunas,* namely, the *Sattwa* (harmony), *Rajas* (activity), and *Tamas* (sloth, or inertia) attributes. The third impulse of the zodiac led to triplication of the Divine Outpouring. The Universal Intelligence (*Mahat*), duality or polarisation described as Male and Female, and as *Shiva* and *Shakti*

Tattwas resulting in triplication of attributes namely, harmony, activity and inertia which enabled concretisation of the Divine Idea, are the basic characteristics of this sign.

Symbolically, a male and a female in sexual embrace, or represented by a male and a female in a boat or even as a pair of human beings bearing a harp and a mace represent the third zodiacal sign. Harp symbolises the feminine aspect of creation while mace represents its masculine aspect. The union of the opposites—differentiation and union occurring simultaneously—furthering concretisation of the cosmic ideation is the main characteristic of this zodiacal impulse.

The geometrical symbol represented by two vertical lines along with their top and bottom crossed over by horizontal lines, reveals its deeper psychological details. The vertical and the horizontal lines refer to two sets of individuals, fully polarised between positive and negative aspects of creation united together in pairs. The juxtaposition of these lines and their shapes (especially the upper line with slight upward curvature and the bottom line with downward curvature) point to the relationship of unequal predominance of masculine and feminine compositions in one's constitution. This enables these characteristics to satisfy sexual relationship, socialise among different types of people and racial propagation. The shape and position of these lines suggest the harmonious blending of dissimilar forces which is the cause of all movements. The two vertical lines enclosed by the two curving lines indicate the delimitation and restrictions imposed on Divine Intelligence (whose primeval quality is unbounded freedom) by materiality of life.

The symbol contains two positive lines representing *Purusha,* the positive or the male aspect of manifestation and two horizontal or *Prakriti* lines suggesting the negative, female or the material component of manifestation. The curvatures towards the extremities of the horizontal lines point to their material and spiritual propensities. The symbol is not phallic, it does not indicate sexual copulation but the conflict arising from the union at different levels of developed intellect. The symbol is asexual in nature. The Hindu scriptures on cosmogenesis talk of a stage of manifestation when certain *Prajapatis,* the Mighty Powers, assigned with the task of human propagation refused to do so owing to their concern for their own purity and chastity. Gemini is not very conducive to human fecundity. The meditational practices of these *Prajapatis* seem to find their correspondence in intellectualism indicated by this sign of the zodiac. The development of the mind principle at this stage of manifestation also leads to the creation of Space and Time which in fact is the result of one's thinking principle.

CANCER

 The concretisation of the Divine Plan takes place under the fourth zodiacal impulse. The four levels of consciousness, the four directions of spatial extension, or the four heads of Brahma are all related with this zodiacal impulse. The relationship of this sign with Moon and its close connection with human psyche point to its basic nature. But crab which symbolises this sign, is very insignificant looking ten-footed crustacean. The geometrical sign of Cancer is represented by two circles joined by two arcs, one of which curves downward, and another upward and the two circles are placed horizontally without any actual interconnection between them; the figure seems like doodlings of a child. Both the symbols, the crab and the circles indicate the great depth of its mysterious impulse.

Crab is an aquatic creature, it dwells in water as well as on the ground. It is neither found in deep water nor much distant from the shore. It sheds its hard crust as and when it grows in size. This suggests the principle of reincarnation which is necessary for the renewal of life and maintenance of the primeval consciousness as the everlasting unifying thread of life. Crab's ten feet are symbolic of the number ten which stands for perfection as well as the ten organs of man—five as sense organs and five as action organs. Its shy nature reveals a kind of other-worldliness, a characteristic feature of this zodiac. Crab is sensitive to the slightest noise or the feeblest movement in its vicinity. Similarly Cancer makes a person very nervy, sensitive and impressionable. Crab is not poisonous, it is even edible. The eyes of the crab are shining bright. The selection of this creature as a symbol for the fourth zodiacal impulse reveals the great insight of the ancient seers in the nature and characteristics of this zodiac.

The aquatic nature of the crab suggests that the stage of manifestation has not yet left its connection with the primeval element, water which it would do when greater materialisation of the Divine Energy occurs. The form of manifestation represented by the crab at this stage shows that the manifestation still exists in nebulous form, partly concrete, partly abstract. The Divine Intelligence pervading through the third zodiacal impulse still continues its way though the concretisation of astro-mental bodies have begun. The adaptability of the manifesting egos and the universe, necessary at this stage of creation is symbolised by casting away of the old hard crusts around the crab as and when it grows from one age to another. The ocean bed which is the great receptacle for the crabs corresponds to *Hiranyagarbha*, the great receptacle for the human souls and other forms of manifestation which the fourth zodiacal sign very appropriately represents. This is the zodiacal sign which stands for all latent potentialities as well as the ultimate destiny of every form of creation. This characteristic of the fourth zodiacal impulse established the various states of consciousness and dimensions of space. The shining bright eyes of the crab looking to the distant objects point to the connection between the fourth zodiacal impulse and the tenth one which represents the ultimate destiny for the entity. This contains within itself the possibility of developing during the course of manifestation what is latent within the entity itself; the past which represents latent faculties and the future which is the archetype are both linked within the fourth zodiacal sign.

The ten legs of the crab, point to the fact that the perfection of creation is an inborn, inherent nature in all forms of creation. Every form of manifestation has the inbuilt nature of perfection in its very constitution. It is this inherent quality which assures gradual successful unfoldment of one's inherent qualities which finally become its ultimate destiny. The action and sense-organs, together representing the number ten, help in attaining this ultimate destiny. All potentials of development lies in the fourth impulse (Cancer) of *kalapurusha.*

Cancer is emblematically two circles each of which is joined by an arc of the circle, one curving downward and the other upward. The first circle on the left represents the latent potential of the individual while the other, on the right, stands for the ultimate flowering of the same. The evolutionary journey of the individual enables the latent faculties contained in the fourth house of the zodiac to finally reach the archetype represented by the tenth house. The course of evolution is from the fourth to the tenth, the passage of which through several intervening zodiacs before finally arriving at the tenth house. The linking arcs represent the impulses which make these circles important components of the total evolutionary journey. The Golden Egg, or the *Hiranyagarbha* of the Vedantic philosophy, contains within itself all the latency as well as the ultimate destiny, both of which taken together constitute the emblem in its totality. The left-hand circle is connected with an arc emerging from its top, proceeding towards the right-hand side and curving downward. This emblem represents the energy contained in the Cosmic Mother's Womb emerging from it on its evolutionary journey. The downwardness of the arc is a pointer to the fact that the evolutionary experiences are primarily stored in the consciousness which is constantly guiding the ego towards the realisation of its ultimate destiny represented by the circle on the right. The left-hand circle contains the faculties to be developed; the course of manifestation results from the attraction of latent faculties to the archetype, the ultimate destiny, represented by the circle on the right. The archetype is always sending impulses to the incarnating ego, guiding it towards its perfection. The circles symbolise perfection, rhythmic movement, wholeness of the being; the fourth zodiacal impulse as well as the tenth, both are, associated with wholeness and rhythmical movement. The right-hand circle is linked by the arc touching it from the bottom suggesting that during the process of its transmutation into the Pure Essence, the latent faculties have to pass through a series of changes. The fourth zodiacal impulse itself constitutes a mini-world of creative energies where the concretised quality of Spirit and Matter, the form and the consciousness, the entire latent faculties scintillating with Divine energy, are awaiting to move towards the ultimate goal. Cancer has the unique quality of extending its realm of operation from the uttermost depth of human experiences to the highest possibility of the Supreme Bliss attainable on this earth. It is the stage when intelligence is churned and the ego is prepared to commence its evolutionary journey further.

LEO

The fifth sign of the zodiac is named Leo which is Latin for lion. Even in Sanskrit the sign is known as *Simha* meaning lion. The geometrical symbol for it is a circle connected by a descending arc which at its lower end is linked to an ascending arc. All these symbols refer to the basic impulse of the fifth sign as the entry of the cosmic creative energy Fohat—the ray of the Primordial Light, which is running through the various planes of manifestation, moving in spirals, established different force centres, which by stepping down the cosmic energy at lower levels finally succeeds in the manifestation of micro as well as macrocosm. At this stage, noumenon concretises; the abstract spiritual principles transform themselves into material forms. The fifth sign stands for the creative impulse at all levels of existence whether in the universe or in the individual.

Almost every ancient religion has assigned special importance to lion, because this king of the forest has several physical as well as occult characteristics well known to the ancient seers which very appropriately symbolised the majesty of the creative urge in Nature. Without this urge the continuity of life-force could be disrupted and the glory of Divine Plan lost. The concretisation of Time-Space dimensions of manifestation only prepared the arena for the action of the individualised entity. The manifestation of individualised entities began with the generation of the fifth zodiacal impulse. There could hardly be any better representation to point to the Divine Spark enshrined in every entity than a lion wherein the inner is always sparkling in its movement and behaviour. The individual at this stage of manifestation is bestowed with the divine creative faculty primarily with the intention of enabling it to reproduce that very nature of the Supreme. Inspite of delimitation, there is the quality of freedom and majesty in this sign. It is however, to be noted that the absolute freedom of the lion inherent in the Divinity of the individual human soul, does not enable either of them to express the same because of external conditions.

The lion does not waste its vital energy, its virility, for non-reproductive purposes. It is said that the lion copulates only once in life and that also only for reproduction. This may merely be a traditional belief, but such beliefs are important for understanding the basis on which a symbol is selected. At this stage, the Supreme has assumed fetters, his spark now lies hidden in the materialistic sheaths, the lion is encircled and delimited in its forest, though it could operate like a king even in its limitations. The power of the lion radiating from it made it associated with many gods and goddesses. Yoga-Maya, Durga, Kali and many other female deities of the Hindu pantheism, representing the Nature's passive creative powers, are often shown with lions as their vehicles. The lion represents the male, the masculine creative power, but the benediction of *Prakriti* can flow efficiently when it is appropriately harmonised and assisted by the *Purusha* energy of equal strength. The masculine creative force represented by Leo, the Lion, can fructify only with the help of feminine creative forces of Nature, therefore the Hindu goddesses ride on the lion for their locomotion. Creativity can be possible only through *Prakriti* but the creativity itself is a masculine attribute.

This idea has been very succinctly expressed by the geometrical sign of Leo. The circle in the symbol represents the wholeness of the Golden Egg, the *Hiranyagarbha*, the evolutionary potential. It takes a first step, and the hard crust of the individual egg breaksdown and the energy contained in it begins to overflow. The individualised energy capsules, known in the language of religions as 'souls' are now materialised. The onward journey is symbolised by downward curving arc of the circle, which for gaining experience has to undergo series of births and deaths and finally to return to its original source. The last phase of the journey wherein the soul looks homeward and takes the path of return is symbolised by the upward curved arc tucked at the bottom of the right hand circle in the symbol. This is the essence of the fifth zodiacal impulse. The wholeness of the *Hiranyagarbha* involves itself in manifestation, that is, descent in matter, but finally it looks homeward. Under this impulse the individualised ego, an independent individual entity, is immersed in material existence. Thereby it gains experiences and then begins its homeward journey. The whole course is intended to provide the necessary knowledge and wisdom of the creative process. At every stage of the journey, the incarnating ego has to involve itself into action, without creativity no progress is possible. This creativity is the essence of the fifth zodiacal sign.

The symbol also resembles to a great extent a living human sperm eager to mate and procreate. One of the features of the Leo born ascendants is to have the great creative urge. The level of creation is not so important as the urge to create. It often results in creation for the sake of creation itself. It may not be directed to any specific goal. If this impulse is functioning at the physical level there could be physical procreation. If the impulse is active on 'astro-mental' plane, one could find much activities at emotional and intellectual levels. The fifth zodiacal impulse is characterised by tremendous urge to concretise that which is in the non-manifest form. This concretisation is also linked with the individualisation process which in fact differentiates one form of creation from another. The symbol contains only one circle but indicates the full course of its creative activities.

VIRGO

 The fifth impulse of the Cosmic Man has been a vehicle for the cosmic feminine creative principles worshipped as Durga, Kali, Mahamaya and others having lion as their vehicle of locomotion. But these energies get further involved and their subjectivity is chained in matter so as to embed the Divine Energy much deeper. Virgo stands for the crucification of the Cosmic Man. He is nailed more firmly on the altar of matter. Virgo represents consciousness in bondage but with an awareness that the shackles can be cast away with right understanding of the relationship between Spirit and Matter.

This zodiac is assigned the emblem of Virgin, but diagramatically, it is three vertical lines joined at the top by an undulating line resembling a serpent but with a cross tucked to its tail. The reference to Virgin in several world religions has almost been identical. The Hindu scriptures considered the celestial virgin in such forms as *Prithvi* (the Earth), *Aditi* (the celestial space), *Parvati* (Lord Shiva's consort who is considered the mother of all gods and men) and *Jagadamba* (the mother of all men). In Greek mythology, she assumes the form of Pallas Athene who sprang from the head of Zeus, full grown and armed. The Romans considered her as

Minerva, the goddess of wisdom and arts. Gospel of St. Mathew and St. Luke described Virgin Mary conceiving Jesus by the power of the Holy Spirit. No less significant is the story of Sita, the wife of Lord Rama, born to Emperor Janaka fully grown while he was ploughing the field. All of these show the Virgin as of immaculate birth; they are all connected with wisdom and are personification of hidden powers in Nature. They have suffered much in their personal life in order to assist in the Divine Plan.

This is the only human symbol among the twelve signs of the zodiac. Gemini is more an abstraction and it refers to the union between positive and negative forces in Nature rather than two human beings, as indicated by it. Virgo refers to a maiden, not a married female adult. It refers to feminine aspects of Nature, unalloyed by any other influence. The primeval female in Nature being *Prakriti,* this sign is associated with virgin nature. In order to maintain her pristine purity, the primeval Nature (as Nature is protective inherently, it is considered as mother) has to conceal herself in several layers of materialisation, and thereby suffer and forgo her independence. In the manifested world, the sixth zodiacal sign points to the Divine Energy lying entrenched very deeply in matter. As a result of this relationship between the inner and the outer conditions of life, the individuals acquire supreme mystic consciousness. If the relationship between the two is uncoordinated and disharmony surfaces at the physical level, the individual suffers from diseases, while any such disharmony in social relationships gives rise to enemies and other social problems. A balanced harmonious relationship between the inner and the outer conditions of life enables the individual to attain considerable power over the six primary forces in Nature.

The diagrammatic representation of the zodiac goes much deeper in expressing the characteristics of this impulse. The three vertical lines, a serpent, and a cross are all very meaningful symbols which can be studied at different levels of existence. The vertical lines refer to consciousness, it is also connected with *Purusha,* the male or the positive aspect of creative energy. The three vertical lines imply pluralities of the levels of consciousness. This refers to stages such as the dream stage (*Swapna*), deep sleep (*Sushupti*) and *Samadhi* or the *Turya* stage. The pure spirit at Virgo stage gets immersed into matter much deeper and undergoes several stages of immaterialisation. The hidden capabilities of the individual are fettered according to the layer of their immaterialisation. The serpent is a very ancient symbol susceptible to many exoteric and esoteric interpretations. It is a symbol of both wisdom and wise. In the present context, the serpent is the 'Fohatic' force itself; it is the universe of manifestation representing the ever present electrical energy with ceaseless destructive and formative power. The serpent on the three vertical lines describes the *siddhis,* the perfections, the creative powers which control, regulate and propel the universe to its different layers of manifestation. The serpent is both the destructive and the constructive symbol, the cause of death as well as of eternal illumination. By establishing right relationship with this power, one can possess great powers and wisdom. The tucking of the cross at the tail of the serpent has reference to the manifestative process itself.

Under Virgo, the Nature's finer forces lie deep under the various levels of manifestation. When the human beings develop creativity (the result of the fifth impulse), they penetrate deeper in matter placed around them. As a result of his enquiring mind and creative involvement, the individual acquires knowledge and power to control one's consciousness and comes face to face with hidden sides of Nature. The sixth zodiacal impulse is the materialisation of cosmic electrical power and expression of natural laws of action (and reaction), which is known in popular parlance as the Law of Karma. With proper harmonisation of various forces, both personal and natural, this impulse enables the individual to attain various *siddhis,* the perfections, resulting from transcendence over material restrictions. The serpent over the vertical lines refers to the possibility of attaining wisdom by transcendence over different levels of consciousness embedded in various sheaths of materiality. In this effort there is always a strong tendency to be weighed down by materialistic propensities as the serpent is loaded heavily by the materialistic cross at its tail-end.

LIBRA

 The Vedic astrology has named the seventh zodiacal sign as *Tula*. Other names given to it are more or less synonyms of this word. The various names such as *Tauli* (weigher), *Vanika* (merchant), *Yuka* (joined) and *Tula* (scale) are more or less related words. Even the word Libra which has Latin derivative, means pound weight or pound sterling in English. But what do they weigh, or what do they balance? Why did the ancient seers suddenly put such an inert symbol at this stage of egoic growth, while all other symbols had been living entities, even the two other inert symbols namely *Dhanu,* (Sagittarius) and *Kumbha* (Aquarius) are action-oriented signs. The geometrical symbol of Libra is a horizontal straight line over which one finds two short straight lines joined in the middle by a semi circle bulging upward. We have earlier examined the significance of horizontal and vertical lines, and the different segments of a circumference. The horizontal line in the way it is represented here, points out that the feminine aspect of the being is not motivated by the craving for further involvement in matter. There is a radical change in consciousness which is receptive. If the male component of the being is interested in immaterialisation, it would not deny or refuse its advance but by itself, it is in the state of neutrality. The urge for any kind of positive activity at the stage seems to be in abeyance; the vertical line is not present in the symbol. The feminine nature of the ego is in the state of complete inertia.

In Libra one horizontal line is of the normal length, but the other one has been broken into two halves. The male aspect of the ego, represented in philosophical discussions as *Purusha*, has almost abandoned its active role. It is very much in the same stage of psychological inaction as Arjuna on the battlefield where he feels the futility of all material attainments. The creativity of the person in the cosmic drama has become fragmented.

The link between the fragmented portions of life is stabilised by the semi-circular segment of the circumference. The segment joins the Great Deep, the *Anant Kshira-Sagar,* the ocean of pure essence, from which all forms of life have arisen, to its ultimate form of manifestation. One end of the segment is at the very end of the beginning, the fragmented godhood in latency and the other end at the final achievement, the fruition, at the end of the journey. The articulation of that which is contained in the egoic consciousness is the very mission of every life's manifestation.

The segment joining the two halves of the line represents the real crux of Libra. It points out to the great upsurge of the inner quest, there is strong dissatisfaction with the existing situation. The individual does not find that the life conditions as available to him are satisfying. He wants to know the purpose of his life. He wants to articulate his inner urges, the inner purpose of his life. He does not wish to abandon the material affluence, he does not wish to give up his material advantages and conveniences, he is still fond of his status and worldly gifts but his heart does not feel satisfied. Such persons wish to have more and more, they want to excel both in material acquisitions as well as in spiritual realisation. Success in either is not possible to the expected level. So Libra gives tremendous dissatisfaction and frustration. Beneath all these psychological complexities what is worth discerning is the lack of satisfaction, and the attraction of spiritualisation of life without feeling the necessity of severe austerities needed for such attainments. Such persons who have Libra as their ascendant would acquire material possession, but would like to feel and often argue that these possessions are incapable of giving them the real satisfaction. They would wish to acquire occult *siddhis,* perfections; they may even attend religious rituals. They would like to have the advantages of both the spiritual attainments and the material affluence. They may engage themselves in meditational practices, go to seers and saints, but they would be unable to renounce the material gains in order to devote themselves completely to spirituality. Libra's geometrical symbol represents this state of psychological indecision resulting from attraction and dissatisfaction from both the material as well as spiritual attainments and requirements.

The more orthodox and traditional symbol of a balance is much more direct than the geometrical symbol. Traditionally, the balance represents Libra. At this stage, we know that the fragmented god-head has immersed itself completely in the deepest layers of materiality and further progress will have to be in another direction. At this stage, the involutionary impulse has reached its deepest point. The movement now would be towards the release of material bondage in order to regain its pristine state of purity and splendour. For this purpose, there will be dissatisfaction with worldly existence, and there may even be flashes of spiritual possibilities. There would be equal attraction towards both the types of life.

In order to represent this kind of psychological duality, the balance has been used to show the wider implications and the seriousness of the situation. The balance is made of a central rod which is hung in the middle. On either side of the rod there are three strings attached. These three strings are of equal sizes. They are tied to a plate on which the articles to be weighed are kept on one side and the weight on the other. This homely symbol represents admirably well the psychological state of the evolving ego.

The single thread in the middle of the rod stands for *sutratma* with which the individual ego is linked with the Universal Energy called *Paramatma*. It also represents the initial spark, the primeval life-force emanating from the universal life. This life in unity, for evolutionary purposes, has to polarise into two though the polarised energy in unity represents the primeval life-force. In its duality it leads to various modifications which induce its further immersion in materiality. At the end of the rod, on both the ends of duality or polarised aspects of life, there are three main motivating attributes, *gunas,* known as *sattwa, rajas,* and *tamas* which by their natural attractive and dispelling qualities create various situations in life which are constantly weighed in order to give further impetus and momentum to life's course. At the Libra stage, the two sides of the balance are bereft of anything, implying thereby that neither there is any material consideration which could necessarily impel the ego towards any course of material involvement, nor the spiritual merits (or attractions) have been important to direct its course. This is the stage where the karma of the individual places him in such a situation that he could take up any road. This is the situation when the calculation of life's experiences and assessment of different values have to be made by the individual himself. This decision being difficult, he could suffer great turmoil or he may be immersed in such attractive material conveniences with spiritual attractions and urges that the giving up of those affluent conditions becomes trying. Whatever decision the person takes, that is going to decide his course of evolution for several incarnations to come.

This situation is well indicated by certain other astrological features of this sign as well. Saturn is exalted in this sign, Venus is in its own habitat, and the Sun is debilitated. The exaltation of Saturn hints at the possibility of austerities and penance needed for undertaking the evolutionary course but if taken up, it would bestow to the individual the blessings of real achievements of life, the articulation of life's real purpose, that is, realisation of one's unity with the Universal Spirit. The voice of spirit, or the impelling force of the Universal Spirit which has guided the ego so far will presently be silent. There will be no suggestions from the Sun at this stage on the basis of which the individual could make up his mind. He will have to depend completely upon the intuition and sensitivity bestowed by Venus which will however not obliterate the attractions of material indulgences. These three planets, Saturn, Venus and Sun have very important role to play at this stage.

SCORPIO

 At Scorpio, the decision of the ego is made; the ego has decided to take serious steps to regain its primeval nature. The geometrical symbol of this sign indicates the trials of the ego, success in which would decide its further advancement and growth. The geometrical symbol of Scorpio is represented by three vertical lines over which is placed the undulating serpent with its tail attached with an arrow. Three components of this symbol are the three vertical lines, the serpent in movement, and the arrow. The basic impulse flowing through the eighth sign of the zodiac is indicated by these three components of the symbol.

The three vertical lines represent the three important *nadis* which are instrumental in arousing the Serpent Fire. *Ida* and *Pingala* are two *nadis* coiled round *Sushumna Nadi*, which are channels for the upward journey of the highly active occult power located at the base of the spinal cord. *Ida* is said to be connected with the Sun or the solar energy and *Pingala* with the lunar energy; these two are twined around *Sushumna*. The three are important constituents of the spinal cord which is often compared with a bamboo rod with several knots within it. The verticality of the three lines in Scorpio refers to the activisation of these *nadis*. The undulating serpent over these lines refers to the arousing of the Serpent Fire. This energy is said to be contained in a serpent-like coiled state during the period of its dormancy and begins to uncoil itself when yogic practices are followed. The undulating position of the serpent over the three vertical lines indicates that the serpent has begun to move within the three *nadis* which has begun to vivify the masculine or the solar and feminine or the lunar energies in him. It is enjoined in the yogic literature that this energy is extremely powerful. It can bestow enormous capabilities to the individual but also to destroy him unless he is well equipped to control the same. The essential safeguard needed to control this energy is altruism. The aspiration towards spirituality is the basic condition for all altruism. This aspect of aspiration towards unity with the universal self is symbolised by an arrow. The combined symbol therefore clearly points to the arousal of the Serpent Fire as indicated by the undulating form of the serpent and its movement through the three *nadis* which form the part of the spinal cord (represented by the vertical three lines) and the cultivation of yogic austerities (as indicated by the arrow at the tail of the serpent). The zodiacal sign of Scorpio is often said to represent the hidden aspect of one's life. It is said to be related to pit, ant-hill, serpent's hill and such other places which points out to the seat of the *kundalini shakti,* or the Serpent Fire.

The emblem of a scorpion assigned to the sign, more clearly describes the nature of this impulse. The scorpion which represents this zodiacal impulse is itself very mysterious in its behaviour and very suggestive in its symbology. The zodiacal sign itself is described as a deep opening in the earth, a cavity, a hiding place or a hole where Vasuki, the *Serpent Naga* used in the churning of the ocean resides. This hole is also referred to as the pit where the scorpion dwells. The pit also indicated the hiding place of the precious jewel. Such allusions suggest that this is a hiding place and a repository of secret aspects of one's life. As far as scorpion itself is concerned, it is described as an insect which stays in secret holes in warmer parts of the world and is as deadly as the serpent itself. A special characteristic of this insect is that a male scorpion finding a female engages in some sort of primitive courtship consisting merely in grasping the hands of the female with his own hands and rubbing her tail against his. But after copulation the male is often attacked by the female and devoured unless he manages to escape. This curious behaviour indicates that the insect is not fond of demonstration of affectionate relationships. The animal instinct attracts the male to the female who in return after the procreative mating is finished, desires to kill the mate. Such a situation denotes the antithesis or disharmony between the masculine nature of the individual and his feminine counterpart. The *Ida* and the *Pingala nadis* are not well harmonised in such cases. In alchemical literature this opposition at the early stages of one's evolution is pictured by the two serpents with their heads facing opposite directions. In predictive astrology, the influence of Scorpio leads to sexual incompatibility and the partners mate simply for the satisfaction of their lustful design.

Another aspect of this insect is its central bony constitution with knots in it, resembling the spinal cord in a human being. The two hands like claws represent the two solar and the lunar *nadis* which require to be energised for the arousal of the secret power. The most important part of this insect is its sting located at its tail. In order to tame and manage this insect, it is important that this portion of its body is well taken care of. In the geometrical symbol this aspect of the problem is suggested by putting the arrow there, but in the traditional presentation that portion of advice is left unmentioned. How one is prepared to manage the arousal of this power and delve deep in the pit will determine his attainment of the *siddhis* and preparation for the future journey on the path.

In providing the suggestions for such preparations, the stellar relationships with this sign are important. Here no planet is exalted. It is important because at this stage no indication could be given regarding the necessary preparations that could be helpful for the individual. Only a kind of warning can be given. That is indicated by suggesting that Moon is debilitated in this sign. The worst situation occurs when the consciousness of the person is left unguarded in a state of complete passivity. Many undesirable influences begin to affect such an individual and he is fatally endangered. Extreme degree of alertness is needed during the arousal of this latent power. When the astrological impact of this sign begins to influence a person, he will be doomed if he does not take necessary precautions against such onslaughts. Furthermore, the sign is owned by Mars. This implies that the personal initiative and the readiness to bear the burden of the sacrifice, ordeals of austerities and such other traits that Mars symbolises would be most helpful for the individual. Scorpio would generally arouse the Martian conditions, both psychological and physical, but how these powers are used is left completely to the judgement of the person concerned. The non-availability of any guidance as to how one should prepare himself makes this sign very dangerous and mysterious.

SAGITTARIUS

 Sagittarius has a special place among the zodiac signs. The simple geometrical symbol consisting of an arrow with a cross attached to its lower portion portrays its essential features. Emblematically the centaur with a horse body and a human head shooting an arrow upwards, represents the ninth sign of the zodiac. The Sanskrit names for this sign are *Dhanvi* meaning an archer, *Chapam* meaning a bow and *Sharasanam* who is an arrow shooter. These concrete representations, or objective symbols of some abstract attributes or features of stellar radiations are not adequate guidelines but are good pointers.

Arrows have been sparingly used in occult literature but whenever they are used, they indicate, one-pointed direction of one's energy for the attainment of some spiritual goal. In some of the Upanishads, mention of *Pranava* and various occult preparations have been connected with this symbol, but essentially, the arrow is one pointed. The two sides meeting at its point, resemble the integration of one's polarised energies for the given objective. During the Scorpio stage, the two polarised energies represented by two aspects of the insect were being harmonised so that they could help the arousal of the latent energy in oneself. At Sagittarius, these two polarised forms of energy have been well coordinated and are perfectly controlled and directed under the human will. The arrow is pointed upward, the energy aroused after careful control of one's hidden powers is now directed towards attaining some higher objective. The nature of this higher goal is still undefined but it is something nobler, something fulfilling. The cross attached to the bottom of the arrow shows that the arrow is trying to extricate itself from this burden. If it could succeed in doing so, its flight towards its goal, the direction in which the arrow is shooting, could succeed. The cross, we have already seen, represents manifestation, the objectified Divine Essence in material sheaths. Seen this way, Sagittarius is aspiration towards spirituality, the urge to release the divinity in man from the various material impediments which are hindering the flowering of his inner spirituality. During the process, there have to be spiritual preparations of which one-pointedness resulting from integration of polarised forms of energies is very important.

The pictorial representation of the sign by a centaur is also suggestive of the same essential features but it adds something more from predictive standpoint. The centaur represented a race of creatures having the head, trunk, and arms of a man and the body and legs of a horse. They dwelt in the mountains of Thessaly and Archadia. They were often represented as drawing the car of Dionysus, the Greek god of fertility, wine and drama, or they were bound and ridden by Eros, the god of love. They often indulged in drunkenness and amorous habits. Their general character was that of wild lawless and inhospitable nature, slaves of their passions with the exceptions of Phobes and Cherian who dwelt at the foot of Mount of Pellion and were famous for their wisdom and knowledge of their healing art. The general features of the race of centaurs show that they were admixture of two widely different character traits. They were human as well as animal-like and many of them were wise but most of them were lawless and amorous. They were slaves of gods but some of them were respected for their helpfulness. Among all these traits, the most important feature of a centaur was its physical form; it consists of part horse, and part human being. The hind part consisted of the animal energy, the horse, while the front constituting the hand which stands for instruments for action, and head which represents the organ of thought, stand for human qualities.

Under Sagittarius there would be enormous vitality which is symbolised by a horse, but this energy has to be satisfactorily utilised as a result of discriminating thought and action. The centaur in the symbol is shooting an arrow, which represents direction of the thoughtful action and thought, the control of mind and control of action and having made them one-pointed, efforts towards the mobilisation of the energy in the service of mankind. Considered this way, Sagittarius stands for potential for spiritualisation. There would be enough of horse sense, animal vitality, and the power for procreation under Sagittarius. But the duality of nature cannot be overlooked. There would be much capacity for spiritual development and becoming helpful to one's fellow beings. There could also be some inclination towards indulgence in the pleasures of life. The cross at the bottom of the arrow is often very powerful. There would be enough of opportunities, enough of God's grace, which if rightly taken, could lead to spiritual growth.

The essential nature of Sagittarius is aptly contained in several synonyms of the sign. *Dhanvi* is an archer and under the impact of this sign whatever the conditions of life, they would conspire to induce the individual to move towards acquisition of spiritual power. He would now feel dissatisfied with his attainments of the material gifts. Even if he is immersed in material pleasures, these would not satisfy him. In case he suffers from discomfort and some kind of agony, the redressal by itself will not satisfy his psychological cravings. He would desire some kind of enlightenment. That is implied by being an archer. He must attain the 'goal'. He must strive for the unattained. *Chapam,* which is the bow itself, refers to the various religious practices in which the individual would engage himself. The bow can be in the relaxed state or its strings may be stretched. Under Sagittarius, the possibility for both are there, which one the individual takes up depends upon the actual conditions of life and his natural karma and will. *Sharasanam* means an arrow shooter. There is every likelihood that the worldly attachments would begin to seem burdensome at this stage and the individual would begin to make the necessary preparations for higher goals in life.

In essence, Sagittarius represents that zodiacal impulse which inspires the individual to move from the earthy to the heavenly direction and in turning his gaze he would be prepared to undertake the various occult responsibilities. There would be a transformation in his nature. The most important characteristic of Sagittarius is its effect in transforming the animality in man to humanliness. Under its impact, the animal in man is transformed into Divine, or at least the necessary preparations for it begin to change his nature and to spiritualise his life.

CAPRICORN

The tenth sign of the zodiac known as Capricorn is more mysterious than the earlier ones. This sign known as Makara, is not a crocodile with which it is ordinarily associated with. It is much more evolved and can be deciphered only with great care. Capricorn is a goat-like creature but many other symbols are also assigned to it. Mythologically, in some schools of astrology, it is represented as a unicorn, a horse-like creature with a horn on its forehead. In Vedic astrology it is known as Makara, which literally means a crocodile but astrologically the word has other significance. Geometrical representation of the sign consists of a horizontal line terminating with a downward moving arc going in the right direction, ending with a loop with an extended arc moving towards left side. Another geometrical symbol assigned to it is a V-shaped beginning whose right side upper end has a horizontal extension with a loop followed by a downward arc convexing to the right. From all these, one at the very outset infers that this zodiacal impulse has a very abstruse influence to impart.

Taking the geometrical emblems first, we find that in one of these symbols there is a prominent horizontal line at the end of which various twists and turns are made. The horizontal line represents passivity or the feminine aspect of one's life. It is associated with receptivity. The horizontal line ending in a downward moving curve looping towards the end of it indicates that this feminine aspect of manifestation, constituting matter and form of creation, having reached its end of the journey is again put to severe trial. It has to make some more efforts towards creating another realm of manifestation and to transcend it again. The horizontal line stops when the individual or the universe has realised its goal and merged with the Divine Intelligences, the *Dhyanis*. But this union devolves further responsibilities. The arc descending from the horizontal end is similar to the involutionary flow of the Divine Essence which at the earlier stage had expressed itself during the first seven zodiacs. These aspects of cosmic ideation are to be replayed at a higher level and at a smaller scale. The loop is the microcosm which the realised individual has to create by himself. The succeeding descending arc showing convexity of the arc towards right side stands for the downpour of spiritual energy. Taken together, the emblem in its entirety represents the individual who has realised his own goal, is now engaged in recreating another realm of manifestation, or cooperating with other Divine Intelligences who are engaged in similar efforts and then again transcending these involvements for another kind of spiritualising transformation. The *Dhyanis* also have to go beyond the realm of their involvement in creative activities.

The other emblem which begins with a V-shaped angle followed by a small horizontal line tucked with a small circle and ending with a downward arc convexing to the right, shows the same aspect of cosmic ideation as the earlier one but from another angle. The previous emblem indicated the position of the realised individual in the cosmic drama, but this emblem represents the situation from the universal side of the phenomenon. It shows the downpour of divine energy for further working out of the Divine Plan. The V-shaped sign resembles the pot in which sacrificial fire is ignited; it stands for the chalice through which the Divine Grace is funneled downward for the furtherance of the Divine Mission. The V-shaped funnel stands for special benediction, guidance and association of the higher powers with the world of manifestation. From the V-shape emerges the horizontal line representing the receptivity of the aspirant and the succeeding looping and the descent of the arc with its convexity are similar to the last part of the previous emblem. Thus, the tenth sign of the zodiac stands for a recreation of the life form, it stands for the downpour of the Divine Essence for the furtherance of the Divine Plan. It also indicates the readiness of the realised being in cooperation with the work of other Cosmic Intelligences who are already engaged in such activities. The involvements of the individual requires him/her to make many preparations and clearing of the various sheaths which he had inherited. There could therefore be much hardships and sufferings necessarily related with this sign.

Unicorn, which is one of the pictorial emblem of this sign, is a mythical creature resembling a horse and having a single horn in the centre of the forehead, often symbolic of chastity and purity. Goat which is said to be another emblem for Capricorn is a harmless, small quadruped herbivores by nature and often representing austere sages. Crocodile is a kind of reptile found in sluggish waters and swamps of the tropics, having a pointed snout. Though Makara as the tenth zodiacal sign does not necessarily refer to crocodiles, yet one can see that there are many features of these animals which are very suggestive. An aquatic creature, crocodile represented the possibility of entering the deep sea symbolising the expanse of the universal life. We shall later on see that fish which represented the twelfth sign is also an aquatic creature. Narrowness of the snout of the crocodile and the central horn of the unicorn suggested a unique one-pointedness of the sign with which all its efforts and impulses function. It is really a very powerful sign which is very effective in creating its impact. But the symbol of the goat goes much deeper. The herbivorous nature of the animal refers to its status among the spiritualised beings. It symbolises the fact that the entity has reached a position where it has succeeded in controlling its physical appetite. Austerity and saintliness associated with goat are indicative of the inner changes that result under the impact of the tenth zodiacal sign.

The true significance of the sign is contained in its very name. When it was referred to as Makara, it had allusion to that area which is related with the Tropic of Capricorn; it is the region where Dakshinamurti dwells and looks after the welfare and progress of this world. That is the seat of occult guidance and wherefrom occult aspirants are directed. The affinity of this realm with the sign of the zodiac is much greater than its association with crocodile, the animal. More importantly, the letters of this sign are connected, according to the science of mantras which deals with the impact of phonetic values and which align the numerical values of different letters with the planets, with the limbs of human beings and so on. The word Makara, in this way, is linked with ten limbs of action and understanding, which under the impact of this sign have to be controlled, integrated and dedicated to the service of the occult hierarchy. The individual life of the person under the impact of this sign begins to be universalised. It has to be impersonal. That is the goal and for this objective, it is necessary to be pure and chaste as symbolised by the unicorn.

In essence, the symbols of the tenth sign of the zodiac represent that stage of cosmic ideation when the individual having purified himself and having attained spiritual enlightenment under the Sagittarius impulse, begins to identify himself with the spiritual needs of the world and begins to cooperate with spiritual powers to alleviate the heavy karma of the humanity. It is a life of much responsibility, much suffering, and denial of personal conveniences and comforts. Purify oneself, do penance, develop intelligence and cooperate with higher powers of nature—these are important requirements at this stage. That is why Saturn is its ruler, Mars which bestows courage and initiative is exalted here, while Jupiter linked with exoteric religion and formal worship is debilitated.

AQUARIUS

 Aquarius is symbolised diagrammatically by two wavy lines whereas pictorially it is symbolised by a pitcher, sometimes simply as the vessel while on other occasions it is mentioned as the pitcher from which water is flowing out. The very word *kumbha* which stands for this sign means a pitcher and is linked with *kumbhaka* associated with *pranayama* forming an essential part of yogic exercises.

Under the Capricorn impulse, the incarnated ego learnt the significance of working with the occult hierarchy for which necessary personal preparations were made. As an active cooperator with occult guardians, the individual has begun working for the universal life subjugating and annihilating his personal predilections. Saturn, the lord of the sign, precipitates much suffering which could be borne only with courage and enthusiasm bestowed by Mars. The next stage in cosmic ideation is the merging of the individual with the universal. This situation is actually reflected by the various symbols of Aquarius.

The two wavy lines present in the geometrical symbol of Aquarius represent water. This is supposed to indicate the great depth from which life began. It is to be noted that Capricorn, Aquarius and Pisces—all three signs are connected with water. This is significant specially after the spiritualising process of Sagittarius.

Now, under the Aquarius impulse, the individual has begun functioning like the universal life-force. The one wavy line refers to the origin from which the life began, the other one represents the individual who has merged in the ocean. As the both have become one, the two wavy lines are of similar nature and they have become indistinguishable.

The symbol of a pitcher is not much different from what has been described above. The Vedantic philosophy has already popularised the mystic significance of a pitcher and the maker of the pitcher. A pitcher is made of the clay which is the ultimate particle with which all forms of manifestation are made of but the idea of the potter who had shaped the pitcher is also present in this symbol. When we know that the Aquarius sign of the zodiac is represented by a pitcher, naturally it has allusion to that pitcher with which the potter is associated. The individual has at this stage reached his archetype. Now, he has to function like the ultimate or the universal life which is represented by the water flowing out of it. At this stage, from the individual standpoint, he has reached the level where the full influence of Aquarius is absorbed, and now he will begin pouring forth the universal life contained within him for the good of the people. This aspect of Aquarius is observed in many of the Aquarius ascendants whose life has been dedicated to the regeneration of some spiritual or occult goals of life which are being forgotten or neglected in the modern world. Such a courageous impersonal work is possible only when the difference between the individual and the universal life-force is obliterated.

In yogic practices, as indicated earlier, *kumbhaka* has an important role. *Kumbhaka* is the retention of breath in Hatha Yoga practices. It implies in the present context that the universal life is retained for some specific purpose in the individual. That is, the individual, as such, has qualified himself for final liberation, but for carrying out the Divine Plan, he has voluntarily accepted certain limitations as a result of which there has been some kind of differentiation between him and the universe. Otherwise there is no essential difference between the two. For this reason, there are two wavy lines in this sign of the zodiac, both being identical. The word *kumbhaka* refers to the regulation of the essential life-force and that indeed is the impulse flowing from this sign. How that life-force is utilised would be dependent upon various other factors.

PISCES

Pisces is the twelfth and the last sign of the zodiac after which the cycle begins once more. In this sense it is difficult to indicate whether this sign relates to the beginning of the cycle or the last point of it. In fact, the circle is always a continuous chain. The zodiacal cycle being a series of cosmic impulses carrying out the Divine Plan of manifestation, is a circular movement necessarily through different stages of development. The twelve signs of the zodiac are all connected together, they are unified together and any one taken separately loses its significance. Even Pisces though it is said to come towards the end of the cyclic movement is in reality merely one link in the chain, one bead among the twelve ones.

The symbol for it diagrammatically is two half circles facing opposing directions but linked by a copula at its middle. This emblem appears like two semi-circles joined together in the middle by a horizontal line. All the essential components of life are present in this emblem. If the two segments of the circle are transposed and brought face to face, they would together represent the circle which is the symbol for manifestation itself in its wholeness. Positioned differently, linking them by bringing the segments in such a way that they touch each other only at a point in their middle, is indicative of the fact that though they are linked together at some important stage of their separate existence, they are seemingly two different entities. At this stage, the involutionary and the evolutionary momentum induced by the manifestative process have become disjoined. They are no longer impelled by the cycle of necessity expressed as births and deaths and the gradual evolution from lower forms of creation to the higher ones. The delinking of the two tendencies, however, does not suggest their complete annihilation. They still repose in Mother Nature, the horizontal line linking the two arcs represent Nature, the feminine aspect of Eternal Life. Thus, the emblem expresses that a balance is attained but there is no compelling force to move forward. The seed for future regeneration is however still preserved. The ego is presently at a stage of manifestation where it can remain in the Great Deep till the next Dissolution, or it could take birth again and embark on the manifestative journey, may be at a higher rung of creation. The two arcs would represent two different births. H.P. Blavatsky equated Pisces with Noah, who appears in the generation as the twelfth patriarch and is the forefather of a new race of mankind. The emblem of Pisces stands for this linkage between the two incarnations, between the two races of mankind, between the two cycles of manifestations.

The other emblem for Pisces is a group of two fish each clinging to the tail of the other and are placed in water. Fish is the symbol of fertility, auspicious nature of events, it is the source through which seed is carried to the future. We have already referred to Noah in the previous paragraph. The fish suggests the procreative potential which enables the beginning of a new cycle of manifestation. Fertility, prosperity, regeneration, auspicious nature of the symbol show that there is no compulsion at this stage but there is willingness to enter into any state of divine action, though that action is not the result of any compulsion or culmination of past karmas. All karmas have ceased and the ego is liberated, yet there is willingness to do whatever is required. The psychological state is similar to that of the avatars. The two fish in deep water symbolise this frame of psychological orientation.

In the symbol lying parallel to each other, lying side by side but the head of one is towards the tail of the other, reminds of the cessation of duality in Nature. We may recall that the creation began with the first zodiacal sign, Aries, symbolised as the vertical line forking into two lines like a newly sprouting seed whose two leaves were coming out of the tiny stem. Having completed their journey, these two leaves have once again united together. The masculine and the feminine poles have ceased their separate existence, they are lying together, as if merging in Unity as a result of which all electrical, magnetic and other kind of energy generations have come to rest. Their identities have not ended which shows that they are capable of being reactivated. Thus, Pisces has quietitude of dissolution, but with the expectation of a new generation.

The three planets connected very closely with Pisces are Jupiter, Venus and Mercury. Jupiter owns the sign and is Deva-Guru. This ownership is indicative of the auspicious nature of the sign. Jupiter is also connected with progeny and that aspect of nature is well represented by fish as the symbol of procreation and fertility. Jupiter is God's Grace, and protection; nourishment provided by fish is well taken care of by placing them in their natural habitat. For the onward march of the soul, it is necessary to have sensitivity and intuitive flashes of the Divine purpose. The journey would involve much engrossment in matter. It would involve compromise of metaphysical ideals for which the virgin ascetics or the Kumaras refused to undertake manifestative functions and Daksha Prajapati had to be created. The new orientation with its possible pleasures and karmic bondages is represented by Venus being exalted in this sign. Mercury is thought, duality, calculated action and it is debilitated in Pisces. At this stage the ego involves itself in manifestation not for its personal ends but to cooperate with Nature.

Recapitulating the last six zodiacal signs, we find that Libra, Scorpio, and Sagittarius were associated with psychological preparations of the individual ego which had reached the stage of material affluence. At Libra, there was a balance between material attainments and the spiritual urge which had begun to impress upon the psyche of the person. The two sides of the balance were equipoised. There was an equilibrium between involutionary and evolutionary impulses. One could expect much dissatisfaction at this stage, but also a kind of equanimity. At this stage there is always a possibility of perceiving the future course of one's life, and immersion in matter. There is balance and complete passivity of action and receptivity of the psyche. This leads the individual in search of deeper meaning of life and he enters into a secret pit. He delves deep within himself, tries to understand the nature of his latent possibilities and at a later stage even attempts to arouse the Serpent Fire. The spiritual aspiration becomes very demanding. This could occur as a result of some misfortune or due to deep reflection but this kind of aspiration, represented by the arrow at the end of the serpent in the geometrical emblem of Scorpio is indicative of this situation. The whole concept is well indicated by the scorpion which dwelt in secret pits, cavities and holes which referred to the seat of the Serpent Fire in man. Then came the transformation and urge to rise higher in the realm of spirituality. At Sagittarius, the animal in man is transformed into a human being and the individual under this impulse takes his journey towards the path of spirituality and unity with Divine workers.

The following three signs, namely Capricorn, Aquarius and Pisces are associated with water in some form or the other.

Representing the Primordial Essence in which all forms of existence dwell, water forms an important aspect of the life of an aspirant. At Capricorn, he comes closer to the occult hierarchy and begins to share greater responsibilities devolved on such higher beings. He becomes associated with Dakshinamurthi and that type of Divine Forces. He could be much misunderstood in everyday life, but he knows his path and goal. At Aquarius, which is significantly, the sign where there is neither any exaltation nor debilitation of any planet, there is no guidance of any kind; the individual is left completely to his own light. There is much suffering, though much enlightenment of the right kind is also possible as these are represented by Saturn, the ruler of the sign. The two wavy lines signified that the individual life-essence has merged itself with the universal life-essence. At Pisces, all polarity has ceased and the ego has the option either to be in the universal life-essence and to wait final dissolution when it could again be activated, or it may take up an immediate assignment and begin the next course of cyclic manifestation. He may in that case soon join his hand with Aries and begin the Divine Pilgrimage again forgetting for the time being all that he has acquired and the spiritual eminence he has acquired. His new cycle of pilgrimage however, begins with greater innate enlightenment and spiritual consciousness which as subconscience constantly radiate the message of the Supreme.[1]

---

[1]A detailed description of these symbols is available in author's *Myths and Symbols of Vedic Astrology,* Passage Press, Utah, U.S.A.

18

SUN AND PANCHA MAHAPURUSHA YOGAS

Pancha Mahapurusha Yoga or the five combinations for human greatness, postulate non-luminaries in their own signs or in exaltation occupying a cardinal house. These planets produce prosperity and happiness of different kinds depending upon the nature of the planet involved. Jupiter, Saturn, Mars, Mercury and Venus under these conditions produce *Hamsa, Sasa, Ruchaka, Bhadra* and *Malavya Yoga.* Each of these imparts to the individual concerned certain special features of its own. They enable the individual to accomplish exceptional results. Yet a superficial examination of their attributes in the classical texts do not reveal any marked differences between them.

The various measurements as given in *Brihat Samhita* for example, of certain human limbs do not provide any clue to greatness of these planetary combinations. Some of the results indicated for these *yogas* are very enigmatic and misleading. Leadership of a gang of thieves, covetous of another's wife, for example, as given under *Sasa Yoga,* cannot in any civilised community be considered signs of greatness. A right appraisal of *Pancha Mahapurusha Yogas* will evidently require a very careful study of the forces involved in these combinations, specially because they are very powerful stellar radiations and have been highly applauded by astrological seers.

The basic features of *Pancha Mahapurusha Yoga* are the involvement of only five non-luminaries, namely Jupiter, Saturn, Mars, Venus and Mercury; their being in strength either by occupancy of their own signs or exaltation; and their position in cardinal houses. This *Yoga* does not require collective occupation, each planet in such a situation will produce greatness of its own kind. The individual uniqueness in any positive manner which makes the person function harmoniously in accordance with the archetype destined for him can qualify him for greatness.

The exclusion of luminaries and the Nodes requires special attention. The Sun, Moon and the Nodes have their special influences, certain inner qualities of the individual do come out under their impulsion. The rationale for separating them from the purview of these *yogas* of human greatness can be better appreciated by studying their unmentioned assumptions. It may even indicate the differences between the working of luminaries and other planets.

The classical texts classified the Sun and the Moon as different from the non-luminaries. They described the Sun as the soul of the universe from which all other planets derived their sustenance. The Moon reflected the radiance of the Sun. Both together provided the nucleus around which the different aspects of human personality revolved. Astrological tenets assigned only one sign to each of these luminaries while the non-luminaries were given two signs each to express their qualities. The first clue to separating luminaries from the non-luminaries lies in this distinction. The luminaries are not polarised; they always function in wholeness of their being.

The second clue lies in the difference in their mode of functioning. The luminaries do not, as a matter of fact, impart anything of their own to the individual. They only burn the dross, dispel the ignorance and enable the individual to function in their own light on their own strength, understanding, viewpoint and colouring. They only provide some kind of support on the basis of which the individual may externalise and develop some of their own latent qualities. There is effort required in this case on the part of the individuals. These differences make the luminaries function on the spiritual aspect of the individual. They work on the Divine Plane where there is no difference between the individual and the universal life-essence. The non-luminaries function on the physical and psychological sheaths which function on the objective plane which can only be perceived within oneself. The physical sheaths are changeable, they reflect the progress of the soul towards its self-realisation whereas on the subjective plane there is no progress but only uncovering, unfoldment and elimination of ignorance to find out that which already existed.

The difference between the basic nature of the luminaries and the non-luminaries results from the differences in their mode of working and the impact they make on the individual. The luminaries which are subjective planets have however their special roles to play. Here we shall restrict ourselves only to some considerations related to the Sun.

The Sun works from within, from the centre of the being; it is the very antithesis of every material covering. Its impact is noticed on the spiritual component of the human personality and in sharpening his psychic faculties. Under the influence of the Sun, the inner qualities of the individual come to the fore. It is a kind of self-illumination. Under it, the individual's effulgence shines forth. The Sun burns the dross and the inner reality is realised, there is less of achieving greatness and little progress from one stage of development to another. This does not characterise evolution, modification, transmutation, ascending a higher level from a lower plane as under the impact of other planets. Rather it suggests realisation of that which already was present within the individual.

A powerful Sun is extremely self-centred. Realising one's uniqueness, one does not necessarily become humble. Humility is a state of the mind. When the outer, the separated individual realises the one universal life as immense, overpowering and exceedingly great compared to his little, tiny, individual self to which his consciousness is still entrenched, he becomes humble. It is in a state of duality. The contrast between the perishable separate outer personality and the permanent wholeness of the inner being alters his psychology. His approach to things and relationships radically alters. He becomes truly religious. Such a realisation occurs when the individual is identified with the centre which reveals the outer illusion of the existence which is a product of *avidya*, ignorance. The Sun merely revealed the truth, destroyed the veil of illusion. Exclusion of the Sun from the *Pancha Mahapurusha Yogas* is in this way understandable. The non-luminaries under these *yogas* indicate the progress of external transient self in accomplishing certain attributes, not in uncovering the individual's real divine nature. Some kind of effort is needed in this achievement, which is not merely uncovering of the already existing inherent attribute.

Furthermore, the impact of the Sun is highly subjective, so this cannot be experienced by itself. It must have some material base to express itself. The non-luminaries being physico-phsychological in their influence can function independently. The dependence of the Sun on non-luminaries is comparable with the light and the wick. Latent fire (Sun) requires some external medium, electric filament to warm wick, oil and inflammable gas (non-luminaries) to be perceived as a flame. For this reason, the astrological texts emphasised the need for support to luminaries for the effective production of their results. The luminaries must be supported by some other planets for the actualisation of their results (on the physical plane). The planetary combinations under *Vesi, Vasi,* and *Ubhayachari Yogas* are based on this basic support theory for the luminaries.[1]

These combinations to support the Sun occur when the planets occupying the twelfth, second or both the *bhavas* are adjacent to the Sun. The presence of any planet other than the Moon in second position from the Sun produces *Vesi Yoga*. Under it, the person becomes fortunate, happy, virtuous, famous and aristocratic. Planets other than Moon occupying the twelfth from the Sun gives rise to *Vasi Yoga* under which the individual is happy, prosperous and favourite of the ruling class. In some texts, the results of the former are given as truthful, lazy, unbiased, prosperous, modestly rich and tall, while the latter makes the individual proficient, charitable, strong and renowned. The difference between the two does not seem to be marked unless one emphasised that the planets in the second position produced righteousness or truthfulness more than affluence while in the twelfth house from the Sun the emphasis is more on renown, learning and proficiency. The distinction is much obliterated in *Ubhayachari Yoga,* where the individual is considered to be a prosperous, kind or one equal to a king.

The enigmatic nature of these supportive *yogas* which also elude the basic nature of the luminaries is explained better if studied in greater detail. The nature of the planets involved in these *yogas* is

---

[1]Similar support is needed even for Moon.

very important. Essentially, the Sun will only precipitate the effect based on the nature of the flanking planets. In case the Sun is flanked by Saturn and Rahu, or Mars and Ketu, the auspicious results of *Ubhayachari Yoga* may be reversed. The individual may lead a miserable existence full of troubles, sorrows and deprivations. Mercury and Venus are always hovering around the Sun. Mercury being within 28° from the Sun and Venus within 60°, these are always in supportive positions. Mercury's association with the Sun produces special *Budha-Aditya Yoga*, making the person highly intelligent, skilful in all work, famous, comfortable and happy. The proximity of Mercury and Venus to Sun does not necessarily produce the results expected from *Vesi, Vasi* and *Ubhayachari Yogas*. Jupiter is the only planet whose placement in second, or twelfth needs special attention. Jupiter in close proximity with the Sun may get its own benefic results greatly reduced, but if it is near the Sun but not very near it, its auspicious effect on the Sun is remarkable. The solar rays are so piercing and destructive that Jupiterian effects may get annihilated if Jupiter is within 11° of the Sun, otherwise the Jovian effect on the Sun adds to its spiritualising and life sustaining force. Jupiter placed in fifth or ninth house from the Sun is excellent. In sum, the auspicious and inauspicious plan ts create different results from that usually given for *Vesi, Vasi* and *Ubhayachari Yogas*. The nature of planets flanking the Sun becomes important in these combinations.

This aspect of flanking planets was appreciated by the ancient seers. They stated that the nature of auspicious planets is important for prosperity and renown expected from the Sun. An inauspicious planet producing *Vesi Yoga* (planet in second from the Sun) will make the individual fond of bad company, evil minded, and bereft of riches and comfort. Under *Vasi Yoga* (planet in twelfth from the Sun), with malefic planets, the person becomes stupid, afflicted, lustful, murderous and ugly faced. He may have to go into exile. From these combniations, it is clear that these *yogas* do not bring out any special auspicious results, they merely emphasise the fact that the Sun is a special planet; it needs support for its impact which depends upon the nature of the planet coming near it to support its results. What needs to be noted in the present context is that the solar impact becomes effective on the physical plane only when it works through some non-luminaries. The Sun does not play an independent role in any horoscope where efforts on the plane of manifestation (as in *Mahapurusha Yogas*) are involved.

Another reason for precluding the Sun from *Mahapurusha Yogas* is its deep acting (subjective) influence. The cardinal houses where the planets must be posited to produce the *yoga,* are connected with physical or the mundane welfare of the individual. The *Pancha Mahapurusha Yogas* lead to mundane prosperity, physical affluence and expansion in social relationships. The Sun is certainly the most effective royal planet, yet its effect in cardinal houses does not lead to satiety on the physical plane, expansion in social relationships and harmony in family matters. The growth and maturity of personality and one's uniqueness in worldly matters (specially in comparison with his fellow individuals) depend upon planetary delineation in cardinal houses. This uniqueness is destroyed by the Sun occupying a cardinal house in strength. It is a very anomalous situation. The non-luminaries such as Saturn, Jupiter, Mars, Venus and Mercury derive their sustenance and strength from the Sun which is the central storehouse of power and energy, yet by itself the Sun is incapable of producing harmony in the individual's life and a sense of satisfaction and glorification in his individual achievements. The cardinal houses play an important role in *Mahapurusha Yogas* where the solar radiance creates much destabilisation which results in its exclusion from this *yoga*.[2]

The four cardinal houses in a natal chart are important for assessing the life pattern and the evolutionary course of the incarnating ego. Among these houses, the fourth has special importance. Astrologically, it links the individual to his hoary past. The exoteric astrology describes the fourth house as the significator of mother, mansion (especially entrance into one's own abode or the loss of it), vehicles which signify royal insignia, garments, land, agriculture, tent, pavilion, temperament and learning as well as the power of comprehension. These features symbolise and represent the primordial essence and its expansion in its manifestative process inducing the ego to traverse different terrains during its downward course of materialisation. They relate the incarnating ego to the very source from which it has been reeled off and which like a

---

[2]Sun even in the tenth house in exaltation or in its own sign, invariably produces inauspicious results for marital happiness and social relationships.

discerning guardian always oversees the activities of the child and sends from time to time intuitive flashes to him for his guidance.[3]

This being the essential nature of the fourth house, the Sun in exaltation (implying thereby the presence of Aries there) or in its own sign (it can happen if Leo is there), will churn the deepest level of the individual. The basic nature of fourth house being encouragement by the Great Depth, Bythos, to reel off the incarnating ego on its materialising process, the Sun in this house will produce resistance to this impulse. It will activate the individual to seek his union with the centre of his being, *Atman,* Brahma, the Universal Self which exists only in the realm of *Arupa Lokas,* the formless planes. When the Sun is in a powerful position to pull the central life pulsating in the individual towards its primeval source which is formless, then the question of involving the involuting self in terrestrial glorification becomes meaningless. Under such a circumstance, there may be great urge in the individual towards renunciation of everything material, everything connected with mundane affluence, material status, physical conveniences, emotional satiety and such other aspects of interpersonal comparison with other human beings. This combination will impart a sense of immense loneliness and an intense urge towards unification with the universal life. *Saravali* states that the presence of the Sun in the fourth house will make an individual devoid of conveyance and relatives, he will suffer from heart diseases, will destroy his paternal house and wealth, and he will serve a bad king. In fact, the very presence of Leo in fourth house makes the individual so radiant that less evolved individuals feel uncomfortable with him. His behaviour is regal but emotionally he is detached. His feelings are so intense that they cannot be expressed externally.

His warmth may be genuine but only very evolved persons can vibrate at his level of awareness. He may often be considered dry and without any emotion. On the social level, his relationships will be curt, and even within his own family circle he will be misunderstood. The presence of Sun in Leo enables the individual to establish a link with the very essence of his being and consequently increase his spiritual knowledge considerably. He

---

[3]See, *A Study in Astrological Occultism,* IBH Prakashan, Bangalore, pp. 10-21.

attains a regal status and acquires property but very few people feel comfortable with him, even his mother is estranged from him. Obviously, such characteristics make him a little of superman, centred more near his *Atman* but farther from his fellow-beings and the world of glamour and sense-gratification.

With Leo in fourth house, the ascendant will be Taurus whose lord Venus will rule over the sixth house and will be inimical with the Sun. The sixth lordship to the ascendant is not conducive to general happiness. Mars, the seventh lord is friendly with Sun but it also owns twelfth house which is bad. Moreover, the Martian lordship of the seventh house is not conducive to marital happiness. The ninth and tenth lordships go to Saturn. The Sun aspects the tenth house which may have destabilising effect on professional career. There may be too much ambition, too little affability and much karmic difficulties. Such a conjuncture of circumstances arising from the Sun in Leo in fourth house may make the individual eminent but not materially satisfying. The churning of the heart leading to emotional turmoil will disturb every important aspect of his material existence and social relationships. Disillusionment and discontent in store for him may in due course lead him to spiritual quest but they will certainly not qualify him for material happiness.

Even the seventh house Sun will not be less disturbing. A person who is incapable of maintaining a coherent relationship with any individual whether it is one's spouse, business partner or social companion and is always craving for the satisfaction of his own personal desires and interests can be considered introvert, self-seeking and selfish. Such a person exercises great pull in his professional career and is materialist to the core. He can be ruthless in execution of his designs. His very nature, Saturn being the lord of the twelfth and the ascendant, will be troublesome. It will rarely lead him to universality of approach which is the basic psychological orientation needed for spiritual greatness. Even Jupiter for such a person will induce him to try acquisition of material wealth and affluence. He will be so much entrenched in egotism that any spiritual suggestion or any ethical injunction will be treated with disdain.

The Sun in tenth house with Leo sign is very significant for material prosperity, social status and official recognition but egoic objectivity and universality of vision, essential characteristics of every spiritually indivisualise person, will be absent from him. He may attain high status in public life and his personality may be well defined but these are intended to make him finally turn his gaze towards the central source from which every form of life has been reeled off. He will have no satisfaction in his domestic life, his children will be disrespectful to him, his wife may have her affection somewhere else. His aggressiveness will not be appreciated; he may be considered callous, fierce and without any milk of human kindness. Such a person may be at the turning point of his egoic journey, but he may not yet be fit enough to be specialised on any ray for undertaking any carefully marked divine assignment. His trials and tribulations in life are not expressions of karmic retribution but they are mere necessary preparations to strengthen his inner self.

The Leo ascendant people are certainly powerful and when the Sun is also there, the sparkling dazzle of his personality often makes him overpowering. The exclusion of such a person from the purview of *Pancha Mahapurusha Yogas* often seems baffling. Leo rising gives a majestic appearance, as if the life-force was vibrating from his every sinew. Such persons are possessive parents, egotistical and selfish in temperament and braggarts by disposition. They are excessively libidinous but not necessarily promiscurous. They are not satisfied with material heights they attain. They always aspire towards greater intellect, greater wealth, greater status in social life and greater respectability. Often they think (inside themselves) that they have achieved more than what they have actually worked for, that is, they exaggerate their own attainments (atleast in their own mind), yet they think that they deserve more than what they have received. They are basically materialistic but they think that they are highly spiritual. The Sun in this position makes the person invincible, enduring, meticulously punctual and victorious over his enemies. He may like to dwell in forests, mountains and in village away from the din and bustle of busy dwellings. He is admirably suited for spiritual studies and practices but his entrenched egotism will not enable him to experience the bliss of his inner quietitude or identification with the universal life of which he is (an insignificant) part. Material satisfaction will be absent from his psyche and spiritual vision will always elude him.

Similar conditions arise when the Sun in exaltation occupies any cardinal house. In exaltation, the basic creative spark of the Sun is so luminous that its fructification on the material plane is difficult. Viswakarma, the Sun's father-in-law, had to block his rays to enable his (Viswakarma's) daughter Tvastri bear her husband's effulgence and live with him.

The allegory of Surya chasing Chhaya, the shadow of his wife, and cohabiting with her and producing several children from her suggests the dependence of pure light of the Sun on non-luminous base for its material manifestation. In its exaltation, it is nearer its radiant self unable to manifest its creativity on the objective plane without any material base which is necessary for affluent and material existence.

Placed in the ascendant, an exalted Sun has an assignment to complete, a mission to fulfil and it has ability and power to execute the same. With such a planet in the ascendant, the individual is ready and fully prepared to embark on a new journey with new energy and new task to perform. In such a person, the Divine Spark is actively functioning. There is unfoldment of divinity in him. As such, there is genuine humility in him, not an external show of greatness and achievements. Aries in the first house endows the individual with a scintillating spark which enables him to leave his mark on whatever the individual undertakes. When the Sun occupies this sign, this situation is greatly intensified. The spark becomes highly active. The spirit in the individual becomes very powerful. The individual may receive political patronage, be invincible in his approach to life, yet his reactions to these attainments are those of indifference. He is not working with any urge for achievements. These reactions are not aimed at or acquired as a result of accomplishments of the present incarnation. They are the aftermath of exertions of past lives. The *Mahapurusha Yogas* assume that the accomplishments are acquired during the present lifespan of the person, for which foundations may have been laid in the past. There is a difference between some power and certain specific assignment already entrusted (at birth) to a person, and some qualities acquired during the lifespan and expression of the same for the good of the humanity. *Mahapurusha Yogas* refer to the latter while in the case of Ascendant with Aries-Sun, the former conditions operate.

When a powerful Sun as evident from its exaltation is located in fourth house, the central core of the individual is churned and all that is latent in him is brought to the surface. Certainly such a condition should have qualified him for the *Mahapurusha Yoga*. The exclusion of the Sun from it in this situation is based on the fact that the Sun in this position is brought about to produce certain karmic results following him from the past so that if he succeeds in meeting the trials and tribulations aroused by it, he qualifies for greater heights. The transience of material existence for the individual is juxtaposed with eternal vibrations from the everlasting Eternal. It makes the divine nature in man express itself in the external or the physical realm. It make the individual very regal, viewing all problems of life and relationships from a pedestal of detachment and universality of approach. It also detaches him from the masses. His nature becomes very selective and no one can establish partnership with him on the basis of equality. Ordinary persons and relatives are often alienated from him. They even become vindictive and antagonistic to him though he himself remains courteous, measured in speech, and dignified in behaviour. He is often faced with persons who are vindictive, jealous, and undignified. These are special conditions confronting him because the materialistic core of his life, evident from the Ascendant being ruled by the grossly materialistic Saturn, needed refinement which can take place only when detachment from the superficial, external and transience is inculcated deeply. The Sun is exalted in fourth house of already evolved souls.

A similar situation is present when the exalted Sun occupies the seventh house. With exalted Sun in seventh house, the individual has lunar rulership of tenth house leading to instability, vacillation and changes in professional career. His sphere of interaction with the world around him will be instable. He will have to learn much diverse lessons from each of these relationships. The Ascendant lord Venus which is a deeply materialistic planet will minimise the importance of his detachment, spiritual vision, development of higher values in life and purification of various human sheaths. The fourth and fifth houses will be greatly tainted by crude materialism of Saturn. A person who cannot establish a harmonious relationship with his spouse and social partners can hardly be well balanced within himself and have a matured personality. So there is ample justification for excluding Sun in seventh house from *Mahapurusha Yogas.*

The exaltation of the Sun in tenth house is important for material success. The tenth house is the only house where the individual manifests results of his latent faculties and general approach to life. It is the house which provides the creative zone where the individual can show what power he has to express. All other houses reveal his past achievements and the already acquired abilities and faculties. In other houses, various aspects of one's life are nurtured, strengthened and opportunities stored for their further manifestation. But tenth house shows the likely interaction of the individual with the world outside with the conditions which are not of his own creation. The tenth house shows the interaction of the *Kshetrajna* and the *Kshetra* (if we borrow these concepts from the Bhagavad Gita). The interaction of tenth house with the outside world creates fresh karmas. When the exalted Sun occupies tenth house, the Ascendant has an even sign, Cancer. It indicates passivity in one's approach. The initiative in man is considerably restricted; he seeks other external support to develop his abilities, to achieve fruition of his efforts. The tenth house of *Kalapurusha,* the Cosmic Man, represents the main purpose of one's birth. Esoterically, it represents the impulse which enables the individual to merge himself in the universal life. In terms of occultism, this house links the individual aspirant with the world's spiritual hierarchy and thereby makes him an agent of the Divine. In this process, the individual personality is annihilated. Prior to his final absorption in the universal life, the individual becomes a channel for the divine outpouring. The tenth house of the natal chart shows the manner in which externalisation of energy is activated and made manifest. With exalted Sun in this house, the individual externalises the highest in him. As the Sun is pure subjectivity, so when the individual expresses in the world around him that which is pure subjectivity, and when he is engaged in externalising the universal quality of nature latent in him, his behaviour becomes impersonal. Whatever his eminence and achievement, there is very little of personal greatness. *Mahapurusha Yogas* accentuate and emphasise the nature of personal achievement, or accomplishments and not the externalisation of any universal quality latent in the person.

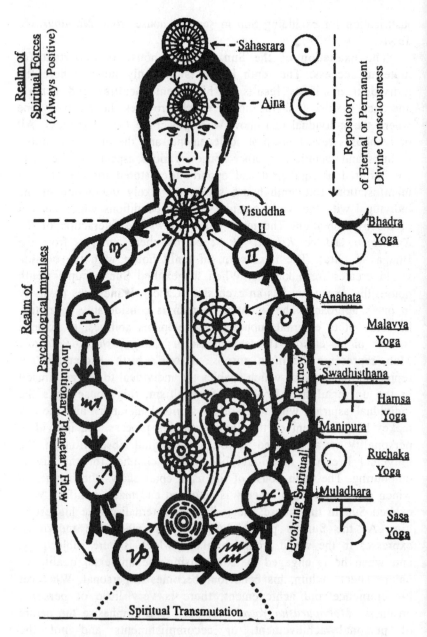

**Relationship Between *Pancha Mahapurusha Yogas* and
Yogic Energy-Centres and Zodiacal Signs**

The primary reason for excluding luminaries in general, and the Sun in particular, from the purview of *Mahapurusha Yogas* is their basic spiritual nature. The Sun and the Moon work on the subjective realms of existence with complete absence of materiality. They constantly radiate divine spiritualising impulses. The absence of any matter in their radiance does not qualify their effects, their basic quality, for any transformation; the impulses in their pure, primeval nature, always remain the same. This aspect is demonstrated by the two highest energy-centres, *chakras,* namely *Sahasrara* and *Ajna,* uniquely tucked above the circularity of the flow of manifesting impulses, circulating and manifesting according to the action of non-luminaries which are assigned two signs of the zodiac, one on the materialising side or on the involutionary side and another on spiritualising or evolving side. *Mahapurusha Yogas* are basically concerned with the world of manifestation. The cardinal houses have their special function in this scheme. The subjective planets require objective or non-luminaries to express themselves on the planes of manifestation; by themselves and in their strength (as evident by their being in their own signs or in their exaltation) their invincible impulses will destroy materialistic impulses and inculcate pure spirituality. This will be the very antithesis of material affluence, sensual gratification and worldly attainments. Material growth and spiritual realisation both cannot exist simultaneously.

The Sun in cardinal houses, whether in its own sign or in exaltation, unveils the latent divinity in man which is different from acquisition of material power, status and affluence. The non-luminaries by their impact in cardinal houses in strength enable the individual to evolve, acquire, and accomplish; there is progression in personal development. The luminaries, especially the Sun, burn the dross, remove ignorance and reveal what is inside the man, who is essentially divine in nature. As real spirituality which aims at unfoldment of divine nature in man is under the domain of luminaries, their presence in cardinal houses which are concerned primarily with material attainments, rightly deserves exclusion from *Mahapurusha Yogas.*

19

BHADRA YOGA:
The Mercurial Greatness

Bhadra Yoga is formed by Mercury's exaltation or occupation of its own sign in a cardinal house. It is a rare combination of human greatness. Varaha Mihira gives a detailed description of the physique of the person born with this combination. Parasara also almost repeats the same results. He says that "a person born in *Bhadra Yoga* is a great man, has large and muscular chest, his gait is like that of a lion, he moves like an elephant, his arms are long, touching the knee, he is an expert in yogic activities, erudite, has beautiful beard, moustache and feet, he is passionate, *sattwic;* his hands and feet are marked with the figure of conch shells, mace, arrow and elephants, as well as those of plough, flag, lotus. He is well-versed in scriptures, has a beautiful nose, his hair is black and he is a scholar. He is independent in all his activities, he maintains his people and lends his wealth to his friends. He has wife and children, rules over the middle region of the country and lives for a hundred years." One wonders whether these qualify a person to be exceptionally great in the modern age. Obviously there is need for a careful understanding of this combination.

Bhadra means gentle, auspicious, gracious, prosperous and socially accepted mores. But a great man is one who accomplishes exceptional feats. Such an individual must be uncommon, unusual, having achieved exceptional positive attributes within the reach of human individuals but not ordinarily attained. The supreme quality of human individual is *thinking,* his expansive *consciousness;* the self-awareness or his unfettered mind is the unique asset of a human being. Mercury is related with *Manas,* human intelligence. When Mercury irradiates an individual in a positive manner, he becomes capable of taking an independent and objective judgement and moulds his life according to such an unfettered, unconditioned thought. But mind has its own limitations, not generally recognised by humans. J. Krishnamurti once stated that "The mind cannot go from the limited to the immense, nor can it transform the limited into the limitless." But the task before the human being, if he wished to transcend the everyday humdrum of life, is to transcend this limitation of mind. Krishnamurti also indicated that a righteous life is not the following of social morality, but the freedom from envy, greed and search for power—which breeds enmity. The freedom from these does not come through the activity of will but through being aware of them through self-knowledge. Such a king of self-knowledge, without any personal thought, or a thought based on social morality or traditional ethics can be the basis of true greatness, which could be rightly considered gracious, noble, auspicious. One has therefore to find out the basic conditions provided by *Bhadra Mahapurusha Yoga* enabling the individual to transcend the limitations of thought and traditional morality without becoming reactionary.

In analysing this *Yoga,* one may consider three of its outstanding features, namely, the occupation of Mercury in Gemini or Virgo in a cardinal house. Jupiter, Sagittarius and Pisces will then be occupying the cardinal houses which necessarily follows the earlier condition; and the Sun's proximity to Mercury assumes this luminary either in the sign occupied by Mercury or in one of its flanking houses. These conditions hold some of the keys to the greatness of *Bhadra Yoga.*

Mercury is connected with the Fifth Principle in Man which represents *Manas,* the bridge between the objective and the subjective realms of existence. Mercury is not only considered a bridge between the higher triad viz., *Atma, Buddhi* and *Manas,* and the lower quaternary but it is considered by certain class of occultists as one with the Sun as well as a step-brother of the Earth. Eulogising Mercury, H.P. Blavatsky mentioned it as an astrological planet more occult and mysterious than Venus, and indicated that "it is identical with the Mazdean Mithra, the Genius of God, established between the Sun and the Moon, the perpetual companion of the Sun of Wisdom: he had wings to express his attendance upon the Sun in its course; and he was called the sharer of the Sun's Light. He was the leader or evocator of Souls, the Great Magician and the Hierophant." She further stated that the Sun and Mercury are One.[1] Referring to the origin of Buddha, in the Puranic legend, where he is mentioned as the son of the Moon (Soma), she characterised Mercury as "the intelligent and the wise, because he is the offspring of Soma, the Regent of the (in)visible Moon, not of Indu, the physical Moon." Thus, according to Blavatsky, Mercury is the elder brother of the Earth, metaphysically his step-brother, so to say, the offspring of Spirit, while she (the Earth) is the progeny of the Body.[2]

The mystic role of Mercury is infinite. Not only its proximity with the Sun makes it the sharer of the Sun's Light, but as a 'messenger' of his father Jupiter, with whom he shares common altar in many religions, and as step-brother of the Earth, it has a unique role to play in interplanetary transmission of influences.

The very name Hermes in Greek means among other things, the "interpreter". As a 'Psychopomorpic Genius,' Mercury conducts the souls of the Dead to Hades and brings them back again. In Alchemy, it is considered as Primitive or Elementary Water, containing the seed of the Universe, fecunded by the Solar Fires. The frequent changes of sex, as given in Puranic allegories, make Mercury suitably adapted to positive and negative, active and passive roles in manifestive process. The winged angel is capable of freely traversing between the completely material and supremely spiritual realms of existence. All these are possible because Mercury represents Mind or the Thinking Principle in man which has unlimited scope for expansion, extension and adaptability. When thought contents resulting from millions of individuals and racial experiences fill the thought of the individual, it is pulled down, earthward, and limits the growth and evolution of the man. The planet expresses its most material aspect in this nature. But when emptied of these crystallised thought forms, in its pure capacity to comprehend, with freedom to look with innocency, as J.

---

[1]*The Secret Doctrine* op. cit. Vol. III., p. 41.
[2]*Ibid.*, p. 56.

Krishnamurti would like to call, Mercury is capable of bringing about a radical transformation in man, a complete regeneration in the individual. In his ethereal nature, Mercury is unique, Messiah of the Sun, Messenger of Jupiter, but in relation to earth it is only a step-brother of the Earth.

In *Mahapurusha Yoga,* Mercury assumes a special role by virtue of its occupancy of Gemini and Virgo signs of the zodiac. Apart from differentiation and polarisation of the cosmic manifestive impulse, Gemini has certain other potential often not very well appreciated. It has been named *Yama* and *Yuga* besides being given several other names. Yama is the god of death, but he is also the teacher of Swetaketu, the Upanishadic seer, to whom Yama imparted the mystery of life and death. This knowledge opens the inscrutable gate to spiritual enlightenment. The knowledge of death enables the individual to empty his mind of its material thought contents. Virgo is said to be the symbol of Primordial Feminine Creative Power. Any ripple in the disposition of Virgo releases very powerful forces in the consciousness. Mercury in Virgo greatly activates the subjective or the subtler impulses providing immense opportunities for the release of latent creative energies. At this level, wisdom is accompanied by personal power.

When Mercury occupies Gemini or Virgo in a Cardinal house, the innercore of the individual is stirred. The Fifth Principle in Man, *Manas,* is activated which begins to link the physical life of the individual as an extension of his inner-beings. Depending upon other planetary dispositions, the individual begins to perceive the subtler forces impinging on his everyday life. The airy element of the zodiac in association with earthliness of the planet Mercury makes the individual very self-centred, if not selfish. In fact, his creativity and understanding of the natural forces and laws give much power to him, but in all his exercise of these forces and direction of them to the good of others, he always remains conscious of his personal gain, both material and spiritual.

As indicated earlier, the nature of Mercury in *Mahapurusha Yoga* is very much affected by its proximity with the Sun and Jupiter's inevitable ownership of cardinal houses. In the case of Mercury occupying Gemini in the zodiac, irrespective of its position in the horoscope, the Sun would be in Taurus, Gemini or Cancer and if Mercury is in Virgo, the Sun's position has to be in Leo,

Virgo or Libra. These solar occupations will have important impact on Mercury. In Taurus, the Sun enables the individual to obtain scriptural knowledge and impart the same to others. In Gemini, the intellect of the person is greatly sharpened by Sun and he attains penetrative understanding of abstract mathematical laws or of complex economic relationships. In Cancer, the Sun makes the individual relinquish its basic idealism and he gets immersed in contemporary materialistic way of life. In Leo, the individualism in man is greatly sharpened and he begins to have an unconscious understanding of his latent powers and destiny though it may sometime express itself in arrogance and egotism. In Virgo, the Sun is fierce enough to burn the dross of materialism, bring forth the individual's latent creativity, but also to make him a little sad, ladden with innumerable personal and social responsibilities. The Sun in Libra is not good for material prosperity. The struggle of the inner spirit to liberate itself from physical restrictions often depresses the man. When the Sun along with Mercury occupies Gemini or Virgo, there is further transformation of their nature. Known as *Budha Aditya Yoga,* this kind of association between the Sun and Mercury makes the person learned, beautiful and strong but fickle-minded. Mantreswara adds to these effects, the possibility of the individual becoming famous as well. These features arise from the solar influence flowing to the thinking principle in man and irradiating it to such an extent that the individual's creativity, specially in the realm of thought, is greatly energised. The fickle-mindedness of the person may occur when Mercury is weak and incapable of absorbing the radiance of the Sun. Occupying exaltation or its sign of rulership, Mercury does not produce fickle-mindedness though under certain conditions, it may make the individual headstrong and sometimes even impervious to thoughts and opinions of other persons.

In *Mahapurusha Yoga,* which arises due to Mercury's special placements, the beneficial effects of the Sun arising from its zodiacal position near Mercury, is available only under certain special situation. With Mercury in the Ascendant and the Sun in the twelfth house, the individual is said to be hated and without any wealth and children, which is the very antithesis of the Sun in Taurus. In the Ascendant also, the Sun's position is not very happy.

In the Ascendant, the Sun makes the individual valiant, impatient and cruel-hearted, but with Mercury it intensifies the thinking capacity of the individual. In the second house, the Sun produces absence of modesty and riches. Such contradictory results accentuate many contradictions in one's life which require explanations in order to recognise the 'greatness' expected under the *Bhadra Yoga*.

Another important factor in the present context is the Jupiterian relationship with Mercury. What message of Jupiter does Mercury carry forth? Under the conditions of *Mahapurusha Yoga* formed by Mercury, the Jupiterian sign of Sagittarius and Pisces would fall in the cardinal house. Benefic planets owning a cardinal house, unless they are placed in cardinal houses themselves are not auspicious. In case Jupiter occupies a cardinal house, there is every likelihood of its forming *Hamsa Mahapurusha Yoga,* or it would be associated with Mercury. In such cases, Jupiter will support and strengthen the inherent qualities of Mercury. In case, Jupiter does not occupy any of the cardinal houses, the individual will experience setbacks in his major aspects of life as evident by physical troubles (Ascendant), emotional and family setbacks (fourth house affliction), difficulties in marital life (seventh house) or difficulties in professional life (tenth house). These frustrations may not make the individual reactionary but would turn him towards spiritualism and religious way of life.

As the *Mahapurusha Yoga* formed by Mercury being in a cardinal house in strength will have the necessary support of Jupiter, it would lead the individual to radically and completely purify the thought process of its past tendencies and make it a fit instrument for understanding the laws of Nature. Mind under its impact becomes sensitive, perceptive and able to receive reflections of higher laws besides understanding the follies of life. Such a person becomes fully self-reliant, both physically and mentally. This freedom will be reflected in all that he does. He would be skilled in every undertaking. The Jupiterian impact on Mercury will make the thinking of the individual and his approach to problems of life *sattwic* or righteous. Ethical influence and sociability, regard for humanitarian well-being with philanthropy will induce him to be supportive of his family relations. But the most important effect of this *Yoga* will be evident in the sharpness of his intellect capable of understanding the effect of the solar radiation in his life. Knowledge of *Shastras,* scriptures, metaphysical philosophies and occult sciences along with *yogic* precepts will make the individual unique in many ways.

Two of the special attributes of this *Yoga* arise from the fact that the special knowledge of spiritual principles would enable the individual to control his Vital Airs, the Pranic Forces circulating around and within him as well as in the world around him. The *Bhuvar Loka* is said to be the middle region of the objective realms comprising *Bhu Loka* (Earth), *Bhuvar Loka* (*Antahriksha* or the Etheric Double) and *Swarg Loka* (the heaven world). The rulership over the middle region of Madhya Pradesh in the classical texts while referring to the effect of the *Yoga*, actually and more meaningfully refers to the individual's control over the *Bhuvar Loka* which is reflected in control over the Vital Airs, the Pranic Vayu. The longevity of hundred years refers to completion of all the four *Varnashramas* including *Sanyasa*. Thus the individual will have the opportunity of completing the full cycle of his life's mission, a rare and unique opportunity for the mortals. In this way, *Bhadra Yoga* enables the individual to complete the various stages of life's unfoldment ending in complete mental renunciation of all the material (and religious) accomplishments. In fact, *Bhadra Mahapurusha Yoga* opens the channel of spiritual communication between the higher nature of the individual for his everyday life; his inner-being begins to guide him imperceptibly so that finally he understands the nature of higher forces and stands aside to let them fill his entire lower nature.

20

MARS:
The Active Male Principle

Mars known as *kuja* (a tree or a demon killed by Krishna), *bhaum* (earthy), *krura* (fierce, invincible), *vakra* (evasive, indirect), *lohitanga* (red-coloured), *papi* (sinful), *aar* (an angle, a corner), *mangala* (auspicious), and *avaneya* or *bhumiputra* (son of the earth) is the most significant vital energy electrifying all forms of terrestrial activities. Being of the nature of fire which gives life-force to all living beings, initiative, enthusiasm and valour for all terrestrial activities, and the generative power for the purpose of human procreation, which induces the male (*purusha*) to seek his partner (the field, the *kshetra,* on which to sow the seed of his productivity) the female (*prakriti*) to make love, unite and bring forth fresh life on the earth, is of the nature of the Sun which is the very centre of the universe at all levels, on all the fourteen *lokas.* Besides getting its life-force from the solar storehouse of energy, Mars also gets its sustenance and nourishment from Jupiter which provides the life-breath, *prana,* to all living creatures. The trinity of Sun, Jupiter and Mars, essential for the growth and development of the living forms, is uniquely integrated with well demarcated functional differentiation between them. Mars is the vital energy, the motive power or the blind power, for creating and vivifying everything, creating and fixing the nature and capabilities of all substances. For this Mars needs the basic solar direction, the ultimate purpose for which the Martian procreative energy can be effectively utilised. Jupiter is the grid, the generator of power at different levels of manifestation which constantly charges the Martian motive force to produce the desired result.

The epithet *Mangala* meaning the auspicious, reveals the basic procreative and rejuvenative characteristics of the Martian planetary radiation inspite of its seeming fierce and formidable nature which led astrologers to consider Mars a malefic planet. The malefic nature, if properly harnessed for divine purpose, leads to the most stupendous achievements. The Yogis in *tapas,* the fire of religious austerities, the penance, having burnt the materialistic proclivities, *tamasic vritis,* or the inertial tendencies, attain release from the bondage of compulsive births and death and thus accomplish their liberation from earthly fetters. This *tapas* is a direct expression of the Martian fire burning within the hearts of every aspirant after true knowledge.

The Vedas did not only consider *Agni,* the fire, along with the Indra and *Vayu* (air) as the trinity of power, but the very first word of the Rig Veda, the oldest written scripture available to the world, is that of *Agni,* and the first five mantras of the Veda refer to the greatness of this cosmic energy. Commenting upon these mantras, Dayananda Saraswati, quoting Niruktakar Yakshamuni states that the word *Agni* does not only mean *Agrani,* the leader, to whom obeisance is offered in all *yajnas* (Vedic sacrifices) and sacrificial rites, but it also refers to the Supreme God as well as the physical fire. Those who lived according to the divine laws and used the fire within oneself for creative purposes can never be destroyed. While offering the oblation to fire, the *homa,* the individual succeeds in irradiating his inner nature and attains his ultimate destiny. The unfailing results of religious austerities which to a superficial mundane individual may seem maleficent, proves highly auspicious for the spiritualists.

The highly abstract teachings of the Vedas often fail to reveal the inner or the deeper content of the mantras to a superficial student. The various Vedic mantras relating to *Agni* do not always disclose their generative power in dwelling and vivifying every terrestrial being. When properly harnessed and directed towards the solar rays, the goal meant for every individual, could result in constant rejuvenation of the being. By dissipating the generative power absorbed in goal-inhibiting inertial activities, he meets his lamentable end. *Agni* is *Agrani* which is also an epithet of Mars. It indicated an aspect of the identity between *Agni* and *Bhauma* which is not described in so many words. Niruktakar Yakshamuni considering *Agni* to be swift moving by which attribute it can cover many continents in no time, associated the god of fire with a horse (*ashwa*) and a bull (*vrisha*) which are embodiments of male virility (which are much discussed in astrological texts in connection with the zodiacal signs of Aries and Taurus). Being of the nature of God, *Agni* spreads divine wisdom, *jnana,* and enables its devotees to acquire valuable skills. Mars is a precursor of new and original ideas, not only in the realm of everyday life, but also in the realm of spirituality; he is also the commander-in-chief of planetary hierarchy. These attributes very well qualify Mars to be an *Agrani,* an epithet given to *Agni* in the Vedas.

The Vedas dealt only in terms of universal principles applicable to a large variety of problems and relationships. They adopted the same methodology even while revealing astrological principles without specifying that these teachings are applicable to astrological understanding of universal laws. Recalling that *Jyotisha,* astrology, was one of the six *Vedangas* (limbs of the Vedas) whose knowledge and understanding were prerequisites for a proper comprehension of the teachings of the Vedas at deeper levels, the student had to obtain oral and indirect guidance from the teacher so as to develop his intuitive perception of the underlying principles. The authenticity of the revelation and its wider applicability had to be tested by the student himself according to his level of spiritual development. For this reason many of the applications of the Vedic general principles were not mentioned in the Vedas and they were left to the growth and perception of the student himself. One cannot therefore legitimately expect the Vedas to be explicitly concerned with individual planets. For this reason, one can understand the absence of explicit statements about the identity of *Agni* and Mars, but every discerning student should take a note of it. The obeisance to *Agni,* which constituted one of the Vedic *triumvirata* along with Indra and *Vayu,* in the process of cosmic manifestation, is full of mystic lore. The present day Hindu practice of invoking Lord Ganesh at the outset of every auspicious enterprise or writing the *Pranava* (Om) before beginning any important work or treatise, is expected to ward off all impending difficulties and receive divine blessings for the success of the undertaking. This tradition is a continuation of the

archaic practice existent in ancient times and followed as a matter
of course in the performance of all religious rituals. The Vedas
followed the same rule. The Rig Veda devoted its first five mantras
to *Agni,* the fire god, who is none else than the presiding deity of
the planet Mars. The reference to *Kumaras* or the Virgin Ascetics in
the present context, identifying them with the fire element reveals the
close relationship between *Agni, Kumaras* and *Angaraka* (the planet
Mars). The initial invocation of *Agni,* indicates the great belief in
the auspicious nature of the fire god, whose close identity with
Angaraka indicated the auspicious nature of *Mangala.* In order to
realise the significance of the planet Mars from the Vedic standpoint,
this identity must always be kept in view.

The Vedas considered the God of Fire, *Agni,* as the primary
aspect of every *yajna,* religious ritual of sacrifice (or simply
speaking, of all significant enterprises). *Agni* provides Light (*Prakasha*),
Heat (*Usna*), and the basic motivating prowess to all human efforts
(*Purushartha*). *Agni* is also the grand priest (*Ritwik*) who officiates
at all Vedic sacrifices (*Yajnas*). Elucidating the attributes of *Agni,*
Niruktacharya Shakamuni indicated three of its important functions
as *ancha* (to light), *daha* (to burn) and *netritwa* (to lead). These
three attributes are basic even to the planet Mars. Leadership is a
special quality of Mars and it is reputed as the planet which burns,
provides warmth, arouses passion and leads to accidents generally
connected with fire. The characteristic of 'lighting' is ordinarily not
very much acknowledged by many astrologers, but realising the fact
that Mars leads to originality, deep penetration in any abstruse
subject and emergence with a radically different interpretation of the
subject, flashes of intuition (specially when supported by Sun, Moon
and Jupiter) are some of the features of Mars which one cannot
justifiably overlook.

The Puranic allegory attributes the birth of Mars to Shiva, the
embodiment of cosmic life-force in whom no dross of materialism
can subsist howsoever subtle its manifestation might be. The Puranic
mythologies are intended to popularise some of the deeper teachings
of the Vedas. These allegories are very esoteric in their implications.
Lord Shiva personifies the central subjective core of all
manifestation from whom emanated even Brahma, the cosmic
creator, to whom Kamadeva owes his origin. Brahma created
Kamadeva and commanded him to afflict human beings with his five

arrows made of flowers inducing them to involve themselves in enduring creative process while remaining himself invisible in their heart. The Indian Cupid thus ever remained subjective, hidden, invisible and residing in the bosom of every man and woman. Shiva's giving birth to Mars symbolises the origin of the active or the male generative principle. Kamadeva and Bhumiputra work together in this sexual creative process. *Shiva Purana* states that Lord Shiva, when in deep anguish experiencing the absence of his consort after her destruction at Daksha's sacrifice, became terribly upset and in desolation went in *samadhi,* deep meditation. The emotional nature of the Lord was greatly agitated. Resulting from such a passionate upsurge, the sweat from his forehand fell on the ground which turned into a small child who began crying. Apprehending wrath from Shiva at this occurrence, Earth not understanding the whole episode, lifted the baby and began nursing it. When Shiva found the child curling in Earth's lap, he blessed them and named the child as *Bhauma* or *Bhumiputra* commanding at the same time that Mother Earth should always protect him as he would always lead to auspicious results. The relationship between Kamadeva and Mars related with terrestrial generative process is indicated more explicitly in several other Puranic stories.

The birth of Kartikeya, who is said to be the presiding deity of Mars (though he is even regarded as the very personification of the planet itself), is woven around the god's plan to destroy the *asura* (the demon) Taraka who had obtained Brahma's boon of indestructibility by any means except the seven-days old child born of Shiva's virility, which was considered almost an impossible condition then. Becoming arrogant with such a mighty boon, Taraka began destroying the religious order of the universe, menacingly usurped the kingdom of gods and dethroned Indra. On their approaching Brahma for redressal, they were asked to take the help of Kamadeva in order to arouse physical passion in Shiva whose fructification in the birth of a child could put an end to Taraka and his misdeeds. Kamadeva shot his arrows which disturbed the Lord but in the process when Shiva opened his third eye, the fire emitted from his third eye completely burnt Kamadeva and he was reduced to ashes. The fire thus released was however a potential danger to the manifestation, so Brahma had to contain it in the form of a horse and made it absorbed in the oceans where it remains for ever in the nature of *Badawanal,* the submarine fire.

The mother of Ashwini Kumaras, the presiding deities of the first asterism in Aries in which Mars has its rulership and the beginning of the cosmic journey, was also a horse, of course, a mare in that case. The arrow of Kamadeva made the virile semen of Shiva flow downwards, which fell into the womb of *Agni* who had gone to him in the form of a dove while he was in the company of his consort Parvati. *Agni* unable to bear the heat of Shiva's vital energy cast into it, deposited the same in the Ganges so as to cool it with the soothing influence of its waters. When the six Krittikas (the third asterism) went to bathe in the river, it was transferred to them each of whom conceived and nurtured the foetuses which on birth were mysteriously joined together to form a person with six heads and twelve hands. Thus he was called Kartikeya.

The passionate nature of Mars and its close relationship with fire are well described in various allegories indicated above, but Mars is not only related with the generative process, the fire and warmth inherent in it, but it also has the concretisation of the solar radiance intended to assist the earthly manifestation at its lower (or physical) levels of creation as one of its functions. In *Brahma Vaivarta Purana,* mention has been made of the birth of Mars in Varaha Kalpa when the sexual generative process was being introduced. It is mentioned that on getting stabilised after its emergence from the Deluge, the Earth wanted the Lord Vishnu who had appeared in the form of a boar, to be her husband, but his effulgence was intolerable to her. So after restricting his power, he came and lived with Earth for a year during which period Mars was born. The identity between Indra, Vishnu, Sun and on the higher level with the electrifying energy latent in Shiva indicates the diverse nature of fire, or the life-giving energy contained in Mars. It is not far-fetched to relate Shiva, the ultimate creative energy with the creative process itself. It is represented during the present life-cycle by the Sun, and the Earth which after its own stabilisation produced all—fruits, vegetables, minerals, human beings trees, animals etc. It owes its manifestive capacity from the solar energy which at higher levels of manifestation of *Arupa Lokas,* the invisible realms, remains subjective and ethereal but on concrete *Rupa Lokas,* the visible realms, functions through the generative power of Mars.

Man, as he is presently constituted, consists of both the solar energy and earthly matter, the Earth being the feminine counterpart of the *Surya Lokas*. The Sun and the Earth together produce electric energy, fire and different generative principles which in unity functioned through Mars. The fire of the *Pitris* presented as electrical fire (*Pawaka*), the fire of *asuras* concerned with physical manifestation represented as frictional fire (*Pavamana*), and the fire of gods (*Suchi*) represented by the Solar Fire imparting inspiration, and the capacity for austere religious observances and martyrdom are, all in some way or the other, in some measure, howsoever big or small, represented by Mars.

Fire is considered the element connected with Mars but such is the case with the Sun also. Any proper study of the Puranic stories will reveal that Mars and the Sun have very well differentiated roles in cosmic manifestation. The difference between the two, also highlights the invisible and the visible counterparts of an integrated unity. The former is often described as the higher self, or the higher trinity and the latter, the lower quaternary representing the man as he is known in everyday life. The higher trinity consists of *Atma, Buddhi,* and *Manas* but these names are given differently in different systems of religious philosophy. *Atma* is also considered as the Individual Soul which is a reflection of the Universal Soul. An individual attains final liberation and is known as *Pratyeka Buddha*. At this level the released consciousness maintains its separate identity before merging itself into the universal flame and thereby losing its complete identity. *Chitta* or *Buddhi* represents the Great Passive Principle or the Spiritual Soul which in several systems of thinking is said to be similar to *Maya* on the universal plane but on the individual level it is the pure plastic state of perceptivity (as distinguished from perception itself) which enables the individual to comprehend the infinite in its multicoloured splendour. *Manas* is also called in some school of thinking as the human or the animal soul representing the breath of the Universal Mind, *Mahat* principle at the universal level. *Manas* carries the message of *Arupa Loka*, the invisible realm, or even the subjective counterpart of the individual to the visible or the physical being, while it has the capacity of abstracting all physical experiences and perceptions into abstract principles linking them with the *atmic* or the highest principle in man.

The lower quaternary has been variously described and several scriptures give much detailed information of different levels of the being. Generally speaking, it can be indicated that the physical body or the visible man consists of physical body (*Sthula Sharira*), *Pranamaya Kosha* or the vehicle through which the Vital Airs circulate and energies the being, *Kama Rupa* which expresses the passionate nature of the individual and *Antahakaran* expressed as egotism. Together these seven, the visible and the invisible counterparts of the human-beings, are the seven flames of fire which have been given different names in *Mundakopanishad.* In the representation of *Agni Deva,* these flames are represented as seven of his tongues, three on one side symbolising the life-essence operating at *Arupa Sharira,* the higher trinity, and four on the other side representing the same life-essence but expressing itself at different levels resulting in different nature of the individual at the physical level. Inspite of such differentiation, all the seven flames are expressions of the same life-essence. One can, in a very rough manner suggest that, the three flames at the higher levels are emanations of the Sun along with the Moon (which is merely the counterpart of it reflecting its radiance) and Mercury, while Mars born of the Sun and Earth functioned at the physical plane (represented by the Venus, Mars, Jupiter and Saturn). All the seven flames are necessary for the sustenance of man.

Their essentiality was explained in *The Secret Doctrine* when H.P. Blavatsky stated that "Man needs Four Flames and three fires to become ONE on Earth as he requires the essence of the 49 fires to be perfect" (Vol. III., p. 67). There is striking similarity between the Sun, and *Angaraka,* the smouldering fire, which is also a name of the planet Mars. The former is carried forth on a chariot drawn by seven horses while the latter splinters itself in seven flames, three on one side and four on the other. The Puranas describe the relationship between the Sun, Mars and the Earth, along with *Agni,* Indra and Shiva and other deities in esoteric allegories whose implications can only be deciphered by deeper knowledge of cosmic and human manifestation and emanation. For general purpose, one can accept that the Sun acts on the subjective or the invisible plane working through the inner principles of man, on the higher trinity of man, while Mars acts on the physical level, but the primary role of it is to externalise what the solar impulse has put inside the man. In psychological terms, one also finds that Mars activating the passionate nature of man, externalises his inner desolation, emotional cravings, personal desires as well as the solar energy latent in him (for example, as it is crystallised as virile semen) to the physical level in several diverse ways. The Sun and Mars both provide light, warmth and vigour but Mars also acts as *Ritwik*, the grand priest who officiates at Vedic sacrifices resulting in spiritualising the physical nature of the man which is evident in *tapas*, religious austerities. The Sun, on the other hand, itself is the representative of the highest deity, the inner ruler immortal, to whom all sacrifices are offered. The Sun and Mars, are in fact, counterparts of one and the same life-essence personified by *Agni* at different levels of manifestation.

The metaphysical literature of the Hindus described *Agni*, the fire god, in great detail. *Swaha*, the oblation given in sacrificial fire, is his wife and he has three offsprings namely, *Pawaka, Pavamana* and *Suchi*. The first is the electric fire representing fire of the *Pitris;* the second is produced by friction and is related with the fire of *asuras*, the demons signifying "dwellers on the threshold" symbolising impediments and hurdles against the pilgrim's path; and the third represents the Solar Fire. Every man living and moving on this earth contains within himself the Electric Fire which is the life-essence obtained from his ancestors, his ever incarnating ego; he has the Solar Fire which enables him to rise higher on the spiritual plane which provides to him the fire evident in penance, the fire of *tapas;* but in him also lies the proclivities which make him lust after physical experiences, indulge in physical cravings and deny the voice of his inner being which results in his *Asuric Vrittis* being aroused by the activities of *Pavamana*. The Sun and Mars together control and regulate the activities of these three types of fire whose precise knowledge could indicate the direction and goal of every common individual.

The Martian fire activating different human principles manifests itself in different ways. Under the influences of Kamadeva, who was given birth by the cosmic manifestative power, Brahma, Mars, functions as a result of command from Vishnu (who was himself produced by Shiva), and in him flows the creative energy which activates the individual's lustful behaviour and physical generative activities. Moving upwards, in association with *Anahata Chakra*, the *Pancha Bhutas*, especially the element of *Vayu*, Air, are harnessed for ascending to the subjective trinity—the higher trinity functioning at the *Arupa* level—in man. The occultists indicate that the function of the fire by friction, *Pavamana,* in the metaphysical sense represents union between *Buddhi* (or *Chitta*) known as the Great Passive Principle and *Manas,* the Breath of the Universal Mind (called by some as the Human Soul) which in its functional operation produces the Creative Spark or the 'Germ' which fructifies and generates the human being in his essential subjectivity.

Elucidating the cosmic creative process and the role of Mars in it, H.P. Blavatsky states that:

> Adam-Jehovah, Brahma and Mars are in one sense identical; they are all symbols for primitive or initial generative powers, for the purposes of human procreation. Adam is red, and so also are Brahma-Viraj and Mars-God and planet. Water is the 'blood' of Earth; therefore, all these names are connected with Earth and Water. "It takes earth and water to create a human soul", says Moses.[1]

Seed or the creative power of Shiva, which working through the passionate nature of man (produced by Kamadeva on the subjective plane which is externalised as a result of the Martian impulse eager to accomplish its goal), flows to the physical level making the individual active in the physical generative processes. When the Martian energy, represented by Skanda, Kartikeya, in the Puranic allegories, is inhibited from sexual relationships (indicated in the Puranas as the denial of marriage to Kartikeya while Ganesh was bestowed the privilege though from the superficial standpoint Kartikeya had the legitimate claim for it), the individual is induced towards spiritual austerities, *tapas,* and turns his back on worldly achievements. Such a reaction is also expected because fire always burns upwards, its flames never move downwards while water has a tendency of going downwards. Mars is the personification of the fire god, so when its terrestrial propensities are denied, it will recoil and proceed on its natural course, which is austerity, penance, burning the dross to purify and bring out the primordial (virgin) spirit. The impact of Mars on *Kama Rupa* or the passionate body of the individual plays the role of a grand priest, a bridge, which has a two way opening. Following the Puranic stories, one has to conclude

---

[1] H.P. Blavatsky, *The Secret Doctrine,* Madras, Vol. III, p. 55.

that the Martian fire is represented by both, the Shiva's glare from his third eye to burn Kamadeva and by the Lord's passionate nature aroused by Kamadeva's arrows and both these will continue in their periodic generative process in each human individual. Both of these are two aspects, the subjective and the objective ones, of the planet Mars, one leads to *tapas,* penance, and the other-animal passion-to generative functions in man.

21

VENUS AND ARTISTIC SENSITIVITY

Examples of a few internationally acknowledged artists—a dancer, a cine artist and a painter would show that each individual had latent in them some artistic talents which if properly nurtured and developed would have been of immense happiness to them. Much personal sorrow could be obliterated by appropriate recognition of one's artistic faculties and nurturing the same.

There is some confusion among some people who consider only a painter, a dancer, a sculptor, a cine actor, or the like, as an artist. A poet whose poems have been published and has charmed his audience is considered a successful artist. Generally one does not go deeper into an examination of those characteristics which make an individual an artist. A Shakespeare, Milton, Kalidasa or Bhavabhuti is recognised as an artist. But those unknown sculptors who surpassed any known such professionals by creating the Ajanta paintings, Mahabalipuram carvings, or by designing and executing the Tanjore temple or the Egyptian pyramids, are often forgotten or at least very few persons go to the extent of contemplating the inspiration which led them to devote their whole life to some cause which made them unknown artists and probably gave them no personal recognition. Even more interesting is the popular approach when a person worships Valmiki, Tulsi, Veda Vyasa more as a great saint and seer but not so much as an artist. One can go one step further. What is it that makes a mother spend so much time, incur physical suffering, and devote time in dreaming the archetype to which her offspring is going to be moulded in. Yet, she is seldom thought of as an artist. Is it because she is creating something living and in which she becomes a part of her creation or the creation becomes a part of her that she is denied the right of being considered an artist? These are not mere metaphysical questions. If we go deeper into astrological principles, we shall find that creativity, specially original production, not reproduction of something already existing, grants the right of being considered an artist. And as such, each individual who can discover his or own creativity, can find the area and dimension of latent artistic nature in him or her. For a serious-minded astrologer, it is a futile exercise to consider Venus related with painting, Mercury with poetry, or Saturn with sculpture. These are very elementary approaches to deeper depths of Hindu astrology.

The word *kavi* which is the common term for a poet, and refers to all artists generally, was used even in the Vedas. Sri Aurobindo translated the word to mean a seer, or even *vipra,* the wiseman. *Kavi* stands for omniscient. It is an epithet for Venus and even the Sun is referred to by it. In astrology, Venus is almost always associated with artists; unless favourable influence of Venus is present in a chart, one dare not predict the possibility of developing artistic faculties. *Kavi,* stands for Venus as well as the Sun. The function of a *seer, kavi,* who possessed 'the illumined mind' was to transcend the physical limitations, the veil of ignorance, *avidya* and to perceive the spirit as the impulse behind all the phenomenal existence. For them, the material objects were symbols of the immaterial; the cows were the radiance or illumination of a divine dawn, the horses and chariots were symbols of force and movement, and gold was lights. The similies and metaphors used by a poet are not necessarily flights of imagination in the sense of describing something unreal for the real, rather the so-called similies were simply an expression of something ethereal, not usually felt so, perceived so, by common man. A seer perceives the reality behind the unreality as he is omniscient, and tries to create that reality in the realm of unreality.

Translating one of the hymns of the Rig Veda, Sri Aurobindo says that "All forms he takes unto himself, the Seer, and he creates from them good for the twofold existence and the fourfold. The creator, the supreme God, manifests heaven wholly and his light pervades all as he follows the march of the Dawn." Commenting upon this hymn, Aurobindo explains thus:

> "For all things have their justifiable cause of being, their good use and their right enjoyment. When this truth in them is found and utilised, all things produce good for the soul, increase its welfare, enlarge its felicity. And this divine revolution is effected both in the lower physical existence and in the more complete inner life which uses the physical for its manifestation . . . The Seer takes to himself all forms, he brings our (creates or manifests) good for the twofold (two-footed), for the fourfold (four-footed)." (Sri Aurobindo has even mentioned that the symbolism of the words *dwipade* and *chatuspade* may be differently interpreted. The discussion of it here would occupy too large a space).

The function of a seer, *kavi,* appears threefold. He has to have the vision of the supreme drama in which everything is an expression of the Inner Reality. He has to perceive the relationship between the cause at the immaterial level and the effect on the material level; and he has to create the inner impulse, manifest the hidden, to the external realm of experience. Thus he is an illumined mind, he is devoutly theistic, he experiences the unknown (to the multitude) reality, and he is superbly creative. When Valmiki perceived the killing of the swan, he had the illumined or the sensitive mind to perceive the inner pain and passion of the mating bird, and he created or manifested his sensitivity in concrete expressions by words. Those unknown sculptors and rock carvers, whose creations still exist at the seashore of Tamil Nadu though nobody knows who they were, they possessed an extremely sensitive mind, their sensitivity to the intonations from the other worlds was exceptional, they envisioned the great cooperation and intermingling of life-force, the birth of Ganges, in manifesting the phenomenal existence, and they had the ability to concretise their vision. These three factors are necessary for all great artistic achievements. The degree of excellence of the artistic achievement depends upon the level of seer-ship attained in regard to these three factors.

When a reader reads *Raghuvamsa,* the poetic composition of Kalidasa, apart from the sensitivity to various details of the rise and fall of the Raghu dynasty, he conveys the undying message of destructibility of every phenomenal form of existence, howsoever sublime it may appear, at one point of time. Every artistic creation conveys a message of the divine which the artist executed and conveyed through physical forms. It is creativity (the fifth house), the perception of the Supreme Light (the Sun) and uncommon sensitivity (Venus) which are essential in all great artistic achievements.

The role of the Sun in all creative processes is very basic. It is so in cosmic evolution and manifestation of geological changes as well as in the expression and unfoldment of all divine qualities in man. If we are not considering draftsmen and plagiarists, it is necessary to give attention to the position and strength of the Sun. Varaha Mihira was one of those astrological seers who had a deep insight in spiritual astrology. In the very first *sloka* of *Brihat Jataka,* he considers the Sun as giver of form to the Moon, who is the pathway for those who are after eternal bliss or salvation, who is the soul of the sages (who know themselves), who is the object of worship among those who perform sacrifices, who is the chief among the gods, planets and stars (the centre of the universe), who is the author of destruction, creation and preservation of all the worlds, who is invoked in the Vedas in various ways. Learned commentators of this verse have very ably suggested that Varaha Mihira in his outer meanings of the verse concealed an inner meaning which indicated their knowledge of the Sun being the progenitor and feeder of all other planets and asterisms. Even in their description of the relationships between the Sun and the Moon, the astrologer-seers left much to the intuition of their readers. The Sun is illumination, an inner spiritual ecstasy which is so intense that it cannot be manifest in anyway in its pristine nature.

Only when it is associated with the Moon that its inner illumination and pure divinity is transformed into cosmic subjective productive principle. The Sun is said to be of the nature of fire. The fire in the Sun requires faggots through which it can be expressed. But the Moon is merely a reflection of the Sun in its downward creative direction. The Moon, as such, is still at the subjective plane. It requires further support for the fructification of its externalisation of the productive principle. This function is performed by the fiery planet Mars. The pristine fire in the Sun which is pure illumination transcending all forms of concretisation, during the process of its downward expression, it is at first reflected in the Moon which gives to the latter the appellation of Mother from which everything has the possibility of externalisation. When Mars is activated and is associated with Moon in some form of relationship, the fecundity of Moon begins to be active. In the case of great artists, the benediction of the Sun, Moon and Mars must be there to give them the characteristics of truly great artists.

The influence of Venus is well acknowledged in the present context since the ancient times. Venus usually known as the preceptor of *daityas* and demons should be an active agent in imparting the basic impulse of artistic talents seems a little incongruous. If the real nature of Venus is recognised, much of the confusion in this regard can be avoided. Venus is certainly the preceptor of *asuras,* but who are the *asuras* in the original sense of the word?

John Dowson related the *asuras* with 'spiritual, divine' beings and stated that in the oldest parts of the Rig Veda this term was used for the supreme spirit. In the sense of 'god' it was applied to several of the chief deities, as to Indra, Agni, and Varuna. It afterwards acquired an entirely opposite meaning, and came to signify, as now, a demon or enemy of the gods. He says that the word originally meant *asu-ra;* according to the *Taittirya Brahmana,* the breath (*asu*) of Prajapati became alive, and with that breath (*asu*) he created the *asuras.* Even Sri Aurobindo has mentioned that *asura* was a word used in the Veda, as in the *Avesta,* for the Deva (Ahuramazda), but also for the gods, and His manifestation; it is only in a few hymns that it is used for the dark Titans, by another as *a-sura,* the not-luminous, the not-gods. Obviously, our present-day understanding of the nature of Venus, the preceptor of *asuras,* is not Vedic; the original deity represented as Sukracharya was a part of divine manifestation. Even the Puranic stories relate the planet with virile semen of Lord Shiva when his consciousness was for some divine purpose directed 'downward' and Lord Shiva was not at all antipathic to the deity represented by the planet. In fact, he is said to have given the name Sukra to it.

In the present context, the association of Venus with the creative impulse of the Supreme Lord, and with the life-breath of manifesting Prajapatis is very relevant. Unless the artist gives a new insight into manifestation which provides a new impetus to life, to have a different perception of life-process, his contribution cannot be much appreciated. Even when one reads Kalidasa's *Meghadutam,* or sees some of the sculptures of Rodin, imperceptibly the sensitivity of the individual is refined. He begins to feel and see differently the human expressions. This change transforms his life to some extent. This is one of the basic truths about the real piece of art. The form of art is not so necessary—it may be a dance performance interpreting a song, or a story according to the understanding, perception and vision of the artist, or it may be vocal music or any other form of art. Once an individual comes in its contact, he must basically change. This is one of the basic impulses with which Venus is connected.

The function of an artist as stated earlier is to down to the mortal world of manifestation, a flash of divine illumination, a vision and concretise the same for ordinary individuals. In this way, he is a bridge builder. The importance of Mercury in this context is great. This is a planet which builds bridges between the subjective and the objective realms of existence. The two luminaries and their rays to the physical realms are expressed through Mercury. Mercury is also related with *Vishudhi Chakram,* the throat or laryngeal energy-centre. Its main function is to purify one's experiences so as to transmit the same to the permanent part of the ego and at the same time it is through Mercury that the permanent intonations are filtered down to the human brain for its everyday use. For an artist who has to filter down in concrete terms the subjective visions and everlasting impressions into a form of expression understandable to a common man, the importance of Mercury cannot be minimised. For a successful artist, it is necessary that the supernal fire represented by the Sun and Mars, and the Moon which reflects the creative potential of solar fire, must be contained in psychological planes, namely, Mercury and Venus. It is therefore imperative that an astrologer concerned with prediction regarding artistic nature of a person does not restrict his gaze to merely a few planets howsoever important these in the present context may be, but he considers the creative faculty and possibility of the individual as a whole.

Let us look at Chart I. E. Joseph was born on 11 November 1911, in India, with superb creative faculty as far as painting is concerned. He was accorded a very high position by the Government of India with several important assignments being given to him. Cancer was his Ascendant with Moon in it; the Moon was aspected by Jupiter. Jupiter was associated with Mercury. No malefic planet aspects the Moon. These are important conditions to make this luminary a good reflecting agent. One is intrigued about the placement of his Sun. It is in debilitation, associated with Ketu, and fully aspected by debilitated Saturn. (There is an exchange of some sort between the Sun and Saturn. The Sun is in the exaltation sign of Saturn and Saturn is in the exaltation sign of the Sun. These two planets are associated with the Nodes). Mars also aspects the Sun. Mars was in Jupiter's house and aspected by Jupiter. This makes Mars very constructive. Its fifth house ownership has made the individual extraordinarily active in a productive manner, increased his sensitivity and made him an eminent painter.

Mars	Rahu Saturn		
	CHART I E. Joseph		Ascdt Moon
	Jupiter Mercury	Sun Ketu	Venus

Chart II is an example of a radically different type of person. It belongs to a cine artist (Raj Kapoor) who had been one of the greatest names on the Indian screen, and as a film director he is known almost in every part of the civilised world. He was born on 14 December 1924. In this case also the Moon is importantly placed. The Sun and the Moon have fifth-ninth relationship. The Moon was associated with Rahu and fully aspected by exalted Saturn which was associated with Venus occupying its own sign. There are two *Pancha Mahapurusha Yogas* formed by the position of Saturn and Venus. The Sun is flanked by Venus and Jupiter both in their own respective signs, and Jupiter is associated with Mercury.

Venus is aspected by Mars from the ninth house. The fifth house in Chart I is occupied by Jupiter and Mercury (but the painter did not have any child) and in Chart II it is occupied by the Sun but he had several children. (Mark the Sun flanked by Venus, Mercury, Saturn and Jupiter). Creativity of the person, with unique receptivity to solar illumination and lunar sensitivity and its reflective capacity strengthened by the position of Venus and concretising planets, Saturn and Mars made the individual a superb actor, story writer and director.

Mars			
	CHART II Raj Kapoor		Ascdt Moon Rahu
Ketu			
Jupiter Mercury	Sun	Saturn Venus	

The third chart is an example of rare qualities—highly spiritual, extremely self-controlled and dedicated to the cause of art. It belongs to Rukmini Devi Arundale, one of the most reputed dancers, born on 29 February 1904, whose entry on the Indian stage created a revolution. She was born in Taurus Ascendant; it happens to be a sign of creativity. The Sun is in the tenth house; she devoted her whole life for spiritual regeneration of India. To her, her dance performances or musical compositions were part of her divine mission. The Moon is in its own sign, aspected by Jupiter, Venus, Mercury and Saturn. The last three placed in the ninth house, showed that much of her talents came to her from her previous life. Saturn's aspect on the Moon gave her tremendous control over her emotions, actions and physical movements. Jupiter's aspect gave her highly spiritualistic values in life. The Ascendant lord Venus placed in the ninth house gave her natural sensitivity to finer forces in life. Rahu in the fifth house gave her no issues, but the strong position of the fifth house (Mercury the

lord of the fifth house in the ninth, associated with Venus, and
aspected by Moon from its own house) gave her tremendous creative
faculty.

Ketu Jupiter Mars		Ascdt	
Sun	CHART III Rukmini Devi		Moon
Venus Saturn Mercury			
			Rahu

These examples are merely illustrative. From these one should
draw a conclusion that in case an individual concentrates on his
fifth house and understands it deeper nature, it is possible to
understand the direction in which his creative faculties can be
effective. Depending upon other planets (the Sun, Moon and Venus)
he should draw conclusions regarding his susceptibility to higher
realms of Nature where vision, illumination, inspiration, search for
light, and such other finer forces operate. An artist is said to be a
disciplined *yogi,* implying his control over his bodily functions,
attunement to higher forces of life, and the capacity to function at
that level. With these preparations, if he begins harnessing according
to his capacity and nature what is destined for him to do, there is
every possibility of his artistic nature to develop further and enjoy a
more satisfying life. It would be highly erroneous to predict artistic
achievements merely on the basis of a few planets without taking
the entire horoscope into consideration. Secondly, artistic faculty is
different from the form in which it can be and is expressed. In
whatever way the individual is engaged, it is possible for him to
express his artistic faculty according to his sensitivity and
inspiration.

22

JUPITER:
The Ruler of Vital Airs

Jupiter is known as Brihaspati or Brahmanspati in Vedic literature. It is primarily concerned with preservation, nourishment and expansion of the outer man. The Rig Veda calls it the Bull of Men and states that "He with his seed spreads forth beyond another's seed whomsoever Brahmanspati takes for his friend."

Jupiter controls the outer form. He is the preceptor of gods yet he does not possess the inner secret of life. He had sent his son Kacha to Shukracharya, Venus, to learn it from him. Blavatsky describes Jupiter as merely the personification of the immutable cyclic law which arrests the downward tendency of each root race after attaining the zenith of its glory. Hinting at the inner significance of Jupiterian influence, she mentions Jupiter as the son of Saturn.[1]

This is certainly an enigmatic statement, much different from the orthodox Hindu view. Yet the students practising austere *yogic* discipline lay a great emphasis on these two planets. They give much significance to Jupiterian signs, Sagittarius and Pisces, which encircle the Saturnian signs, Aquarius and Capricorn. The Sagittarius impulse towards spiritual aspiration and self realisation leads the soul to material depth followed by psychophysical trials and tribulations. Saturn finally arouses the thirst for inner wisdom.

---

[1] H.P. Blavatsky, *The Secret Doctrine*, Madras, Vol. V, p. 441.

Jupiter intervenes to arrest the downward movement of materialising tendency. Jupiter is unable to bestow the secret wisdom; it can however sustain and nourish the individual to bear the heavy burden of such an arduous task of attaining self-illumination.

The ancient religious myths and allegories reveal the special contribution of Jupiter to yoga students. Jupiter's father, according to Indian tradition, was *Angira,* a Vedic sage who occupied due to his spiritual penance the revered position of the presiding deity of one of the stars of Saptarishi constellation, the Ursa Major which moved around the pole star. *Angira* married two daughters of Daksha Prajapati and begot Jupiter as one of his sons. As a son of *Angira,* Jupiter is concerned with generative propagation in an important manner. He belongs to a big family; he has two brothers and a sister, and from his two wives he had seven sons and seven daughters, besides *Swaha* which meant the sacrificial offerings to the fire in a *yajna.* He also begot Bhardwaja, another Vedic seer, from his brother's wife. *Swaha* is personified oblation in sacrificial pit and indicated the role of Jupiter as the one who interceded between the sacrificer and the gods.

Jupiter's preoccupation is with preservation of manifestation and social order. It is revealed by various allusions in ancient literature. Dowson mentions that an ancient code of law bears Jupiter's name. Jupiter is said to be the Vyasa of the fourth *Dvapara* age. In second *Manavantara,* a sage of the same name is mentioned as the founder of an heretical sect. In *Matsya, Vishnu* and *Bhagwad Puranas,* there is an esoteric story about some ancient *rishis* having 'milked the earth' through Brihaspati.

These allusions show Jupiterian influence on stability, generation and preservation of life on the Earth. Jupiter intensifies the life-force pervading our planet. It strengthens the energy inherent in every being. It helps them to absorb more of the solar vitality. It does not impose any design of its own. It provides merely the protective cover so that the individual is strengthened to live his own life and gradually proceed towards his own spiritual goal. Jupiter will not, by itself, produce any material deprivation or psychological sorrow to disillusion the person with outer goals in life. Yet if the aspirant is ready, Jupiter helps him in harnessing the spiritual forces for the attainment of his enduring goal.

Jupiter nourishes both materiality and religiosity. It does not possess the secret of life, the power to give immortality (cf. Kacha's mission to obtain the secret from Venus). Yet Jupiter knows the method to harness the nature's finer forces. It makes Jupiter an able priest. *Swaha,* one of his daughters, sometimes considered as one of his wives, represents Jupiter's ability to make the sacrifices of his worshippers to fructify. He is an efficient supplicant, a sacrificer, a priest who intercedes with gods on behalf of men. Yet his influence does not extend to inner comprehension of the secret wisdom. His knowledge concerns the outer form only (otherwise the gods would not have frequent trouble with the demons in which gods were generally vanquished. Their position was generally retrieved only after higher intervention). Brahmanspati is the deity in whom the action of the worshipper upon the gods is personified. It represents materialisation of the Divine Grace, so to say, by means of rituals and ceremonies and the exoteric worship.

Tara's[2] fascination with Soma arose from her dissatisfaction with exoteric rituals and religiosity. Jupiter's religiosity leads to disillusionment when mind-principle is developed. Mind leads the individual to the domain of Saturn, materiality, and frustration, which finally enables the individual to merge in universal life represented by Jupiterian Pisces sign.

Jupiter is closely related to higher principles of man. It has special relationship with the luminaries. Jupiter imbibes the liberating influence of the Sun and the Moon. The ancient Egyptian sages noted the special impact of Saturn and Jupiter's transit over a sign. What the Sun and the Moon did annually for a month and two and a half days every month respectively, these two planets, namely Jupiter and Saturn intensified during their transits over them. The Sun transited a sign every month annually for twelve years what Jupiter does during a year after a gap of twelve years while the Moon transited every sign for two and a half day every month for about thirty years before Saturn transited the sign for about two and

---

[2]Tara was the wife of Jupiter, who is related with exoteric ritual practices. Soma, the presiding deity over the planet Moon, is associated with celestial nectar symbolising inner wisdom. Tara felt dissatisfied with the outer forms of religion so she left Jupiter and went to the company of Soma to receive deeper understanding of divine wisdom.

a half year. The ancient Egyptian teachers taught the inner significance of these situations to their selected disciples.

The relationship between Jupiter and the Moon in Hindu predictive astrology is discussed under several planetary combinations. *Gaja Kesari Yoga* formed by auspicious placement of Jupiter in relation to the Moon protects the individual from many difficulties. *Adhi Yoga* constitutes Jupiter's favourable position in relation to the Moon along with Mercury and Venus so as to funnel to the physical level the lunar nectar for the nourishment of the individual. *Sakata Yoga* impedes the flow of lunar psychic preservative influence through Jupiter and produces periodic sorrow. These refer to Jupiterian impact on the outer life of the individual. The story of Tara's abduction by Soma and birth of Mercury emphasises Jupiter's preoccupation with outer religiosity which failed to satisfy Tara thirsting for inner insight. The special feature of Jupiter-Sun relationship as observed by the Egyptian teachers provides a clue to the basic nature and function of Jupiter in the life of a man.

Jupiter's main task is consolidation, preservation and nourishment. It derives energy for these functions from the Sun. The Sun imparts its specialised influence to each sign annually for twelve years which Jupiter consolidates and objectifies during its transit every twelfth year. The Sun imparts noumenal life-force on the subjective plane which fructifies on the outer realm under the consolidative and preservative influence of Jupiter. Jupiter consolidates and diffuses the solar attributes and potential throughout the body. Jupiter by itself is powerless. It is effective only in doing someone else's work. The specialised solar energy accumulates in every sign every month for twelve years. The solar energy is so radiant and effulgent that the total in one instalment can be destructive. The beneficent radiation of Jupiter carefully consolidates the total solar energy and transforms it as nourishing influence during its twelve-yearly transit. Jupiter carries during its transit the solar impulse to the outer life of the person for his welfare. The Sun provides the spirit, Jupiter provides the channel for its expression.

Jupiter's harmonious relationship with the luminaries was known to Vedic astrologers. Yet its role as the carrier of Sun's life-giving energy on the physical plane needs special emphasis. Jupiter is exalted in the Moon's sign Cancer. Jupiter's influence in Leo is markedly auspicious. Its transit over Leo activates in the individual his highest spiritual aspirations. There is a perceptible twelve-yearly auspicious cycle in everyone's life. Jupiter's transit in Leo consolidates and nourishes the best in the individual. A fine thread of spiritual relationship is forged during this period between one's higher triad—*Atma-Buddhi-Manas,* and the physical body. From Leo, Jupiter aspects Sagittarius which arouses spiritual aspiration, Aquarius which enables the individual to endure the trials resulting from his spiritual aspirations, and Aries which provides him courage, initiative and strength for beginning a new life. The Sun is the storehouse of life-giving energy. It is this energy which Jupiter objectifies and diffuses over the various physical sheaths for the nourishment and welfare of the individual.

Saturn concretises the solar energy. It stops the same from diffusing itself in the wide expanse of the cosmos without manifesting itself in any form. Saturn assists it in manifestation by producing hindrance against the solar flow of life-essence. In this process, the physical sheath of the individual gets concretised. The role of Jupiter is different. It consolidates, preserves and nourishes the solar energy. It breathes life in the form concretised by Saturn. Jupiter brings to the physical sheath that energy by which it becomes alive. Jupiter is called *Jiva,* life entity, because of this function. *Jiva* implies the principle of life, the vital breath, the principle in man which lives and moves during a life period. *Jiva* is the power enshrined in the human body that imparts to it life, motion and sensation. It is a synonym of Maruta, the god of winds. The god of wind, the vital air, *prana,* all represent an aspect of the Sun essential for the life of a person. Jupiterian contribution in consolidating the solar essence deposited annually in every sign refers to this function of Jupiter. This energy is deposited and consolidated in the individual's physical and subtler body, the *Sthula Sharira* or his etheric double. The subtler body is directly controlled by Jupiter. The symbiotic relationship between Jupiter and the Sun through the vital air, *Prana Vayu,* is "critical" involving risk and suspense especially during the process of spiritual exercises.

Prana is one of the three energy forms radiating from the Sun which sustains the universe and the man. The other two are the cosmic electricity, known as *Fohat* in Tibetan occult literature and *Daivi Prakriti* in Vedanic texts, which pervades the entire universe, and the Serpent Fire, *Kundalini,* latent at the root of the spinal cord whose activation gives enormous power over Nature. *Prana* is life-breath, it is differentiated in five channels for its various functions in a human body. As vitality, it originates from the Sun, expresses itself as wind and enters man as his breath. It surrounds man as his health aura which is expressed as etheric double to clairvoyant seers. In Vedantic literature health aura is known as *Sukshma Sharira*, the energy in *Pranamaya Kosha*. *Prana* is described as the "invisible" or "fiery" energy which supplies the microbes with "vital constructive energy" to enable them to build the physical cells. Health of a person is directly related with the absorptive capacity of his *Pranamaya Kosha*, the etheric double. Jupiter's role is to strengthen, preserve and nourish the etheric double. Jupiter plays a passive role in an average person. It receives the solar energy, transmits it to the physical body which employs the same for its several gratifications and experiences. Excessive flow of vital air may disrupt the psycho-physical balance of the individual and make him depraved and over indulgent in sex. This involuntary tendency is reversed under the practice of *Yama* and *Niyama*. These disciplines prepare the individual to fruitfully employ any excessive inflow of vital air when it so occurs. Jupiter takes sway over such aspirants when they wish to dedicate themselves to work for the Divine Plan. Jupiter is the priest who intercedes with gods on behalf of men. Jupiter is yellow in colour which symbolises one's conscious decision to sacrifice oneself to higher forms of life. In everyday life we put on yellow clothes on religious occasions. Jupiter prepares the devoted persons to imbibe greater solar vitality if they so try. Jupiter is helpful in such activities. It requires purity of purpose and cleanliness in personal life.

Yogic literature describes right postures (asanas) and controlled breathing (Pranayama) necessary for imbibing and assimilating larger amount of vital air. Fasting, meditation, chastity of thought, word and deed, silence for certain periods of time, governance of one's animal passions and impulses, utter unselfishness and even the use of certain incense and fumigations are said to be helpful. These are exoteric preparations. They are only initial physico-psychological preparations. The Jupiterian influence provides the helpful milieu, the real efforts at this stage will lie in maintaining right postures and controlled breathing. The intake of vital air consists primarily of inbreathing, *Puraka*, withholding the breath, *Kumbhaka*, and outbreathing or *Ruchaka*. Depending upon individual requirements, eight varieties of Pranayama have been listed. The eight horses yoked to the chariot of Jupiter possibly refer to these eight forms of Pranayama (besides the eight *siddhis,* yogic accomplishments which also result from Jupiterian beneficence).

The vital air received at the splenic force centre, *Swadhisthan Chakra,* absorbs *Vyana Vayu* to diffuse it throughout the body after differentiating the air coming from the Sun. This *chakra* sends *Apana Vayu* to *Muladhara,* the basic force centre situated near anus. *Samana Vayu* concerned with digestive system goes to umbilical force centre, *Manipura,* near navel. *Udana Vayu* goes to laryngeal or *Vishudhi Chakra* near throat and *Prana Vayu* goes to cardiac or *Anahata Chakra.* The control and regulation of breath intensifies absorption and distribution of vital airs to different *chakras* nourishing and strengthening them for their specific functions. The solar fire represented as Vital Air, on differentiation moves through different *nadis,* artilleries, and burns impurities. Different types of Pranayamas make the practice a cleansing operation specially suited to the specific needs of the person. The circulation of Vital Airs specially activated *Ida, Pingala* and *Sushumna,* the *nadis* around the spine and make them fit for the Serpent Fire, *Kundalini,* to flow upwards. A favourable Jupiter reveals the possibility of undertaking this arduous task of spiritual preparation.

Jupiter's extreme friendship with Sun and Mars reveals its role in spiritual unfoldment for the individuals. Jupiter absorbs the solar energy to preserve and nourish the subtler body, the etheric double of the individual and provide them the necessary impetus and conditions so that he may have martian initiative and courage to proceed towards unification with the universal spirit. Any one desirous of undertaking the arduous task of voluntary spiritual development must look for well harmonised Jupiter, Mars and the Sun.

23

SATURN:
The Spiritualising Planet

Predictive Astrology describes Saturn as a powerful malefactor. It is a bitter enemy of the luminaries. Its aspect is destructive. Saturn produces laziness, difficulties, distress, sickness, opposition, old age maladies, weakening of the nerves, and ugliness. It makes an individual crippled, poor, and servile, devoid of manliness, and downcast. Saturn makes one wear dirty rags, lie and live among the thieves, outcastes and menials. Happiness of the company of respectful women is denied to him. He mixes with maidservants, appropriates others' money and is unethical.

When Saturn transits over the Moon and its two adjoining signs, much unexpected troubles meet the individual.

To consider such a planet as the saviour of mankind and a guide on the path of spiritual return requires a very different understanding of the nature of Saturn. It will require an investigation into the inner motivations and basic impulses of the planet.

Shani Stotra eulogises Saturn as the bestower of kingdom if happy with a person, while destroys it instantaneously if dissatisfied. All troubles vanish on praying to it for succour.

Saturn's occupation of cardinal houses, whether in exaltation or its own sign, produces one of the five *Mahapurusha Yogas* indicating the maturity of the soul. These characteristics of Saturn reveal a very different aspect of the planet.

Such contradictory indications of Saturn on the outer life of a person are in fact expressions of its basic spiritual nature.

Saturn is represented as a black fat man with ugly appearance, and ruffled hair, riding on a vulture with a bow, a trident and an arrow in his hands. He moves slowly, stays on dust and garbage heaps, always looks down, is dissatisfied and his nature is feverish. He is born of Chhaya and Surya and is a brother of Yami, the river Yamuna. He is *tamasic* in attribute. He is concerned with ash, iron, lead, wind and the mendicant's bowl. While Saturn's form is described in such symbols, his eyes are said to be of wisdom; for gods and mankind he is said to be divine or an adept Naga, the serpent teacher. All these are deeply suggestive symbols revealing the spiritualising effect of Saturn.

The ancient seers knew the inner side of Saturn. They associated Saturn with Yama as well as with various animals to indicate that the Saturnian impulse is concerned with transformation, rejuvenation and nourishment. The different animals of which *Uttara Kalamrita* has mentioned, dog, bull, buffalo, horse and goat represent its procreative energy and its power of yearly rejuvenation. The Pharaohnic teachings contain much reference to these animals in imparting the inner impulses of the universal life. The generative power in these animals in Egyptian religion was identical with the force by which life is renewed in nature continually and in a man after death. Yudhisthira's refusal to part company with his dog before his entry into the heaven shows that the ancient Vedic sages were aware of the symbolic significance of these animals. It is worth remembering that the deity associated with Saturn (its *Adhi-devata*) is Prajapati, a progenitor of mankind. Behind the fierce appearance of the planet, its great concern for the evolution of mankind was known to the ancient sages.

Vulture, the carrier of Saturn, belongs to the same feathered species as Garuda, the carrier of Vishnu, the preservative principle. Both of these were born of the same Vedic sage; the Sun was also born of the same sage Kashyapa. Garuda represents the Great Cycle during which the material sheaths of the person are periodically destroyed until they are able to merge back into the perpetual motion, the Eternity. The various allegories about the vulture make it the emblem of the Great Cycle, the Mahakalpa, coeternal with Vishnu, one with the Time and the Sun. What Vishnu does by nourishing and sustaining life, Saturn does in darkness through death and biological transformation. The vulture, like a dog or jackal, swallows even the bones and flesh of the dead and changes putridity into life-giving substance. When Saturn inflicts sorrow, sickness, deprivation or even death, its aim is to liberate the soul from its physical weaknesses, psychological attachments and decrepit physical sheath and transform the same into life-giving energy.

The spiritual impact of Saturn is often overlooked due to its special operational method. It provides appropriate channel for the outflow of the solar radiance. Without Saturnian veil, its materialisation, the Sun cannot create and succeed in its evolutionary mission. The Sun being a pure spirit, a subjective orb of life and light, it needs primordial matter, *Mula Prakriti,* embodied in the Moon, and objective, material sheaths, restrictive material and resistance represented by Saturn in order to project itself in the world of manifestation. This also shows the special relationship between the Moon and Saturn. The epithet's downward vision (*Adho Drishti*) westward looking (*Paschima Mukhi*) and the attribute *tamas* (darkness, inertia) refer to concretisation and materialisation of the life-force as an impulse of Saturn.

Saturn provides opposition to the Sun. But it is so to help the Sun in its mission of cosmic evolution. The Sun's light can shine only against the darkness of Saturn. The Sun's life-force can energise an ego and give it rebirth only when there is old age and death caused by Saturn. The regal splendour of the Sun can look impressive only against the Saturnian rags, shabby clothes and ashes on the body and garbage around one's house. The Sun's gold is precious only in the presence of Saturn's iron. Saturn and the Sun are two poles of the same function; they represent *Prakriti* and *Purusha;* the East and the West. Both of them work for spiritual evolution. Saturn does it through its vulture who swallows the putrefied corpse, absorbs within itself the dead matter from which in it extricated life-force to initiate a fresh life. Transformation and rejuvenation by releasing the spiritual essence in man from his sickness, sorrow and death is the goal of Saturn.

If this feature of Saturn is properly appreciated it will change our approach to man and conditions of his life, and will enable us to transform the malefic impact of Saturn into a spiritualising impulse. Saturn always looks for producing inner wisdom and imparting secret teachings provided the human beings are willing and prepared to receive them. Saturn consumes all in the sacrificial fire of death so as to prepare men to be open to divine wisdom. Saturn's fall in the serpent's world *(Naga Loka),* his wanderings in wood, forest and the mountains and the smearing of ashes on the body refer to the quest for inner spiritual wisdom. Vishnu's Garuda is an enemy of the serpent; it implies that one's involvement in matter, mundane existence, succeeds in the absence of esoteric wisdom and occult vision whereas Saturn's falling amidst the serpents refers to destruction, deprivation and afflictions arising from material attraction, experiences which produce clarity of vision, disillusionment and the realisation of pure Brahma, enlightenment. The placement of Saturn in relationship with the zodiacal signs and its rulership of different asterisms indicate the various stages in the Saturnian transformation process. The luminaries namely the Sun and the Moon, are pure subjective planets, one represents Brahma, *Purusha* or the Spirit and the other *Mula Prakriti, Buddhi* or the reflection of Brahma itself. Their impulses are always directed in one way, towards fulfilling the divine destiny. Only subsequently, with differentiation of Mahat Principle and *Manas* in the evolving soul, the cyclical evolutionary journey commences for the incarnating soul. Immersion in matter and withdrawal of divine consciousness from it begins with the Saturnian impulse.

The Sun and the Moon are assigned only one sign each which belongs to them. All other planets have two signs to rule. The dual nature of these planets, one on the outer plane on which the materialisation of the soul takes place and the other on the inner plane where the soul is enabled to extricate itself from mundane existence, can be understood better by studying their relationship with the two signs owned by them.

Each of these planets, except Saturn, have their rulership signs separated from each other. Considerable time period must elapse before the materialisation impulse is transformed into withdrawal from the outer life. But Saturn owns Capricorn and Aquarius which form a continuous belt of the zodiac. The wide spectrum of influence flowing through Saturn is perceived under five asterisms covering this area. The transformation caused by Saturn does not need incubation: it is direct, fierce and invincible. At the initial stage intensification of matter occurs. In the process the deepest

layer of materialisation is churned. Spirit embedded at the innermost core of the being is unable to express itself on the outer life
that gives an impression of its being dead and absent. But the soul
cannot permanently stay at this position. Inertial motion of Saturn
takes it further. The slow moving donkey is sometimes so slow that
the distance covered seems negligible. Saturn is slow but there is
always movement, that is its inertial motion, the *tamasic* proclivity.
The material sheath gradually thins, losses its hold and crumbles
down, and the inner spirit begins to assert. This is the spiritualising
process produced by the malefic Saturn. At this stage Saturn is
painful but the inevitable realisation of the final destiny becomes
clear during the soul's sojourn through Capricorn to Aquarius.

Capricorn churns to intensify materiality at initial stages so as
to produce complete disenchantment with its fruits. At this stage the
individual is gradually, in one continuous chain, developed; he
becomes the image of God on the earth; his action organs and
wisdom senses are well-formed. What use he makes of them is his
consideration. The inertial impulse of physical self leads him to seek
sensual gratifications, psychological satisfaction, personal ambition
and social status. Often his cravings are fulfilled. Yet towards the
end of this fulfillment dissatisfaction awaits him. This is the kind of
special transformation produced by Saturn. The material acquisitions
must end in frustration, this is the spiritual lesson Saturn imparts. It
has brought the individual at Capricorn to this situation to inculcate
in him the desirability of spirituality. The three quarters of *Uttara
Ashada, Shravana* and first half of *Dhanistha* gradually destroy the
personality and pave the way for further progress. *Uttara Ashada*
produces psychological orientation for discharging the ultimate
responsibilities and karmic debts. It involves us in intense physical
activities accentuated by a sense of personal fulfillment.

Under *Shravana* the physical exertion for personal fulfilment
continues but the voice from the distant vision begins to sound
louder. The sense of frustration from material acquisitions grows
deeper. *Dhanistha* produce trials, sorrows, frustration. It impels the
individual to give up demands of one's own self and begin working
for others. The sprouting of the seed of altruism begins here. During
the soul's journey through Capricorn, Saturn makes the person seek
personal gratifications, a natural phenomena under intensification of
materiality of man, then it begins to produce frustration and

psychological dissatisfaction not due to non-fulfilment of personal ambition but due to inherent inability of material goals to satisfy the inner man, and finally Saturn under Capricorn prepares the individual for spiritual trials and tribulations awaiting every spiritual aspirant.

Saturn continues the impulse in Aquarius. Under the Aquarian impulse, the individual is carried further by a gale of past karmic forces. This special impulse produces an important psychological orientation in man. He can now acquire a new outlook, a new direction in life and a new psycho-biological transformation. The sign consists of *Dhanistha* later half, *Satabhishaka* and first three quarters of *Purva Bhadra* owned by Mars, Rahu and Jupiter. These asterisms are intimately connected with powerful past karmas. They create conditions through which personal vanities, sensual gratifications and self-seeking ambitious activities give way to considerations for others, altruism and spiritual values. The continuity of Saturnian signs aims at producing the spiritualising impact without any time interval that makes the lesson arduous and Saturn a planet of great hardships. Saturn has inherited invincibility from its father the Sun, spirituality from its grandfather sage Kashyapa and its method of working conditioned by matter with which it is surrounded.

Saturn represents *Prakriti,* the manifestation around us. Nature does not restrict the power of Original Cause, but it provides channels for its ultimate expression. The Sun is the original impulse while Saturn is the final expression. Saturn fulfils the destiny of Brahma, *Atman* or the Sun for our universe. We form a part of this universal manifestation, Nature, and are not much different from minerals, plants and other animals. All are unitedly trying to express the quality of Brahma, the original impulse of manifestation. Once the process has begun, it can end only on final accomplishment of the goal. The soul relinquished its undifferentiated state of cosmic subjectivity in order to manifest its latent (spiritual) qualities. The multicoloured dome reflecting the One Radiance constitutes Nature; it is the alchemical crucible in which newer forms are evolved, basic transformations are achieved and base metal lead (associated with Saturn) turned into the solar gold. The man exists to participate in this natural process of universal transformation and Saturn assists man to do so.

Saturn represents *tamas,* darkness, but inertia is its inherent attribute. The universe moves under the impulse of inertia. Matter always operates under inertia unless some other impulse is exerted on it. Inertia rules supreme in Nature. In fact, at the root of all earthly manifestation, there must be the powerful impact of Saturn for its growth and development. Under the inertial impact of Saturn, the minerals unite and basic atoms constituting them and taking advantage of surrounding conditions, heat, pressure and chemical affinity, one form of mineral is transformed into another. Under this process coal becomes diamond. The transformation process in plant depends upon the nourishment secured by it and transforming the fertiliser into sap and imbibing the sunshine and air to grow into plant, leaves and flowers. The plants take nourishment from earth (*Prithvi Tattwa*), grow in the luxuriance of sunshine (*Agni Tattwa*), nurtured by the spring wind (*Vayu Tattwa*) and open themselves in the fullness of sky (*Akasha Tattwa*). They flower, produce seeds, decay and finally mingle once again in these elements.

Similarly each animal fulfils some special task, develops certain special qualities and adapts itself to some special purpose. The Pharaohic teachings considered Anubis, jackal, as one of their gods and attributed it to represent digestion. Jackal swallows even the bones and changes putridity into life giving substance. The digestion of seed that kills and decomposes it in order to form a new creature belongs to the female principle that give life otherwise, that is to say, without giving corporal volume to the life impulse that the seed carries. If the fecundated female principle does not have the capacity of putrefaction, Nature itself will cease to function. Saturn is assigned *tamas* as its attribute so that it can check the solar radiation from moving only in subjective (or spiritual) realm, concretise it in different multicoloured forms, and then transform it into its useful properties and role in manifestation finally leading it to the original cause. Under these basic factors, Saturn creates conditions for man so that he can pass through various situations imbibing from each condition what is helpful for his nourishment and growth. If the female principle is dead in him, he will rot, putrefy and nature's digestive function will not be operative. Without the Saturn's vulture, neither Nature can exist nor the individual will fulfil his destiny.

Saturn's role in cosmic evolution is to check spiritual impulse from dissolving into nothingness. Concretisation of spirit by putting *tamasic* impediments is its one aspect; Saturn's aim in its final phase is spiritual transformation. Its malefic nature is evident during its middle phase of operation where the soul extricated itself from its material sheaths. It is a painful process. Such a situation can be avoided and pain minimised by willingly cooperating with the Saturnian impulse and helping in its digestive function.

The malefic nature of Saturn results from its natural tendency to push the soul towards self-awareness while the personality clings to attractions of matter and physical indulgence. Yogic literature indicates *Yama* (self-restraint) and *Niyama* (psychological orientation by self-discipline) important to reverse the trend and direct the course of spiritual unfoldment. Saturn ascendants are invariably selfish, egotist, and always seeking gratification of their own sensual and other gratifications. They embrace others with their arms not to give themselves to others but to hold others to themselves. They are possessive, acquisitive and personification of power seekers. This tendency will finally have to be transformed to their opposites, if the trials of Saturn are to be minimised and results easily achieved. This tendency can be reversed by deliberate regulation of one's arrogance, vanity and superimposition of one's desires and wishes on others. Five indicators of this reorientation are non-aggression (*Ahimsa*), truthfulness (*Satyam*) non-appropriation (*Asteya*), continence and pious living (*Brahmacharya*) and non-possession or non-acquisition (*Aparigraha*). These attributes reduce the importance of personal nucleus of the individual's activities, reduce desire to use others for one's own gratification and establish voluntary control over inertial movement of one's inclinations.

This is the first set of rules that create an emptiness in the individual. He feels a sense of loss; he feels that there is no purpose in life and all efforts are senseless. Such a psychological situation marks the turning point in the life of the individual. The individual must now give a new meaning to his exertions. He must purify himself. Natural inclinations under the Saturnian impulse are towards all that is dirty, discarded, depressive, putrid, decrepit and deprave. A conscious inculcation of cleanliness of the body, emotion, thought, dress and personal dealings with others will weaken the impact of Saturn. The planet produces dissatisfaction, craving and thirst for life; cultivation of contentment, control over prying curiosity in other person's personal matters, and acceptance of one's shortcomings and limitations, failures and poverty in life will extricate the individual from the mainstream of materiality. One must stand aside to watch the various personal and social attachments. One's attachment with one's physical body, social status and relationships and even with one's scriptural prejudices involves oneself to materiality of subtler kind. Reversal of such psychological proclivities will need austerity, self-discipline, introspection, and surrender of oneself to God or to some higher impersonal force. These will give a new direction to one's life. These will dissolve the hold of matter on the personality of the person. The fire of *Tapas,* austerities, will burn the dross of past karmas. In this process, the individual will suffer physical pain but there would be psychological transformation. Whether the individual does it willingly, voluntarily in the spirit of conscious cooperation with his ultimate destiny, or is forced into it by the 'malefic' impulse of Saturn is his choice.

24

SASA YOGA:
Saturn's Impulse
for Human Greatness

Sasa Yoga is one of the *Panch Mahapurusha Yogas*. It is a planetary combination on the basis of which the stature of one's personality is assessed. This combination is formed by Saturn in strength occupying one of the cardinal houses. In a general way, it can be stated that *Sasa Yoga* is formed when Saturn is in Capricorn, its own house, Aquarius, its Moolatrikona, or in Libra, the house of its exaltation and it is placed in the ascendant, the fourth, seventh or the tenth house. This *Yoga* is distinguished from other *Raja Yogas*. In this case, the results indicated relate the individuals to greatness rather than to wealth and riches. In general parlance, the astrologers, while indicating the results of these combinations, however, talk of such gifts as wealth, social status, affluence and so on.

The results of *Sasa Yoga* are variously stated in classical texts. In essence they are the same as stated in *Jataka Parijata*. The person born under this *Yoga* would be:–

a king, a minister, or a military general haunting woods and mountains; he is cruel-hearted, and would even defraud others in his eager pursuit of material wealth; has wrathful eyes, he is bountiful, spirited, lovingly devoted to his mother; brave, has a dark form and lives for seventy years. He is a voluptuary, inclined to play the paramour with the objects of his guilty love.

Most of the descriptions of *Sasa Yoga* have been made on the same lines. How could these results, excepting that "the person may be a king, a minister, or a military general" be considered signs of superb eminence, which really constitutes 'greatness' in man is beyond the comprehension of a common-man. The application of *Sasa Yoga* to different persons who in their actual life have this *Yoga* in their horoscopes, also does not support the contention very much. V. Subrahmanya Sastry translated *Jataka Parijata* into English and commented upon and gave many charts in connection with this *Yoga*. But they also did not exactly agree with the actual life conditions as indicated in this combination. The charts given here belonged to the affluent sections of the society, but this feature is not universal. In actual life, the *Yoga* appears even in cases of ordinary persons somehow eking their living. One should therefore overlook the characteristic of affluence resulting necessarily from *Sasa Yoga*.

The Chart I belonged to a high officer in the teaching profession, the second (Chart II) was of person who was 'a very, very wealthy person', son of a celebrated *diwan* in an important native state, the third (Chart III) was a renowned South Indian astrologer, the fourth (Chart IV) was a remarkable statesman and the fifth (Chart V) belonged to a very efficient judicial officer. From these it can be seen that the list consists of persons who are not only "kings, ministers or military generals," but belonged to other

			Moon
Sun Rahu	CHART I		Jupiter
Mars Venus Mercury	3 Feb. 1896		Ketu
		Ascdt Saturn	

			Jupiter
Ascdt Saturn	CHART II 16 Jan. 1907		Rahu
Sun Moon Ketu			
Mercury	Venus	Mars	

	Ascdt Sun Moon Mercury	Venus	Jupiter Mars
Rahu	CHART III 26 April 1895		
			Ketu
		Saturn	

professions as well. The professional indications therefore should be taken merely as indicator of powerful individuality resulting from much inner potential, capabilities and power. The age is given by Sastry for only two persons. The fourth individual was born on 1 June 1845, who died at the age of fifty-six, while the fifth one died at the age of sixty-two; none of these persons died at the age of seventy years as given in the text. The age of seventy years as assigned to *Sasa Yoga* should not be considered definitive. The first individual suffered much mental disturbance particularly caused by native's partner. The fourth one was not cruel-hearted, he was "a very liberal and broad-minded person". He had a hard struggling life which qualified him to deserve respect and sympathy. Greater acquaintance with persons of *Sasa Yoga* would reveal that it is in

	Jupiter Moon Mercury	Ketu Sun Venus	
	CHART IV 1 June 1845		Ascdt
Mars Saturn			
	Rahu		

	Rahu	Venus	
	CHART V 24 July 1873		Ascdt Sun Moon
Saturn			Jupiter Mercury
		Ketu Mars	

the realm of psychological and psychic experiences that the real greatness of the person is perceived. It would not be revealed through the social status or through the individual's fondness for the forbidden love. *Sasa Yoga* is rather a rare *yoga*. Out of the thirty years of Saturn's cycle round the various signs of the zodiac, it is possible only when Saturn passes through Libra, Capricorn or Aquarius. It therefore implies that *Sasa Yoga* can be formed only during 7½ years of the thirty years cycle. During these years the planet could be in cardinal houses only approximately during one-third of this duration. During the hours of solar rotation causing day and night, the *Pancha Mahapurusha Yogas* are formed only during those periods of extreme sensitivity, that is, when any of the non-luminaries is crossing either the rising or the setting horizons or during the time of mid-days and midnights. It is during these periods of sensitivity that the Moon causes upsurge and swing of tidal waves; ebb and flow tides occur during these sensitive points of relationship between the Sun and the Earth.

In occult literature these periods are reckoned as very important. On these special occasions, when Saturn comes in special relationship with these highly magnetic cosmic regions, certain special kinds of egos are born. Because of this uniqueness, it is possible that the egos born under *Saga Yoga* are intended to discharge certain special responsibilities, quite distinct from those with the other types of *Raja Yogas*. *Raja Yogas* are dependent upon special planetary relationships which do not necessarily occur under these magnetic durations, rather they are only individualistic planetary combinations. It is possible that some individuals endowed with special *Raja Yogas* are born at any specified period of time when special planetary configuration takes place, but *Sasa Yoga* can occur only to a group of exceptional persons born during certain selected epochs. For this reason it is permissible to consider *Sasa Yoga* more as inherent astrological nature of the individual concerned, while other *Raja Yogas* could be considered as pointers of certain specific conditions under which the individual has to pass. If an individual with *Sasa Yoga* becomes wealthy, kingly, renowned, cruel-hearted, and lives for seventy years, or so, these could be recognised as dependent on other astrological conditions whereas *Sasa Yoga* (or for that matter any other combination of *Pancha Mahapurusha Yogas*) would indicate the inborn nature of the constitution of the individual showing his inherent capabilities. On the basis of these characteristics there could be the possibility of fructification of certain specified results (as given in the text). The nature of 'constitution' of the individual under *Sasa Yoga* would depend upon special conditions under which this *Yoga* is formed.

Saturn in Capricorn could have three quarters of Uttaraashada, four quarters of Shravana, and two earlier quarters of Dhanistha. These constellations are intimately related to the basic nature of Saturn. This planet in Vedic mythology is known as the son of the Sun; it implies great spiritual status to it. Besides this, Saturn or Shani, this planet is also known as *Kona, Manda, Krishna,* as well as *Yama*. Apart from being a corner, an angle, an intermediate point of the compass, the word *kona* also means the bow of a lute, a fiddlestick, the sharp edge of weapon or of a sword, and a drumstick. *Manda* means slow, tardy, lazy, cold, as well as the dissolution of the world. *Krishna,* apart from being the son of Vasudeva and Devaki, was also an incarnation of Lord Vishnu; the word itself however means the black, dark. *Yama,* apart from being the name of the God of Death, also means restraining, controlling, any great moral or religious duty, the first of the eight *angas* or parts for attaining perfection in *Yoga*, the union between the human individual and the Supreme Power. From these suggestive meanings of the name of Shani, one could probably see that the *Sasa Yoga* may be related to the Vishnu-principle of creation as well as the Shiva aspect of destruction expressed as a great disciplining force leading to unification with the highest which could suggest a corner in one's life leading to a new orientation. Saturn is also the bow of a lute, a drumstick which signifies that the planet resounds some deeper purpose inherent in the individual. In achieving this purpose, Saturn never hurries, very patiently moves towards the allotted goal, the goal of carrying the individual to the kingdom of One Universal Life, the Sun, around which everything moves. In this way, one can understand that Lord Krishna as a manifestation of Lord Vishnu resounded in the world of materiality the message of the Divine Life; his prime purpose was to objectify, concretise, and to make perceptible the Divine Principle in life. The God of Destruction, in one way a destroyer, is a great instrument in breaking the shell of one's physical nature thereby becoming a potent power in the evolutionary process. Under the impact of Saturn, one changes the course of one's life: the Pure Subjective Principle becomes objective and the gross materiality is turned towards spirituality. Under *Sasa Yoga,* Saturn functions in an effective manner in this direction of unifying the individual with the Universal, and the objective to the Subjective Realisation.

In order to play its role, Saturn functions on *Annamaya Kosa,* or the physical sheath of the human individual as well as of the environment. The planet is also related to mystery schools, elemental worship, ceremonies. Temperament of human individuals under which the subjective concepts of beauty and harmony are transformed into concrete aspects of manifestation such as paintings, architecture and the like is also under the control of this planet.

The exoteric and general characteristics of Saturn can be considered as the expression of inner or the esoteric purpose of the Saturnian influence. The manner in which this concretisation could take place may depend upon various details of the individual destiny. The fact that this great mission is assigned to Saturn which under very special conditions forms *Sasa Yoga* justifies its inclusion among the Great or *Maha Yogas*.

The three quarters of Uttaraashada occupying a portion of Capricorn are very much overshadowed by Viswadeva, who presides over this asterism. He primarily arouses humility. When the colossal cosmic presence overshadows the nature of a human individual, the quality of this immensity would inevitably destroy the materiality of the gross physical nature. Under such a condition, the individual would become a philosopher in his personal life, knowing and feeling the futility of material existence. Saturn and Jupiter owning the last three quarters of this asterism, while the ruling planet of the same is the Sun, would influence the individual importantly under the *Yoga*. The glory of the Sun, the Father, swaying and overshadowing the life of the person would fill his Saturnian disposition and the Jupiterian religiosity. These would enkindle in him the dejection of the burial ground and *sanyasa* aroused under the Saturnian influence and devotion and compassion arising from the Jupiterian influence. Uttaraashada is merely an extension of Poorvashada which is closely linked with water and symbolised by the tusk of an elephant. These two asterisms taken together suggest purity and the latent valuable qualities inherent in the individual. Such a realisation must have been undergone before the influence of Viswadeva, the Cosmic Reality, is revealed. The special impulse flowing through Uttarashada portion of Capricorn has the power and quality of the Sun which is the very source of the sustenance of all forms of manifestation. The deity presiding over Uttarashada represents the Universe or the Cosmos itself while the first quarter of it is linked with Jupiter which enables expansion, growth and sustenance of material forms so that the spiritual impulse could later on work itself through it. The formation and strengthening of the earlier form could be disintegrated under the later influence of Saturn leading to the disenchantment from the formal existence thereby enabling the last quarter of the asterism in instilling pure subjectivity by assimilation in the Divinity under the impact of the

Jovian ownership of the last quarter of the asterism. This would complete the universalisation process which can certainly be considered true attainment of greatness. Under the influence of this asterism, the individual is sympathetically attracted by the bond of mutual affinity to the suffering masses, a tendency which is highly accentuated if Saturn happens to be present in this part of the zodiac. It is a condition under which the self-centredness of the individual is greatly reduced, if it is not already completely eliminated. In this process, the individual learns the great lesson of humility which indeed is a reflection of one's real greatness.

Under *Shravana,* the whole of which lies in Capricorn, and which is symbolised by an ear and is presided over by Vishnu or Hari, the sensitivity of the person is greatly intensified. The quality of listening implies receptivity, discipleship and harmony with the song of life enabling the world and the words and deeds of the individual to come nearer the goal of Divine Perfection. The occult literature laid great stress on this quality of listening. *Mandukya Upanishad* begins with invocation of the teacher and the students together praying "O Ye Gods, may we hear with our ears what is auspicious." In another scripture it is said, "Before thou set'st thy foot upon the ladder's upper rung, the ladder of the mystic sounds, thou hast to hear the voice of thy inner God." Explaining the mystic nature of this injunction, the same scripture further elaborated, "When he, the disciple, has ceased to hear the many, he may discern the One—the inner sound which kills the outer. Then only and not till then, shall he forsake the region of *Asat*—the false to come unto the realm of *Sat,* the true." In order to enable the gross physical nature of the individual to attain quietitude or tranquility, *Yoga Sutras* of Patanjali emphasised the importance of *sanyama,* or control (an important aspect of Shani or Yama) which is a sort of physico-psychic harmonisation with the universal or cosmic nature of the deity.

Shravana as an asterism is the seat of the downpour under which the individual rises to the great heights of right meditation. For this very reason, probably, an arrow has been assigned as an alternative symbol of this asterism. In order to attain one pointedness, symbolised by an arrow, one must undergo considerable orientation in one's various sheaths. Saturn does it by stifling the physical proclivities and making the activities of sense perception inward turned, which in actual life may happen by a process which could seem to make the individual cruel-hearted (a quality suggested under *Sasa Yoga*) but this stifling would be a restraint, an abnegation, a sacrifice in order to realise one's real self, or one's true greatness. The various planets, Mars, Venus, Mercury and the Moon, owning different quarters of this asterism show the direction from which the stifling or the disciplining influence would flow in.

The end portion of Capricorn consists of the first two quarters of Dhanistha owned by Mars and symbolised by a drum, presided over by Vasu and the quarters connected with the Sun and Mercury. Vasus are eight in number all representing different aspects of the Supreme. Vasu also stands for Shiva, the God of destruction as well as for Kubera, the God of riches. As a matter of fact, Vasu even means wealth and riches, water and gold; it also stands for salt and a medicinal root. The lordship of the asterism makes it a sign of auspicious transformation. In esoteric astrology, Dhanistha stands for the influence which guides the individual towards perfection, implying that the imperfections of the human individual are considerably eliminated and his consciousness is merged in the Universal. When that happens, the individual does not remain conscious of his failings and the little self, rather he begins to reflect the glory of God. This characteristic is well symbolised by the symbol of *mridanga,* a drum, which stands for Dhanistha whose main function is to resound the tune played by the Great Musician. When this influence begins to flow through the individual, he becomes a truly great man reflecting some glory of God.

In case Libra is the ascendant and Saturn in Capricorn happens to be in the fourth house, it would be one of the outstanding features for revealing the primordial nature of the individual. The fourth house represents mother, the Divine Mother, the primordial Matter, Moola Prakriti, from which every form of manifestation gets its brick-block and thereby the essential potential for manifestation. Being linked with *Laya,* the state of Eternal Quietitude, in which everything ultimately merges and ultimately rests, and from which all levels of objectivity are aroused, the *Hiranyagarbha,* the Golden Egg of the Hindu Cosmogenesis, the house represents the Primordial Essence, the Soul of the Matter, Mind or the seat of all impulses which later on manifests elaborately in time and space. This is the state of manifestation, the Great Impulse, contained in the fourth *bhava,* from which objectification begins in a concrete manner. The archetype of things, the noumena, contained in the Mind of the Lord ready to become the phenomena under favourable conditions are contained here. It has the Cosmic Ideas, the basic seeds, that finally in time and space grow into the trees of the World of Manifestation. Being the earliest source and potentiality, the archetype and the root-matter functioning as the means of transformation and becoming the vehicle of creation, growth and development, Saturn's placement in this house is indeed of tremendous importance for the incarnating ego. It links the native with its basic root. Saturn being the planet which acts on the gross physical plane, while the fourth *bhava* is the seat of Primordial Matter, the Mother principle, Saturn in the fourth *bhava* has a mysterious invisible thread connecting the subtlest with the grossest, transcending all barriers and illusions of intermediate stages of manifestation. The strength of Saturn under *Sasa Yoga,* ensures that its placement in this house does not upset the mental balance of the individual, rather makes him uniquely linked with his basic nature.

Connected this way, Saturn might give a kind of intense desire for unity with the Essential Nature of Oneself, unity with one's soul which at some stage of manifestation may seem a sort of incestuous love for one's Mother. Having no regard for worldly traditional social codes and external behaviour, eager to express and always compelled by the inner primitive feelings and emotions, the behaviour of the individual may seem cruel, ruthless, disregarding the canons of social manners and courtesies. The characteristic cruelty of nature stated as a result of *Sasa Yoga* arises from this planetary disposition under whose impulse the external becomes subordinate to the inner.

Moreover, Saturn from the fourth house aspecting the sixth, the tenth and the Ascendant would create a devastating influence on the external relationships of the individual. His enemies, his difficulties and other kinds of impediments would not be able to stand before him. This supremacy may also be considered the result of the individual's ruthless disposition. Saturn's aspect on the tenth house would also create disarray. The individual would like to take destiny in his own hands, a quality essential for a military general, another quality attributed to *Sasa Yoga.* Aspect of Saturn on the Ascendant would enable the individual's petty self to be destroyed and his real self to emerge, which need not be a very pleasant and happy change, but it could resemble the enthronement of a king. When Saturn in Capricorn bestows these qualities, there could be a mysterious atmosphere around the individual which would force him to give up the coil of his petty self. He is now a part of the Universal Self.

For Libra Ascendant, when Saturn is in the fourth *bhava,* it becomes a *yogakaraka* creating an auspicious situation. Saturn under this situation is the lord of the fifth *bhava* as well and thereby he comes to be the lord of cardinal and trine houses. The destructive nature of Saturn under this condition is transformed into beneficial influence particularly for bestowing riches and wealth. When *Sasa Yoga* is formed with Capricorn, Saturn in the tenth house, the individual's destiny (Karma as the tenth *bhava*) synchronises with that of *kalapurusha*—the Heavenly or the Cosmic Man—thereby leading to a unique sense of Divine Fulfilment. The realisation of subjective spirituality, which can even be considered the disenchantment of the burial ground derived as a result of loss of every possession, specially of the gross physical kind is the Divine Purpose awaiting every individual. It is greatly facilitated by this placement of Saturn. The tenth is the house representing the violent churning of the past karma but guiding the resulting forces to lead the individual to the irresistible future glory awaiting him. Under the impact of this sign, the outer vehicle of consciousness is so changed as to make it an appropriate medium for the expression of the inner—the psychological and the psychic being. Such is often the process of breaking the shell of human pettiness; humility, realisation of divine splendour and complete surrender to the Supreme are some of the expressions of this process of destruction of the physical outer shell. It is often possible for the common man with all his rich attainments, wealth, status and personal glories destroyed to have an insight into his real destiny under that cloud of sorrow. With this realisation, when his feelings and emotions become dry and barren (Saturn aspecting the fourth house) and the pleasures of material life gone (destruction of the seventh house) and the sexual pleasures denied (as a result of Saturn's aspect on the twelfth house), he would be in a situation of restlessness, unable to rest at any place and roaming from one place to another (thus becoming addicted to wanderings in forests and mountains).

He would derive no personal pleasures at any place or in any situation. He may become heartless—cruel-hearted, and having seen the futility of material acquisitions he could become bountiful and sacrificing with whatever he has. An example of this kind of native has been Sardar Vallabhabhai Patel, who had Capricorn Saturn in the tenth house.

With Aries in the fourth house, Libra in the tenth, when Saturn forms *Sasa* by remaining in the Ascendant, it provides a unique example of concretisation of the Universal Power in individualised physical self. The individual's psychological and psychic sheaths become very firm and his egotistic nature so much accentuated that the individual begins to consider himself extremely powerful, a kind of miniature divine self. He is very ruthless in attaining his objective; thus Saturn aspecting fully the tenth house makes his method of functioning in life and adoption of the means of livelihood completely unorthodox, verging on unethical nature. His attitude to marital relation follows the same tendency of unorthodoxy. Such an individual would care primarily for his own self-fulfilment and self-aggrandisement. Saturn thus placed would have the lordship of the second house as well, and it would be friendly with the lord of the tenth house but extremely disharmonious with the lords of the fourth, the seventh, and the eleventh. The individual would consequently acquire much wealth, would achieve high (social) status, but contentment and personal happiness would be denied to him. This contradiction would exist primarily to show that the personal self, though containing within itself much power and capability, is futile and devoid of satisfaction and happiness unless the individualised physical self is completely harmonised with the universal or the cosmic consciousness. When such an individual begins to realise that he is the world, that the sorrows and miseries of the world are his personal problems, not the other way round, then and then only the fruition of *Sasa Yoga* could be final under such a situation.

The occurrence of Saturn in the seventh house with Cancer Ascendant is very different. It is here that the individual experiencing enormous universal downpour through his gross physical sheath is unable to find adequate outlet for this force. His central focus of attention being the field of his expression which has considerable limitation in providing appropriate outlet for his creativity, and the plane of his concentrated activities being the gross physical sheath, his mind is stormed by surging emotions making him sway from one extreme to another. He is fond of sex, desires to enjoy marital bliss, learns the art of love-making, but the conditions being as they are, his thirst is unquenched. This leads to some imbalance in his life. It is accentuated further by the fact that his religious background is different from the unconventional sex life, but he cannot adhere to traditional approach to life to which he by birth and upbringing belongs. He evolves a philosophy of his own where he postulates a kind of universal cosmic hand behind every living form, every action, deed and in every kind of approach to life. He visualises in his philosophy every kind of deed, even the brutalest and the most unsavoury ones, as an expression of some universal energy. As such, there would be nothing according to this philosophy worth despising or discarding in the scheme of things. Many might find this philosophy too revolting. Consequently, he would be left to walk alone on his lonely path. There would be few to share his innermost feelings. A strong interconnection would exist between his physical, emotional and psychological life. Though in his own mind, he would be absolutely candid and leading an honest life, people in general would not see him as such. They would be unable to appreciate his philosophy and approach to life. They would generally misunderstand him and consider him a hypocrite. In this kind of misunderstanding, when his individual self and the world at large, as well as his words (his philosophy) and his actions are opposed to one another, he would begin to take his life in a different way and in this process his individuality would begin to emerge and would gradually begin to assert himself. In this process his greatness would be revealed. He may not be rich materially, he may not be a king of material kingdom, but in his own mind he would soar high and above others. In his own way, he would be kingly in his uniqueness.

In whatever cardinal house Saturn may be placed and in the above examples we have seen so only in the case of its being in Capricorn, the planet would contain within itself tremendous disciplining force acting on the gross sheath of the individual. This makes the physical world the centre of the individual's activities. Under Capricorn, *Sasa Yoga* would provide enormous downpour of universal force channellised through the individual. This connection expressing itself in different cardinal houses may make the individual psychologically dissatisfied and uncommon but, it would make him a vehicle of tremendous downpour of universal energy. This special relationship leading to concretisation of the cosmic power on the gross physical level in whatever little measure it may be under the *Sasa Yoga*, would make the individual blessed.

25

MAKARA:
The Most Mystic Sign

Makara considered as one of the treasures of Kubera, the guardian of wealth of heaven, is the most sacred and mysterious signs of the zodiac. It is ruled by Saturn, the lord of time. Mars, the personification of power is exalted here and Jupiter, the High Priest of religious rituals is under debilitation in this sign. Interestingly, Kamadeva, the god of human desires, has the insignia of Makara on his flag. T. Subba Rao, the great Advaita philosopher of the nineteenth century, indicated the numerical value of the sign as five; Makara was intended to represent the face of the universe which was bound by a pentagon. The tenth sign of the zodiac is esoterically related to five and it symbolises at one and the same time the spirit of Eternal Life and the spirit of life and love terrestrial in the human compound. It includes divine and infernal magic, and the universal and individual quintessence of the being.

The ancient Indian sages were fully aware of the mystic connection existing between Makara represented by a goat or a half fish and half-human figure and the Kumaras, the *manasa-putras,* mind-born children of Brahma, created for manifestative purpose but instead of engaging in such unspiritual activities, disobeying the Brahma's injunctions remained as Virgin Ascetics. The meaning of these highly occult references incomprehensible to uninitiated individuals, in deeper mysteries can reveal deeply embedded and intensely subjective characteristics of this sign, provided the

individual is interested in one's basic motivations and the ultimate
destiny awaiting him.

Makara, the tenth sign of the zodiac, is gentle and mild
(*saumya*) and feminine having *tamasic* attributes, earthly element,
living in the southern direction, powerful during night, roaming in
forests and wilderness and expanding in water. These are certain
characteristics only superficially interpreted in predictive astrology or
simply overlooked as insignificant features of the zodiac. Careful
students would find that these features reveal many operational
details of the sign which can unveil the conditions under which the
planetary inpulses have to pass through before precipitating their
impact on the individual. The very qualification of gentleness
indicates the unobtrusive manner in which the zodiacal impulse
spreads and makes the individual look for its causative factors
somewhere else. Very often the individuals are so much impressed
by the unassuming nature of the Capricorn, that they look for the
causes for many unhappy influences precipitated by it somewhere
else. The sign is feminine, it provides opportunities for effective
operations of active, directly effective forces, fierce planets such as
Mars, to be effective under this area of zodiacal influence. By itself
Makara may prove ineffective, without making any impact on the
life of the individual. Once it gets support and material impetus
imparted to it by any planet either by association, aspect or
otherwise, the concretisation of the result becomes evident.

The astrological classification of the sign as 'even' does not
make much sense with many astrologers. But the occultists attach
considerable importance to this classification. The odd signs are
reckoned as divine and the even ones as terrestrial, devilish and
unlucky. Only one is good and harmonious because no disharmony
can proceed from one. The even or binary numbers are different.
The Pythagoreans hated binary. With them it was the origin of
differentiation, hence of contrast, discord, or matter, the beginning of
evil. In the Valentinian theogony, according to Blavatsky, *Bythos*
(Depth, Chaos) and *Sige* (Silence) are the original binary. With the
early Pythagoreans, the Duad was that imperfect state into which the
first manifested being fell when it got detached from the Monad. It
was the point from which the two roads—the good and the evil—
bifurcated. All that which was double-faced or false was called
binary by them. Invariably one finds the Capricornians are much torn

between serious conflicts. When they are materialists, the vision of spiritual goals is not dim before them, while those struggling for spiritual unfoldment find that their material attraction is very acute. Such contradictions in their psychological make-up make them schizophrenic.

The personal life of Capricornians is invariably full of turmoil, disharmony and inner emptiness. Only under strong spiritualising influences under the impact of other planets such as Sun, Mars and Rahu/Ketu can one expect the latent spiritualising influences under this sign to arise. The inherent inertial attributes (*Tamasic Vrittis*) and earthly elements (*Prithvi Tattwa*) of Makara have to be countered prior to enabling its divine qualities to blossom. As long as the Capricornian individual is functioning on the earthly level and is attracted by terrestrial attractions, his intellectualism caused by Mercury, the lord of its ninth house, attraction for social and sensual pleasures due to Venusian lordship of the tenth house, and his extramarital liaison produced by Martian connection with its eleventh house will stand in its way towards the deeper layers of unfoldment and attainments of higher realms of universalisation. The possibility of attaining both the goals is signified by such characterisation as wanderings in forests and wilderness (symbolising active pursuit of higher knowledge and mysteries of Nature) and expansion in water which referred to material attainments and eagerness to enjoy interaction with physical aspects of life.

The possibility of attaining spiritual heights under the tenth sign is suggested by such references as living in the southern direction, powerful during nights, and wanderings in forests and wilderness. The characteristics of Makara given in exoteric astrology are 'blinds' often aimed at deflecting the attention of the students from deeper possibilities under the sign. The precious pearl hidden within the dirty oyster shell can be exhumed only when such a rich treasure is suspected within. The ancient astrological seers were aware of the spiritual latency of Capricorn but realising the dangers and trials inherent in such an unfoldment, they considered it expedient to camouflage the highly spiritual impulses flowing through this sign. It was done to protect the unprepared from venturing into the perilous terrain of spiritual quest.

T. Subba Rao explained the exoteric content of the Makara *Rashi* in much greater detail. He acknowledged that there was some

difficulty in interpreting this word which revealed the inner essence
of the sign. He indicated that the word contained within itself some
clues to its correct interpretation. The Sanskrit language being highly
integrative, each letter and word of it contains within itself hidden
mysteries and meanings at different level. The occult significance
and numerical values of different letters and even their phonetic
values reveal so much of hidden wisdom that the seeming simple
statements can lead serious students working at many highly
abstruse planes to many precious revelations.

T. Subba Rao shows that the word Makara, "flippantly"
translated as crocodile, refers to simultaneous representation of both
microcosm and macrocosm, as external objects of perception. He
indicated that the letter *Ma* is equivalent to number 5 and *Kara*
means hand. In Sanskrit, *Tribhujam* (i.e. *Tri*=three; *Bhujam*=arm)
means a triangle. Bhujam and Karma both being synonymous,
triangle is also the first possibility of any moving point in a straight
line enclosing a space and such triangles together forming
tetrahedron[1] can produce any solid figure. *Ma* as equivalent to
number 5 and *Kara* representing the sides, Makara or *pancha karam*
means a pentagon. In occult literature, it is generally used to
represent the five limbs of man, the symbol being variously used as
the five-pointed star.

Having established Makara to represent the human being—the
first indication of the sign to the full stature of man in his outer and
inner qualities, the man with five *karmendriyas,* the organs of
action, and five *jnanendriyas,* the organs of wisdom, T. Subba Rao
extends further the sign of the zodiac to the manifestation itself. He
states that Makaram is the tenth sign and the term *Dasadisa (Dasa =*
ten; *Disa* = direction) is generally used by Sanskrit writers to denote
the faces or sides of the universe. Makara is intended to represent
the faces of the universe and he suggests that the figure of the
universe is bound by Pentagaon.

In esoteric astrology, there is a very intimate relationship
between Makara, the microcosm and the macrocosm. There is Vedic
affirmation of the identity between microcosm and macrocosm. The
ancient philosophers held that macrocosm was similar to microcosm
in having even a *sthula sarira* (physical body) and *sooksma sarira*

---

[1]Triangular-based pyramid.

(subtle body) and they held that the visible universe was the physical body of *Vishwa*, the universe, and that was the substratum of the visible universe. There is another universe which is the real universe of noumena, the soul as it were of this visible universe. This universe of Astral Light, according to Subba Rao, is hinted in certain passages of the Vedas and the Upanishads as such, it is represented by an icosahedron (a solid contained by twenty plane faces). If pentagons which represent Makara are taken as regular pentagons, then on the assumption that the universe is symmetrically constructed, the figure of the material universe will be a dodecahedron, solid figure of twelve faces, the geometrical model imitated by the Demiurges in constructing the material universe.[2] The possibility of extending the significance of Capricornian impulse to human individuals, the material universe and to the Demiurges engaged in manifestative mission opens many new vistas of astrological relationships of great metaphysical significance.

Elaborating the comments of T. Subba Rao and giving further details on the tenth sign of the zodiac, Capricorn, Blavatsky stated that "very few are those who know, even in India, unless they are initiated, the real mystic connection which seems to exist, as we are told, between the names of Makara and Kumara." She further indicated that "the first means some amphibious animal, flippantly called the 'crocodile', as some Orientalists think, and the second is the title of the great patron of *yogis*, the sons of, and even one with, Rudra (Shiva) who is a Kumara himself. It is through their connection with man that the Kumaras are likewise connected with the zodiac."[3] These Kumaras who are variously described as being four, five, and seven in number, and their names being an anagram for occult purposes, as *yogis* they are five in esotericism because the last two names have ever been kept secret. In the Puranas, four names of Kumaras have been mentioned and are said to remain ever vigilant, watching the evolution of the world without themselves engaging in physical generation and ever remaining in their *loka*, situated much higher than that of the Saptarishis represented by the Great Bear. The Secret Doctrine described them

---

[2]T. Subba Rao, *Collection of Esoteric Writings*, Madras, pp. 10-12.
[3]H.P. Blavatsky, *The Secret Doctrine*, Vol. IV, Madras, pp. 147-8.

as the fifth order of Brahma devas and the five-fold Chohans having the soul of the five elements in them, water and fire predominating for which reason their symbols are to be aquatic and fiery.[4] The esoteric rationale of the relationship between the Kumaras and Makara is based on the principle of *manas* as essential ingredient of the thinking and conscious five limbed (represented as pentagaon) Man. The relationship between Makara, Man and the Kumaras discloses many of the qualities of Capricornian impulses which exoteric astrology fails to unravel.

The rulership by Saturn imparts to Capricorn a quality which no other sign possesses, the quality of slowly and sweetly grinding the angularities of the individual, bringing out in the process his inner attributes. Like the careful chiseling by the sculptor to carve out from raw, unhewn stone, the slumbering image within it, Saturnian Capricorn unravels the latent divinity in the individual.

The process is certainly inconvenient, often accompanied by excruciating pain, but the end is glorious. In order to accomplish the inner divinity, one has to renounce many of the terrestrial pleasures. It is this quality of Capricorn which makes the sign unwelcome to a large number of persons. The association of the Kumaras with this sign also aims at the same goal. One of the objects of careful vigilance by the Virgin Ascetics is to develop the inner spirituality of man. They are interested in the real, enduring, and long-lasting Manness in the individual. The special spiritual quality unique in individuals is their *Manas,* the thinking faculty, mentation possibility and expansion of consciousness. It takes into account the possibility of integration between *Manas, Buddhi* and *Atman* which requires, as Patanjali suggested, *Dharana,* concentration; *Dhyana,* contemplation; and *Samadhi,* deep meditation. Unless the materialistic tendencies of the individual at the crossroad of spiritual progress are completely eschewed, the other road leading to spiritual heights as a result of conscious, voluntary process, often activated and accompanied by personal sorrow and terrestrial sufferings open under the Capricornian impulse, would be difficult to tread.

Jupiter is debilitated in Makara. The universalisation of consciousness is the goal of Capricornian impulse. The basic nature of Jupiter popularly considered as religious, is not in harmony with

---

[4]Ibid., p. 149.

this planet. Jupiter accentuates physical life. It intensifies indulgence in material affluence, strengthens physical health, induces the person towards formal religious, exoteric rituals, austerities and sacrifices. Jovian influence does not lead to nihilistic philosophy and the doctrine of complete annihilation of matter prior to achieving the final spiritual goal of life. This approach to life is the very antithesis of the influence of Saturn as a personification of Yama, the Death god, in everyday life.

On the other hand, Mars' exaltation in Capricorn is based on the foundation of Saturn, which externalised intense passion of renunciation or the fire at the burning that by which the mortal coil of the being is dissolved to nothingness. Fire as the representation of aspiration and martyrdom does not stop the planet to undertake the severest penance, the greatest sacrifice and renounce personal considerations for the sake of an ideal. Capricorn presents the conditions under which the individual is not entangled in personal achievements howsoever religious or laudable they might appear on the surface, but it makes the individual dissolve into his universal element, a kind of *Nirvanic* experience. Such being the martian influence in harmonious affinity with Capricorn, martian exaltation in this sign is understandable. Under Capricornian impulse, Saturn provides the sorrow and psychological base for liberation while Mars lends enthusiasm, courage and sacrificial power for the attainment of the goal. Mars finds its best use under this situation.

Esoterically speaking, Makara imparts to the individual the force whereby he begins to merge in the universal flow of life-essence. At this stage, after passing through the troubles of life, the individual begins to aspire that the Will of God, rather than his own desire's fulfillment be accomplished.

Makara reorients the life of an individual in such a way that through his various vicissitudes, he is made one with Demiurges of the world and thus flows in him the current of universal life. It is the sign of the zodiac in which the entry of the Sun, after the winter solstice produces warmth and the spring wind for the germination of the life within every seed. It is the gateway through which the life eternal flows towards its ultimate destiny. He who bathes in it, has to leave his terrestrial, temporal life back and be one with eternal life and begin to function like the spring wind which enables latent spiritual potential in each seed to grow and fructify. Evidently, this is the most sacred and the most mysterious influence in life. It is the most precious jewel of the celestial world kept under the treasures of Kubera; and this is the intense flow of energy with which Indian Cupid, Kamadeva, is also related. Makara is also a gateway to spiritual enlightenment.

26

SHADOW PLANETS:
Rahu and Ketu

The Moon's nodes were well known in India even in pre-Vedic times, over 4,000 years ago. Rahu, the Moon's north node, and Ketu, its south node, were frequently invoked in the Vedic scriptures for their blessings, wealth, abundance and happiness. The ancient hymns eulogised Rahu as "always ready to bestow on his devotees riches and plenty, and surrounded by all *shaktis* (powers)," while Ketu was "decked with silk, flowers, garlands, sandal paste and an umbrella—all of variegated colours," seated in a divine car travelling around Meru, the sacred mountain which formed the center of the ancient Indian universe. Legends represented the nodal axis as a Great Serpent which served as the churning cord used to extricate nectar from the Ocean of Milk. In yoga literature, this Great Serpent is the *kundalini* coiled at the base of the spinal cord. Its activation brought enlightenment and liberation to the Yogi.

Vedic Astrology, however, considers the nodes primarily malefic, and their effects are much dreaded. The nodes are not visible or objective planets; these mathematical points orbiting the earth are therefore called "shadow planets" whose effects are primarily felt in the psycho-mental attitudes of the individual. Despite their "shadowy" nature, they are considered very powerful and their effects are enduring. One of the most serious afflictions noted in Vedic Astrology is caused by the nodes when they trap the other planets within their axis, that is, when all other planets are hemmed in between Rahu and Ketu. This is known as *Kala Sarpa Yoga* and restricts the fructification of auspicious results present in the chart.

The great nineteenth century occultist, H.P. Blavatsky, once rightly remarked that nothing exists in this objective and illusory world of ours that cannot be made to serve two purposes—a good one and a bad one. This is very true in the case of the nodes. Any result precipitated by them, however dreadful on the physical plane, has the potential for producing a good result, also depending on the attitude of the person concerned and the milieu in which he or she functions. The nodes' influence takes place not in black and white, but over a wide spectrum of different hues, ranging from highest spiritual to grossest material. Therefore, many favourable results are also attributed to these shadow planets. Rahu can lead to much material gain, preferment in a foreign land and important activities among alien people, while Ketu may produce renown, enlightenment, and honour. Whatever the planetary results of enlightenment and honour, whatever the planetary results of these nodes may be, they are sudden, unexpected, and lasting.

The serpent symbol assigned to the nodes further amplifies their dual characteristics. Venom kills, but life-saving drugs are also made from it. The nodes can degrade a person to a sorrowful existence, but this very sorrow can be psychologically transmuted into soul-power for confronting life's challenges thoughtfully and confidently. The hypnotic quality of the serpent's eyes is irresistible and rules with impelling power. Just so, the nodes' impact is invincible and cannot be avoided, but can serve as a powerful instrument of one's psychological regeneration. The forked tongue of the serpent refers to these bi-polar effects.

Vedic astrological texts state that Rahu produces sorrows and frustrations, duplicity and disputes, bad and insulting speech, gambling and intrigues, and journeys to distant places. It also gives proficiency in the physical sciences, psychology, espionage, and astrology. Depending on how its energy is harnessed, it can impel one towards suicide or towards renunciation and spiritual mastery. Ketu is associated with diseases in general (especially smallpox and illnesses associated with itching), and can intimate attack from social outcasts or depraved persons. But Ketu also leads to abstract thinking, philosophy and complete dedication to philanthropic activities and spiritual liberation.

The Moon's nodes represent a karmic axis around which all planetary forces impinge so as to bring radical transformation into one's life. They play an important role in every horoscope, revealing the psychological problems of the individual and the evolutionary course earmarked for him or her. Rahu represents the serpent's head which "swallows" depravity, cruelties, sexual perversions, financial deceitfulness, physical illness, and personal sorrows. Within its body (i.e., during the process of the individual's reaction to them) these qualities are changed into intelligence, enlightenment, and life-giving substances expressed as the spiritualising effect of Ketu.

These basic results of the nodes are modified according to the signs in which they are placed, the houses they occupy, and the aspects they receive. Rahu in Taurus, Cancer and Aries produces auspicious results. If the nodes are placed in the third, sixth or eleventh houses, their beneficence is pronounced. The nodes vivify the characteristics of whichever house they inhabit. The effects of the nodes will be especially perceptible during the periods (*dashas*) of their main planetary rulership as well as during their sub-planetary cycles (*buktis*).

Rahu in the first house/Ketu in the seventh house intensifies the material urges of the individual. It drives one to seek prosperity, personal prowess, greater work skills, higher social status and to leave one's mark on society. Yet these individuals fail to satisfy their thirst completely. This leads to disenchantment with the people or groups with whom they come in contact. Self-conceit greatly vitiates their interpersonal relationships and these individuals may experience great anguish and psychological frustration at many levels. They may then begin to analyse the working of their inner mind. The psychological changes arising out of this situation makes them more introvert. As their frustration is transmuted, these persons gradually begin to immerse themselves in humanitarian activities, and become useful members of society and helpful and understanding workers.

Rahu in the second house/Ketu in the eighth house may give the individual a sense of mission, a feeling that he or she is functioning as an agent for some greater power. In extreme cases, this can lead to megalomania. More often it makes one so opinionated that it may be difficult for them to establish a positive rapport with others. These persons have unrealistic expectations of others and want to change them to suit their own specifications. They may not feel content with their achievements, and become obsessed with securing even more. The promise of acquiring greater physical or spiritual merit often brings radical changes in their thinking. They may become interested in occult sciences as they become increasingly aware of the immense psychophysical possibilities inherent in the process of expanding their consciousness.

Rahu in the third house/Ketu in the ninth house gives many responsibilities along with a tendency towards reclusiveness. These individuals come out of their isolation when their assistance is sought and they are thrust into leadership roles. The leadership may be in philanthropic activities, dissemination of the wisdom of the past and sacred scriptures, or in the realm of political organisation and philosophy. They may impart guidance in psychological exploration or industrial organisation. They suffer when they have to follow routine duties; otherwise they do not reject hard work, penance and contemplation. Gradually they realise that public and charitable work is the best goal in life and they embrace the principle of right action: selfless activity with no expectation for reward.

Rahu in the fourth house/Ketu in the tenth house may bring emotional suffering and the frustration of desire. These natives often enjoy many physical comforts and opportunities for sense gratification, but first they may pass through heart wrenching situations of utter hopelessness. Their despair may not appear on their faces; indeed, others may accuse them of insensitivity or of exaggerating their troubles. These emotional setbacks may seriously affect their relationships. Those with extremely weak egos may suffer from schizophrenia; those with exaggerated egos may become ruthless and pursue their objectives without consideration for others. When they begin to deal with their inner issues constructively, they prepare themselves to meet any situation without giving undue importance to their personal conveniences, dislikes, or troubles. They begin to realise that life is not for idleness, but for working simply for the work's sake, without wasting time in licking one's wounds.

Rahu in the fifth house/Ketu in the eleventh, activates the person's creativity in a paradoxical manner, restricting material creativity in order to impel the creative forces to higher levels from which beneficence of different kinds can be radiated. These individuals may experience difficulty in having offspring of their own, but on the mental plane they are very active. They keep themselves extremely busy. Material creativity may suffer, as may sociability, and there can be anxiety about financial security. Despondency due to such experiences makes them seek compensation on the mental plane where they attain some degree of satisfaction. Ultimately they may become both impersonal and quite successful in relationships. They attain significant social status and may make a great deal of money. They eventually realise that their happiness and peace of mind does not depend on specific work involvements but on a trust in the law of Karma. Even in small, everyday activities, their actions are now guided by an attitude of helpfulness.

Rahu in the sixth house/Ketu in the twelfth house makes these people intensely concentrated in material pursuits. Often their dreams, psychic experiences and spiritual contacts affect them at deeper levels, producing radical transformations in their mental attitude. They feel unhappy about social differences and may face illnesses, litigations, and personal accusations, but they confront them with courage and confidence, and the final outcome works in their favour. The experience gained during these confrontations gives them inner confidence. Their dream experiences, increased sensitivity, and psychic visions initiate them in the knowledge of supraphysical realms. The perception of higher realities now becomes more meaningful to them than the enjoyment of physical comforts and social acclaim. They gradually establish greater control over their psycho-physical functions.

Rahu in the seventh house/Ketu in the first house may produce restrictions in one's relationships. Psychologically, the person can be self-centred; socially, he is sometimes lonely. He expects the world to conform to his terms, while he himself is reluctant to compromise. Such individuals may find their partners in life, whether in business, social life, or in marriage, not working in harmony with them. Enduring amiability or happiness are difficult to establish. Marital problems do not necessarily arise from any lack of desire to achieve harmony and adjustment, but could be caused by an illness, voluntary or involuntary separate living arrangement or divorce. Such experiences may lead the individual to extreme degrees of loneliness; he feels that no one understands or appreciates him. These people have a tendency to relapse into seclusion, to keep away from others both physically as well as in thought. When they begin to develop self-awareness, they then find themselves well prepared to undertake severe austerities and to assume a spiritual course of life.

Rahu in the eighth house/Ketu in the second house attracts superphysical powers. Such individuals often display tremendous energy which they utilise to achieve extraordinary results. They make their mark on society. Under favourable planetary conditions they create a niche for themselves and may become great scientists, exceptional police officers, politicians, or doctors. If the individual is preoccupied with a sense of gratification, he or she may be drawn towards socially unapproved activities such as smuggling, drug trafficking, or gambling. The results of Rahu in the eighth house are difficult to predict because the range of the unseen world which this house represents is very extensive. Whatever their achievements in life, this placement will lead to the sudden psychological transformation of these individuals.

Rahu in the ninth house/Ketu in the third house produces a psychological storm which may be religious in nature. These individuals become charged with ideas that could seem idealistic, unconventional and provocative to others. Rahu makes the individual absorbed in his or her thoughts, perhaps with some sympathy for others but often without external demonstration of it. They may appear as if some superior spirit has taken possession of their personality which, under malefic planetary influences, could make them ruthless in executing their nefarious programmes. In large numbers of people, this placement of the nodes creates attraction towards religion, holy places, *tantric* rituals, and austerities—all of these with the intention of securing greater personal advantages. There is a gulf between the secret aspirations of these individuals and their external activities, which may make them insecure, temperamental, peevish, or irritable. Coordination between their hidden ambitions and aspiration for psychic power and their actual deeds may be difficult to achieve. But this is the stage where, with some guidance and luck, they can obtain much spiritual merit. They are well prepared for a psychological metamorphosis, which could radically change the direction of their life course.

Rahu in the tenth house/Ketu in the fourth house impels an individual certainly to affect the society in which he or she lives.

These natives are able to concretise abstract ideas, channeling their inspiration to socially useful purposes. They enable society to experience new truths, new visions, new sensitivity, or even new and radically different patterns of living. Rahu in the tenth house produces much social interaction with substantial gains. These experiences vivify the psycho-mental capabilities of the person but may make him or her somewhat unstable. The achievements and frustrations which inevitably arise during their social and professional interactions teach them a sense of detachment. At this stage, the ego is ready for psychic transformation, leading from a sense of utter desolation to a level at which they begin to surrender themselves completely to the unknown universal spirit.

Rahu in the eleventh house/Ketu in the fifth house is very powerful. It enables the persons concerned to acquire physical and social conveniences and power. They are often members of the social elite. An aura of righteousness and morality surrounds them. In materially inclined persons, these impulses are favourable for the acquisition of wealth, social and political status and opportunities for disseminating spiritual and occult knowledge. Opportunities like these come in profusion and may upset their personalities, making them vain, egotistical and self-opinionated. If they maintain their psychological balance, however, they may explore undiscovered laws of nature, clearly describe latent motives of others, and extensively externalise their own inner powers.

Rahu in the twelfth house/Ketu in the sixth house produces an unusual and powerful impact, providing much psychic power and enormous physical strength to carry out any special mission in life. Sometimes these individuals are found living in abnormal or trying conditions, but they produce extraordinary results. These results may be highly propitious or socially undesirable; this depends on the disposition of Rahu in the particular chart. These individuals are great organisers and leaders of large numbers of people. Their leadership may be along bizarre, abnormal, or nonconventional lines. When their psychic faculties weaken, these people feel baffled. It is of utmost importance that they are guided properly so that they can take advantage of their opportunities to gain deeper understanding of the laws of nature, using their powers for constructive purposes.

In delineating the results of Rahu and Ketu, it is important to recognise that they operate as a unit, and their axis is the fulcrum around which the other planets revolve in such a manner that our lives are appropriately prepared for the next phase of evolutionary growth. This axis is an expression of the law of Karma, as it operates in each of our lives.

The effects of the two nodes become especially manifest during the periods of their planetary rulerships called *dasas* and *bhuktis*. When the shadow planet Rahu enters its period, the intensity of affliction arising from its unique disposition in a particular chart becomes pronounced and the individual feels the strain of its churning operation. When the period of Ketu comes to rule over one's life's unfoldment, the benefits of these sufferings are experienced and the expected psychological transmutation takes place. If the individual is aware of the psychological possibilities inherent in this period, the planetary impulses, which otherwise might not be so easy to absorb, are creatively turned to one's immense advantage.

PART-V

Predictive Principles

27

PATTERNS OF HOROSCOPE

An important aspect of every individual's life is to identify the area which would be significant for him. The horoscopic division of twelve aspects of life is very general. For an ordinary person whose life has not evolved in any special way, all these twelve aspects of life may be important in a general way. When the ego or the soul begins to carve out its special destiny, it moves away from its general course and begins to evolve in a special way. In such horoscopes, it should be possible to decipher certain uniqueness.

This uniqueness is not the only various combinations which are mentioned in astrological texts. Often we find that many auspicious (as well as inauspicious) *yogas* occur in a horoscope but their impact is not decisively felt. Sometimes one also comes across certain very interesting horoscopes in which the individual possesses every desirable qualities and conditions in life, but one or two unhappy things destroy much of the pleasures of life. Many persons are obsessed with one or two major aspects of life around which their whole life-pattern is cast. In short, in case we wish to find out the central driving force in a person's life, we shall have to search for indications beyond the usual combinations.

When a person begins to function at higher levels of the evolutionary spiral, there are certain other factors which also operate. For example, Shankaracharya was important because of his religious mission, Shivaji was known for his bravery and sacrifice to uphold the dignity of his faith, Akbar was a great empire builder. Albert Einstein was born probably to reveal certain so far hidden laws of nature. In order to find out such uniqueness in anyone's life, one has to understand the celestial forces working on the individual so as to enable him either to learn certain special lessons of life or to reveal to the world certain special feature of the divinity or of Nature. Some persons are born to suffer because they have to pay back some karmic debts, some individuals are there for the upliftment of the society, some individuals live a life in which certain special qualities of their soul are developed. Thus each individual when he begins to evolve rapidly, gets specialised. Patterns of horoscope would indicate this special fulcrum around which the entire action of such an individual revolves.

Chart I belongs to a person who has been a successful person in life in an ordinary way. He is happily married and is blessed with two sons and a daughter, all are well mannered, healthy, good at studies and so on. He himself has very good academic degrees, foreign trained and educated. He has a good job and is in the higher category of income earners; his wife is also employed, earning a good salary. He has a house and a car. But, and this is a big *BUT,* he does not feel happy. He thinks he should have risen higher. He thinks he should have acquired more money; he wants a bigger house, a better car. His health is not good but he is more concerned about his promotions, more money and self exaltation. He belongs to an educated family where almost everyone is religiously inclined, but his interest in life's deeper aspects is superficial.

Ascdt Rahu Moon			Jupiter
			Mars
	CHART I		
Saturn	Venus	Sun Mercury	Ketu

Now, let us look at his horoscope to find out whether it is possible to discover the special features which are propelling his life. Telling him that he would be dissatisfied in life is not enough; unless the astrologer is able to give him some insight into his deeper psychological complexities and the importance of the same in his evolutionary course of life, astrology would be showing merely the superficial aspects of the person.

In this chart, the individual has Pisces as the sign of his Ascendant with Moon and Rahu in it. Mars in the fifth house is debilitated, but the planet which owns this sign is Moon, and the sign where Mars is exalted is Capricorn which is Saturn's sign, and Saturn is in an angle from the Moon. This combination is good for affluence. The Sun and Mercury together gave *Budda-Aditya Yoga* which is a very good combination for fine intellect, but Sun is debilitated and that also in the eighth house. These planets are aspected by Mars from debilitation. The person has all his quadrants inhabited by planets and so are the trine houses. The eighth house is occupied importantly by two planets. These are indications to show that the present incarnation of the person is very significant for the growth of his soul. But we have to find out the manner in which nature wants him to learn his next lesson.

There are no specified rules by which the pattern in a horoscope could be identified. One has to use one's intuition for it. In this case, the planets whirl around Moon and Saturn in a significant manner. From the Moon which happens to be lord of a trine house, Mars yielding to auspicious *yoga* and Venus in the ninth house unaspected by any malefic planet, are placed in an important manner which would suggest that his personal affluence is vouchsafed. There is no evil aspect on Moon except its affliction by Rahu.

Ascendant has Rahu. One axis of the horoscope is formed by Ascendant-Descendant combine and another axis by Rahu-Ketu. In this case both coincide, which implies that the life of the individual is very much the result of karmic forces. Scrutinised in detail, most of the important events would be taking place without his conscious control over them. Another important axis is formed by Saturn-Jupiter opposition. From Jupiter, debilitated Mars is in second from it, debilitated Sun is in fifth, Venus is in sixth and Saturn is in direct opposition. These locations imply serious impediments to the fructification of his creative impulses. In other words, he has not yet learnt the lesson of altruism. The Moon is tenth from Jupiter, indicating that the altruistic urges will be greatly impeded by his self-centredness and emotional instability which would cloud his intelligence. This would haunt him throughout his life. Second, his Saturn itself will often be brushed by Jovian ideas. Saturn itself is in Jupiter's sign which will make it realise the desirability of giving up its selfishness, but Venus is twelfth from Saturn. The native may be inwardly in the clutches of Venusian urges. The Sun is eleventh from Saturn and will often make his personality churned, he will feel immensely frustrated; because with Mercury his intellect will be shadowed by his personal considerations. Thus Saturnian impulses of narrowness will dog him persistently. There will be conflict between Jovian ideals and Saturnian materiality. This would be the basic pattern of transcending transitory events of his life. The horoscope reveals the basic character of his life through this kind of horoscopic pattern. He has to understand this basic trait, if he hopes to transcend the limiting factors in his life.

We may take another example of Chart II. In this case, one finds that Saturn is exalted in the Ascendant, Jupiter is debilitated in fourth house, Mars is in its own sign, while Mercury is exalted in the twelfth house. Moon is exalted in the eighth house. Thus, there are three exalted planets, one planet in its own sign and one debilitated planet. Three of his quadrants are occupied by planets which are important in their own way. Venus, the Ascendant lord, is in the eleventh house which by itself forms an auspicious combination. Rahu is in ninth and Ketu in the third house. On the very face of it, the chart is very powerful. It implies that the

	Mars	Moon	Rahu
		CHART II	
Jupiter (R)			Venus
Ketu		Ascdt Saturn	Sun Mercury

individual's soul had taken birth to complete some special task he had left undone in his previous lives. These forces should guide the course of his most important life-stream. The pattern of this horoscope gives an indication to the direction of his life.

The native had been a Central Government officer and was considered very efficient in his work. He did not rise in his career as much as others in similar situation did with comparable qualifications and efficiency in work. The native remained unmarried throughout his life. He had a few brothers whose education and settlement in life had been arranged by him, but they did not share his burden in shouldering the family responsibilities. The marriage of his sisters as well as maintenance of a few of his other family members who were mentally unbalanced were attended by him. The responsibility for maintaining his old parents had also been his responsibility. Personally, he has been unhappy about his service condition; his health too, had not been normal. He could be a very loyal friend but he had very few friends.

With this background, if we examine his chart, we find that the primary axis of his horoscope formed by his Ascendant-Descendant axis, and by Saturn-Mars are very important. The other axis formed by Rahu-Ketu also affects his horoscope in an important manner. From the Ascendant-Descendant axis, the Sun is placed in the twelfth and the Sun happens to be the lord of the eleventh house thus becoming inauspicious. His exalted Mercury which happens to be the ninth lord also has given him the gift of the pen but as a lord of twelfth and partially as a result of its proximity to the Sun, has been stripped of any sparkle that it should have displayed. From this axis, the Moon is also not very favourable as it is placed in the eighth house. The two exalted planets namely Mercury and Moon have become spoilt. The two luminaries are also weakened. Implication of these conditions is that the natural benefic rays coming to the native from the luminaries have been withheld for the person's upliftment and unfoldment of his opportunities. Rahu-Ketu form the axis joining the third and ninth houses which implies that his family circumstances specially the collaterals, that is, brothers, sisters and colleagues will not be helpful to him. He has suffered his karmic limitations from them. His spiritual unfoldment has not enabled him to grasp the inner forces working on him so that he could understand the occult forces operating on him and consequently overcome the detrimental influences. Saturn's aspect on Ketu and Jupiter's placement in relation to this axis also strengthen this tendency. The Ascendant lord Venus is left unaspected by any planet while it is placed in an enemy's sign and is also the lord of the eighth house as well, so it has not bestowed pecuniary benefits to him as much as one would have expected. Such hardships arise when the individual in his past lives had neglected his personal responsibilities blinded by one's self-seeking sensual gratifications and neglect of social relationships. Absence of altruism and of sacrifice of one's personal conveniences generally lead to such situations when the mind-principle has evolved to some extent.

Let us examine another horoscope (Chart III). It belongs to (E. Joseph) rather an eccentric person, but a very eminent painter whose paintings contained superb mystical implications and on many occasions his merit was recognised by the Government and was awarded many prestigious assignments. But in his personal life, from the worldly standpoint, he was a failure. His family members had almost abandoned him and he was without a wife or a child. He had no home or any settled existence. He would however always remain well clad and in European dress. His manners were extremely polished and moved in the topmost echelon of the society. He was almost always penniless, but he would not beg or borrow, but subsisted on help from others. He was unmarried but women were not wanting in his life. There were many persons who would crave for his friendship and association. He had psychic potentialities and had studied much occult literature.

Mars	Rahu Saturn		
	CHART III E. Joseph		Ascdt Moon
	Mercury Jupiter	Sun Ketu	Venus

In his horoscope the Sun is debilitated and so is Saturn. The Moon in the Ascendant is also the Ascendant lord, Jupiter and Mars, lords of the ninth and fifth houses, the two important trines in a horoscope have exchanged places. Excepting Venus, all other planets are placed in quadrants and trines.

The horoscope shows two kinds of major formations: the first one is the Ascendant-Descendant axis and the Rahu-Ketu axis, all these are based on special relationship with Saturn and Mars. The second pattern in this horoscope is that of triangularity. Ascendant and its lord formed the apex of the triangle, and the first base line was formed by debilitated Sun-Saturn as well as malefic Ketu-Rahu axis joining the fourth and tenth houses, and the second base line was formed by Mercury and Jupiter on one base angle and Mars on the other which joined the fifth and ninth houses. The triangularity of the pattern is a special feature of this horoscope.

The fourth and the tenth houses are karmically related. The person is selfish to such an extent that all his altruism and artistic expressions and decent behaviour are linked with his selfishness. His abandonment from his family relations and not getting married or not having any regular income resulted from his selfishness represented by his debiliatated Sun and Saturn. This tendency carried from his past lives has resulted in its relationship with fourth, fifth, ninth and tenth houses. In his tenth house Rahu and Saturn have created all the problems. The lord of the tenth house is twelfth from this house and in tenth house are placed the two most materialistic planets in order to teach him certain lessons which should direct him towards real occultism. Presently, because of debilitated Saturn which also happens to be the lord of the eighth house or the house of latent faculties, he has acquired knowledge of occult laws but in the absence of benefic influence from Jupiter he has not received any spiritual training. The placement of Mars has also denied him the courage to undertake the perilous path of occult austerities.

Thus this powerful ego will have a wasted life; one should mark, Jupiter is eighth from Rahu in the Rahu-Ketu axis and Mars is twelfth from it. His sensibilities for higher perception of inner and deeper aspects of life have been destroyed by the placement of Venus as twelfth from the Ketu side, of the Rahu-Ketu axis. His Moon, the Ascendant lord and Ascendant occupant, remains a silent spectator of all the painful events of his life. Occasionally the individual gets an impulse from Jupiter that he should alter his life-pattern but the general pattern of his life does not enable him to embark upon such a pilgrimage. He always remains moving in circles. He is given all opportunities for getting a settled existence, for getting rich, for getting married and for gaining renown, but his Rahu-Ketu axis in relationships with the Ascendant-Descendant axis forms special relationships with other planets, which do not let him cut the shroud on his life. He therefore remains caged in his own cocoon. Sex (Venus) and egotism (Sun) are his problems.

The ego on getting specialised, having gained much experience and maturity, begins to evolve in a special way. The various events in the life history of a person are woven in such a way that he proceeds according to the plan chalked out by his soul in order to teach him his lessons, meet the karmic nemesis and proceed towards his ultimate destiny. This is expressed by the various patterns in which the planetary configurations take place.

Each individual at every level where he is positioned, is evolving. That course of evolution is reflected in the planetary configuration. Once the individual begins to progress in a special manner and becomes differentiated from his fellow brethren, he becomes different from them and his horoscopic pattern begins to assume special forms. These forms are of numerous kinds. The various planetary combinations, the *yogas* given in astrological texts do not refer to these patterns, they primarily indicate the planetary disposition. They also reveal the relationship between certain planetary situations from which certain forces and influences flow. The causes and purposes at the back of those forces are not indicated in astrological treatises. It becomes the subject matter of metaphysics to delve in those relationships.

The working of the law of karma is also not a simple matter. Many forces impinge on the individual. Therefore sometimes one finds several patterns emerging in a horoscope. In such cases, one has to be very careful. The same individual may be confronted in his life with one set of conditions which have resulted from his meritorious deeds done in his past, whereas he will also have to meet the repercussions of his gross omissions and neglect of the opportunities in other areas which produce karmic impediments. In ordinary course of an individual's life, such cases are numerous and therefore no special pattern is observed in their cases. But when the personality begins to specialise on its special Ray of Perfection, its karmas also begin to be intensive. When the progress is accelerated, the retribution also takes place in a massive way. That is one of the reasons why many great saints suffer acutely. Ordinary persons have many acts of omission, as a result of which, opportunities for those virtues which could have arisen in case they had undertaken the opportunities which were offered to them, are reduced in their present birth. On the other hand, minor opportunities leading to special virtues which otherwise would have remained undeveloped if such opportunities were not utilised in past, are offered to them abundantly in the present birth. In astrological terms, we find that in some charts, a large number of planets are in adverse signs from their own signs of rulership. This shows that the individual concerned in his past life, had not adequately cared to develop the corresponding virtues. When such cases are accumulated *en bloc,* it is necessary to counterbalance them so that the path for the onward journey is smoothened. Such afflictions will however be experienced as great handicaps. In case, one could understand these karmic problems, much of the physical and psychological pain emerging from these terrible restrictions causing miserable existence could be overcome and the future assured to be better and harmonious.

This type of karmic bondage can be illustrated by the following horoscopes.

Chart IV pertains to the Duke of Windsor. The story of his abdication is well known. Born a king with a keen sense of duty and feeling for his subjects, he abdicated his kingdom and went

Mars Rahu		Jupiter Venus	Sun
Moon	CHART IV Duke of Windsor		Mercury
Ascdt			
			Saturn Ketu

almost into a kind of oblivion. His autobiography showed his great skill in authorship as well as his ethical and moral strength to face the hardest ordeals including that of penury. He could have incited a civil war, but he went almost into self-exile, away from his relations and country and lived almost like a hermit.

A look at his chart shows that except Sun and Mercury, all other planets are placed in a mysterious sequence. The Moon which rules Cancer occupying the seventh house is placed eighth from this sign. Mars which owns Aries occupying the fourth house is placed twelfth from this sign. (We are presently highlighting some salient features of the pattern of horoscopes and therefore are overlooking such considerations as Mars owning Scorpio which even rules the eleventh house in this chart, which has special significance in this case).

Jupiter which is the most auspicious of the benefic planetary hierarchy has also occupied a very inauspicious place. It owns Sagittarius and Pisces signs which constitute the adverse twelfth and third houses in the present chart and the lord of these signs (Jupiter) is placed sixth and third from these signs. Saturn, the most dreadful of all the planets whose signs of Capricorn and Aquarius occupy the Ascendant and the second house is placed in the eighth house from its *Moolatrikona* house of Aquarius. We are not drawing any specific conclusions resulting separately from these planets but are trying to decipher the mysterious nature of their placements. On an overall consideration, such situations suggest that all his friends and other aspects of life have abandoned him except the Sun and Mercury. He must have made the best use of his intelligence from his difficult phase of life, but there was obviously some bad karmic burden arising from the misuse of his past general opportunities.

Chart V belongs to a person who is no more. His life had been a glaring example of adverse karmic forces. He died in government service in a very miserable situation.

He was basically a good man, but his habits and his attitude to life created a very bad atmosphere around him. His own children and family relations did not have much respect for him. His income was not very low but his expenditure on drinks made him awfully miserable. Often the family did not have anything even to eat because of this habit.

Venus Mars	Ketu	Ascdt	
Moon Mercury	CHART V		Jupiter (R)
Sun			
		Rahu	Saturn (R)

His Ascendant lord Venus exalted in the eleventh house and *Gaja Kesari Yoga* should have enabled him a comfortable position, but the general karmic forces were more powerful in producing his general state of sorrow. His Ascendant lord (whatever it is and howsoever strong it may seem to be) is with the lord of the twelfth house which is placed twelfth from its own sign. The Moon is eighth from its own sign of Cancer. Mercury is sixth from its own sign Virgo and is in the tenth house along with Moon. Jupiter is in sixth from its own sign Pisces. The Sun is sixth from its sign Leo. Saturn is eighth from its own sign Aquarius. Such a pattern of adverse relationships nullifies all goodness, even if they were feeble, his life became an utter failure. He never realised that the past karmic forces were forcing him to waste his opportunities. He always blamed others and felt that gambling could yield him a fortune. In such cases, horoscopic studies along with its occult interpretation could have helped him immensely.

Against such adverse placements of planets, there are others in whose cases the very opposite is in evidence. In their cases, most of the planets would be so favourably placed that whatever they touched would turn into gold. The case in view is that of a former Prime Minister of the United Kingdom, Mrs. Margaret Thatcher.

Chart VI shows the planetary positions of her natal chart in which Ascendant is occupied by exalted Saturn.

The Sun is second from its own sign Leo, Moon is second from its sign Cancer, Mercury is second from Virgo and Venus is second from Libra. This array of planets is supported further by Jupiter in

	CHART VI Margareth Thatcher	Rahu
Ketu		Moon
Jupiter	Venus	Saturn Mercury Ascdt	Sun Mars

its own sign Sagittarius. Only Mars is sixth from its own sign Aries, which happens to be second from Moon, representing creative potential of the person. We can very well understand the tremendous creative impact of Margaret Thatcher not only on the British economy, but on the world as a whole. The second and the fifth houses in a chart are concerend with creative potential and creativity of the individual. She is uncompromising and ruthless, but has a unique position in the British history. In her personal life, there is nothing which she lacks. She has an adorable family life, a loving husband, a powerful professional position, a handsome personality, a fine sense of diplomacy, adept in refinements of culture and above all God's grace.

Let us examine another example (Chart VII) of a very glorious person in whose chart all the planets are placed in such a way as to make him highly creative; he came to the top of every enterprise or activity he undertook. Such horoscopes have naturally many auspicious combinations, but the most outstanding feature in them is a central direction to which all the stellar impulses contribute their forces. The special pattern these planets form does not supplant other combinations, but supplements them. Earlier we have examined the aspect of forward placements of planets, which could be adverse if they are in adverse houses such as third, sixth, eighth and twelfth from their own signs. They could be favourable if they are advanced in favourable houses from their own signs. For this, we gave only one example in which several planets were placed one house ahead of their own signs making the person extremely lucky, socially desirable, and making best use of his or her latent creative potential, so that his or her life would make an impressive impact on society. In the following example (Chart VII) another kind of pattern of planetary configuration is indicated wherein relationship is established between the planets themselves.

Ketu		Moon Saturn (R)	
	CHART VII		
Ascdt			Jupiter
Mercury Mars	Sun	Venus	Rahu

In Vedic Astrology, the importance of quadrant and trine houses is immense. It is because the planets increase their creative capacities if they are placed in trine houses and those planets connected with quadrants make the corresponding aspect of life very active. Such relationship between the planets themselves will very much arouse their energising and creative faculties. This kind of planetary impulse is seen illustrated in Chart VII. In this case, every planet is either in a quadrant house with some other planet or in trine positions. The Ascendant is Capricorn which itself is in a trine position from the sign occupied by its ruler Saturn which occupies the fifth house from Capricorn. The Ascendant lord is tenth from Jupiter, and is in seventh house from Sun. Mercury which is in a quadrant position from its own sign Gemini and Virgo, is associated with Mars, which itself is the lord of a quadrant house, Aries. The Sun is in a quadrant house from its own sign Leo and is placed seventh from Moon and in a quadrant relationship with Jupiter. The Moon is in an angle vis-a-vis the Sun and is in tenth from Jupiter. Jupiter is in a quadrant position with the Sun, trine to Mars and Mercury; Venus in its own sign and quadrant to the Ascendant. As far as Saturn is concerned, it is in quadrant vis-a-vis

Sun and Jupiter, and in trine position vis-a-vis Ascendant. Thus we find that the planets are supportive of one another. Added to other auspicious combinations, such a configuration made the person most likeable, brilliant in academic career, captivating in his manner and the very incarnation of politeness and the most intensive in his search. Dalai Lama once called him Buddha-like. The chart belongs to Dr. Rajendra Prasad, the first President of the Indian Republic.

These examples show that the karmic influence on individuals in very special cases, with adverse placements show their karmic impediments which ought to be counterbalanced so as to pave a better future. It can be done by understanding the nature of planetary impulses and their relationship at different levels·of one's personality. In some cases, the favourable placements enable the individuals to put forth their best foot forward, as a result of which, they can make an impact on society. From the horoscopic pattern it is also possible to predict the possibility of making one's impact on the society in which one lives and with that discovery, the responsibility of the astrologer and that of the person concerned is immensely increased. An important contribution of this way of approaching horoscopic pattern is to find out the purpose of one's birth, to identify the impediments in achieving the same, and the method of overcoming those impediments.

A study of horoscopic pattern enlightens us in some, though it may be in a limited way and gives us an insight in the short-term goal for one's specific incarnation. Before we proceed further in this study, it may be necessary, even if it is in a brief way, to mention that the birth conditions of an individual are decided very carefully by the Lords of Karma. We may not go into the metaphysical question of this subject, but here it may suffice to mention that the Lords of Karma know the future of every individual organisation, community, country, and so on. They also have the knowledge of the destiny of other human beings and what results could follow by their interaction with other influences. On this background, they arrange the planetary influences in such a way that in the Alchemical crucible of Nature the desired results take place. An important stage in this transformation is to counterbalance the disharmonious forces generated by the individual in such doses that it is bearable to him, at the same time each manipulation has to be such that it guides the individual a little nearer his goal. In all these arrangements, the Lords of Karma have the future of the individual distinctly in their view. So from the astrological factors of the horoscope one has to, so to say, indirectly work out the goal of the individual's life. How this indirect method is applied is the task before the astrologer, but the individual seeking the guidance from the astrologer would be more interested in the final result. We should, therefore, try to adopt a method which could enable the individual, if he knows the astrological rules and principles, to come to some understanding with his own goal. It is felt that some gift of insight and intuition of the individual in his own life and his astrological knowledge should enable him to make some helpful use of a few hints available to him. But firstly, let us try to see how the planetary configuration can point to the goal.

How difficult is this exercise is known by the famous story related to the birth of Lord Buddha. Tradition lays down that the royal priest, on seeing the planetary configuration of Lord Buddha burst into tears after congratulating the king on his begetting such a glorious child. He knew that the child was a Divine Being taking birth to eliminate the sorrow of the world and to lead the world to the path of liberation, but how would he do so? Whether he would be a mighty emperor or a travelling mendicant, he did not know. The priest also knew that he would not live to see the acme of the achievement of the newly born child. The royal astrologer could clearly comprehend the mighty purpose behind the birth of the child and he would have also foreseen the severe penance and physical hardships the child would be undergoing. To the astrologer of that eminence, the royal wealth, the beautiful princesses, the lovely child born to the prince and his popularity were not of so much significance as his destiny to liberate the world from sorrow.

Chart VIII pertains to Lord Buddha. He was born in Cancer Ascendant. Rahu occupies Gemini, Ketu Sagittarius, Moon Libra and Mercury Taurus; all other planets are in the tenth house, Aries. Obviously, the centre of gravity in his horoscope lies in the tenth house where the five important planets namely, Sun, Mars, Saturn, Jupiter and Venus are located.

The most important aspect of the horoscope is the most formidable combination pertaining to the tenth house of *Karmasthana*. The exalted Sun at the meridian cannot rest till the individual has attained the peak of the position. Unless Buddha could attain the very centre of his being, he would not pause.

	Sun Mars Saturn Jupiter Venus	Mercury	Rahu
			Ascdt
	CHART VIII Lord Buddha		
Ketu		Moon	

His misfortune and his trials were indicated by the karmic influences which arose from the fact that he was born a prince, brought up in affluence (Venus twelfth from its own sign Taurus) and his intellect (Mercury occupied twelfth from its own Gemini sign).

Not based on polarised *Manas* (lower-mind); his karmic compulsions were also evident from his renunciation of the royal palace and all those aspects of life which go with Venus, and by immersing himself in severe meditational penance to overcome his 'mental limitations' (Mercury). When these forces were overcome, Jovian creative influence (Jupiter is second from its own sign Pisces) could enable him to propound his doctrine. Saturn is in fourth place from its own sign Capricorn under which impetus he could enlighten his disciples to renounce the material bondages and be objective or unattached with their own emotions (fourth house). In doing all these, the Sun and Mars showed the internal achievement of Buddha reflecting themselves on his *Buddhi* represented by the Moon. These planets could enable Lord Buddha to align his various sheaths so as to be in direct communion with the universal solar message which led him to his *Nirvana*. This is a very short and terse delineation of such a great personality, but it perhaps highlights the central fulcrum in the horoscope. In this horoscope, the tenth house becomes the central nucleus around which all other aspects of life get linked.

Let us look at another example of an outstanding Aquarius Ascendant and examine the possibility of deciphering his destiny through his chart. Abraham Lincoln was probably one of the most bizarre, at the same time the most outstanding President that the United States ever had. As a boy, he was born sick, was ugly, poor, whose father was illiterate and of no help to the child; his mother died when he was nine years of age. He had such chequered career, that nobody with the slightest (worldly) common sense could imagine that this person would be the one whom everybody would respect and of whom today every American is proud of.

But nothing happens in Nature as a freak. Astrologically, his greatness was as much ingrained in his stars as the particular destiny imprinted towards which he moved persistently. His natal chart shows that he was born to be crucified for the maintenance of democratic principles in society. In his horoscope, Saturn in Scorpio in the tenth house holds the key to his future mission. Mars in the seventh house from its sign Aries along with Rahu forms a karmic combination while Saturn is in the sign of Mars and in that way gets karmically linked with Mars (whose significance lies in the way he ended his mission in life). Saturn aspects the Moon, his mind, which occupies a Saturnian sign Capricorn, the Sun and Mercury are in Saturn's sign Aquarius. Jupiter from its own house Pisces along with exalted Venus aspects Saturn. The supremacy of Saturn in this way is clearly established. All the planets therefore will contribute their mite to the furtherance of the mission assigned to Saturn. It is Saturn in the tenth house, in Scorpio, which was responsible for Lincoln's sacrifice of everything he possessed for upholding the banner of the anti-slavery and crucifying himself in the mission. It is said that he knew his fate but never demurred from it.

Jupiter Venus	Ketu		
Sun Mercury Ascdt	CHART IX Abraham Lincoln		
Moon			
	Saturn	Rahu Mars	

A missionary assignment to Sardar Vallabhbhai Patel is also evident from his horoscope. His has been a controversial chart. Many persons have assumed many different Ascendants for him. But on the assumption that Sardar Patel was born under Capricorn Ascendant, his natal chart is given as Chart X. In his tenth house, we have the Sun in debiliation, Venus in its own sign, Mercury in retrogression and Jupiter in an inimical sign. The Moon in debilitation is in the eleventh house. Saturn is in its own sign, namely Capricorn in the Ascendant along with exalted Mars. Rahu is in the third house in Pisces and Ketu is in the ninth house within which all the planets are enclosed.

Rahu			
Ascdt Mars Saturn	CHART X Sardar Patel		
	Moon	Sun Mercury Venus Jupiter	Ketu

Rahu			
Ascdt Mars Saturn	CHART X		
	Moon	Sun Mercury Venus Jupiter	Ketu

Sardar Patel had a very special chart which reveals the complexities of his character, but here we are concerned with finding out the possibility of forecasting his destiny on the basis of his chart. In his case, the pattern emerges in a very subtle manner, which can be appreciated only on the basis of deeper significance of different houses. On the very face of it, the chart shows that the tenth house holds the key to the chart, but the way it shows this can be observed if we carefully note the houses within the control (ownership) of these planets.

As evident from the shaded portions of Chart X, except eleventh house, second house and the quadrants beside the tenth house, all houses are owned by the planets in the tenth house. The eleventh and second houses are the houses of income and financial status and the three houses among the quadrants left out of this relationship in the chart relate to personal convenience. All other houses have mystic implications linking the individual with the hoary past and the evolutionary impulses. This linkage with his past karmic potentials presents Patel's life as a series of dedications to higher causes. Acting as the agent of the Supreme, aligning himself to evolutionary forces, he acted as a mighty force towards achieving Indian independence, and building a strong and consolidated country. And the beauty of the situation is that there are three *Pancha Mahapurusha Yogas* and two *Neechabhanga Raja Yogas,* all these point to the fact that the soul inhabiting the personality of Sardar Vallabhbhai Patel was a very highly evolved one which was given this opportunity of taking birth to help the emergence of a strong and unified country which could have been difficult, but for him. His personal deprivations were the small sacrifices his soul had decided probably to counter the past-indulgences and enjoyment for which he had not utilised his powers and resources for others. His destiny is pointed by the emerging pattern of the planetary placements.

The knowledge of emerging patterns in a horoscope cannot be had from exoteric astrological texts. It can be learnt from one's own intuition and understanding of the life's evolutionary process in which important egos, based on several spiritual considerations, are assigned important roles. This role is to be deciphered from planetary alignments which can be observed only indirectly. The various examples given here merely show the possibility of doing so based on understanding and experience of the astrologer and the evolutionary life-process.

28

ENIGMA OF PLANETARY EXALTATION

A successful prediction depends upon an understanding of the purpose for which the incarnating ego has been sent to this world, and his past karmas. The past karmas of the individual are as important as his future destiny.

The past is adjusted in the present so that the future becomes easily accessible. This adjustment is made according to certain natural forces of harmony. Some of the astrological tenets point to this adjustment mechanism. The astrological *yogas*, under which the different combinations of various planets yield a particular result, are merely indicators of the adjustment forces operating on the individual. Their final result depends upon the whole conjucture of circumstances confronting the native.

Certain astrological principles which have been prominently laid down as powerful factors in bestowing good luck to the native do not always bear fruit. Realising such failures in prediction, many astrologers begin to seek explanations due to the presence of certain nullifying *yogas*. But, in astrology, nothing is ineffective. Every planet precipitates its impact but the sum total of the effects becomes different according to their interrelationships. By this, it is meant that an exalted planet could be effective alone as well as in association with other debilitated planets or in association with other inauspicious combinations, but the native will experience the total impact differently. The exalted and debilitated planets will impart their respective influences in the usual manner though the nature of the ascendant or the placement of the planets in question in different houses will vitally alter their results. This is what is shown in a few examples given below.

Chart I belonging to a person born on 7 February 1925, contains exalted Saturn in ascendant, Mars in its own sign in the seventh house, Jupiter in a similar position in the third house and Moon in Cancer in the tenth house.

	Mars		
	CHART I	Moon Rahu	
Sun Mercury Venus			
Jupiter		Ascdt Saturn	

Apparently, there are two important *yogas,* namely *Ruchaka* and *Sasa,* and powerfully-placed Jupiter aspects the seventh, ninth and the eleventh houses. One can expect that the person would have a life quite distinct from the average people. Moon as the lord of the tenth in his own house, should give him a good professional status though there could have been some difficulties in his official career. What is important in this horoscope is not that the various aspects of his life should have been comfortable and pleasant, but that his life and status as a whole should have been quite important. But in actual life, the native had been a very ordinary person. His family life cannot be considered very happy; he had three daughters, none of them in his life time got married. He had to be separated from his brothers; and eked out a living from being a teacher in an ordinary primary school with very meagre salary. His personal health was also very bad. One may explain these individual events of his life, but one wishes to draw the readers' attention to the ineffective impact of Saturn's good results as indicated in *Sasa Yoga* and the benefic influences of Jupiter, Moon and Mars.

Similarly in Chart II *Ruchaka* and *Sasa Yogas* are prominently present. Besides, Sun the lord of the fifth is in its own house along with two benefic planets, namely, Mercury and Venus. Jupiter in the tenth is fifth from Moon, thus *Gaja Kesari Yoga* can also be assumed to be present. But what is the actual result? The debilitated Jupiter in retrogression considered by many equivalent to an exalted planet has not given him the status commensurate with such an assumption. His intellectual attainments are almost nil though he has a large number of offsprings. His physical health, in spite of an importantly placed Mars in the ascendant which should have made him stout and strong, is not so. His physical constitution is lacking in many things; he is even hard of hearing. What is still significant to note from an astrologer's standpoint is that the native does not enjoy even the respectability ordinarily associated with such a Jupiter in the tenth house with strong ascendant lord in the ascendant itself.

	Ascdt Mars		Rahu
	CHART II		
Jupiter (R)			Sun Venus Mercury
Ketu		Saturn	Moon

The third chart is still more enigmatic. Chart III has Ascendant lord Sun placed in ascendant itself. This is even flanked by two benefic planets on either side of it. In the second house is Mercury which is exalted and it is also the lord of the eleventh house. The lord of the tenth house is a benefic planet and it is in its own sign placed along with a friendly exalted planet. Moon is seventh from Jupiter. The native has neither a good academic career nor has he ever set his feet on a foreign land. He is born in a simple family and his profession is also not very honourable. His parents tried to get the best possible education for him but he failed to qualify for higher

			Ketu
			Jupiter
	CHART III		
Moon			Ascdt Sun
Mars Rahu		Saturn Venus	Mercury

education. He possesses two exalted planet, two planets in their own signs. The native moves among lower class people; he is psychologically not happy with his life though he has much money, a beautiful wife and good number of offsprings. His parents are very loving. One finds that the usual expectation that the person with such planets will have an enviable status is absent here.

Another example of an enigmatic horoscope is Chart IV. In this case, there are exalted Mars, Sun and Moon. Some astrologers think that the exalted planets give auspicious results only when they are accompanied by some planets in debilitation. In this case, even Venus is placed in its own sign, so where can one find a planet in debilitation?

In cases of great historical and mythological personages like Raja Harishchandra, Rama, Ravana, Bharat, Krishna, Muhammad

	Sun Merc	Ketu Moon Venus	
	CHART IV		
Mars			Jupiter
	Saturn Rahu	Ascdt	

and others, one can see that all of them had exalted planets without any debilitated planets in their charts, yet they were renowned and living in the higher echelons of life. But the native of Chart IV is a miserable spectacle.

He has neither satisfactory education, nor happy family relations, nor an income on which to subsist. He was not even married for a very long time.

The above examples should suffice to indicate that there are some missing links in these horoscopes which defy the superficial consideration of their auspicious nature. The mystery to a great extent could be resolved if we observe two guidelines; first, the nature and strength of Ascendant has to be ascertained with great care. In such an examination, the main purpose is to discover the purpose for which the person was born and how much of his past merits have been allotted as his wherewithals to encounter his life's battle. Second, one must understand the significance of exalted planets. R. Santhanam, an eminent astrologer and the founder editor of *The Astrological Times,* once stated that an exalted planet in the birth horoscope shows that the native had highest achievement in previous births relating to that planet and that potential is carried forward in the present birth. This is the crux of the exaltation.

Applying these two guidelines, one may get a radically different view of the charts cited above.

Reviewing the given charts, on these guidelines, we find that the first horoscope has its Ascendant in the exaltation sign of the most occult planet Saturn. Moreover the Ascendant is with Sun and Ketu. Venus is the planet of worldly enjoyment. Saturn itself has been chastened by the direct aspect of Mars. It is therefore natural to expect that the native was not born to enjoy a life of affluence. The tenth house contains Moon and Rahu. The individual was born to learn the elementary lessons of a professional career. Saturn aspects his tenth house. Every job needs perseverance. Every act in this world needs certain sacrifice, without stability one cannot fulfil any task. The native has been very impatient, he has no respect for the status of others. Under such conditions, the exaltation of Saturn would show that he had to learn the lesson of penury and he can stand that trial now. In the past he had used his physical power for the destruction of others as a result of which Martian force is denied and restricted. In the second horoscope, the new factors of debilitation and retrogression both are present. Many learned astrologers believe that a retrograde planet denotes restrictions over the planetary impulse in a previous birth of the individual, while in the current birth it tends to overcome this deficiency to some extent by giving him better conditions about the same *Karakatwa*. Truly, Jovian influence of arousing attraction towards the occult has been an important feature of this native. He has been making astrological forecasts and even telling the persons concerned as how to ward off certain inauspicious influences in their lives. He was born to break a new ground in his life's cycle. His Venusian characteristics are being modified, and the nature of Jupiter which is the lord of his ninth house placed in the tenth, has to be accentuated in the present birth.

In the third case, the native had developed very high anti-authoritarian feeling, but the penury he had suffered did not tame him. He has been denied the material status to show that authority should be respected, and used for the good of others. If he was given an authority in the present birth, he would have become arrogant because of the various tendencies he had already acquired during his previous births. His Saturn is extremely important in his chart; it restricts his creativity, his Martian spirit, as well as his Jovian proclivities. With such restrictions he would learn in this life the use of intellect for others (Ketu in the sign of Mercury). Such a powerful chart would have been very devastating, if it were not restrained by Saturn and the Nodes. The moment the native learnt to utilise the radiation of these two planets towards spiritualism, the purpose of his life could be fulfilled and the various restrictions could fall to their respective places.

In Chart IV, the Ascendant lord Venus is in the eighth with Ketu and fully aspected by Saturn. He has bottled-up energy; exalted Mars and latent altruism. But the exalted Moon and the Ascendant lord Venus have to be properly understood. When he would have learnt the lesson of not feeling jealous; not be secretive about his own talents, he would be a powerful person. His emotions are very powerful, his capabilities enormous, but the situation of the Ascendant lord and the Nodes reveal the lesson he has to learn. Once this veil is removed, he could again be a powerful ego.

In conclusion, one would like to emphasise that there are many horoscopes in which exaltation of planets does not give straight textbook results. In such cases, it is important to consider exaltation as a signpost of the native's past achievements. The various aspects of his life which are related to those exalted planets will be powerful and developed and they would form the latent capabilities of the person. Unless these planets are given free play for their fructification, they would veil the real personality of the ego. These conditions very much depend upon the mission assigned to the person in this incarnation. Ordinarily, it is only the powerful persons who are assigned important tasks in life. The importance of the personality is revealed by the number of exalted planets, and the purpose of the birth is indicated by the disposition of the Ascendant lord and the tenth house (in association with the ninth). When a balanced judgement has to be taken, it is important not to depend only on the exaltation of the planets, but one should also take the total horoscope into consideration in which context the ruling period, such as *Dasha* and *Mahadasha* prevailing during the lifespan of the native also becomes important. What one intends to emphasise here is that the astrologer should take extra care of the horoscope with abnormal characteristics in it, such as, exaltation, debilitation, retrogression, combustion and the placement of Nodes and at the outset examine whether the present incarnation could be taken as a karmic birth. If so, he should approach predictions with the help of esoteric astrological principles and apply the occult astrological guidelines in examining such charts.

29

REAL EFFECTS OF
EXALTED PLANETS

The popular assumption that exaltation of a planet invariably gives joyous results does not stand the crucial test of pragmatism. Three or four exaltations do not invariably make the individual a king or even an equivalent of a king, though it may be true that important kings and the like would have a number of exalted planets in their charts. This experience often leads to frustration among the expected claimants.

Inspite of such apparent contradictions, astrological texts abound in much praise for such a planetary situation. It is very interesting to study the mystery of exaltation and probe a little deeper in its nature.

Jataka Parijatam states that a king is born with six planets in exaltation. For the effect of five in exaltation, it has stipulated that Jupiter must be in ascendant in order to make the person born under it a ruler over "all men and all lands". For two or three planets in their exaltation, it stipulates that Moon must be in Cancer and the rising sign in possession of strength to make the person a king honoured everywhere. Such references are available in other texts too.

Of the various combinations that are indicated to produce happy results, the exaltation of planets forms one of the most important conditions. It is also noteworthy that the references to exalted planets are often made along with the occupancy of their own signs.

It implies that the difference between the exaltation of a planet and its ownership of the house is merely a matter of degree.

The astrological texts have also mentioned a special *yoga* relative to debilitation of planets popularly called *Neechabhanga Raja Yoga,* that is, cancellation of debilitation in order to bestow affluence. But there is no such counteracting combination for the cancellation of the good effects of the exaltation of a planet. Studied in this way, one would see that the nature of exaltation of a planet is something special in order to correctly apprehend the effect of such planets.

It may be useful to examine certain illustrative horoscopes to see the enigmatic nature of the problem. These horoscopes should be examined carefully because subsequently we shall be trying to indicate that these planets in spite of their not bestowing the popularly expected, good results of making the persons kings or the like bestowed on them something unusual.

We shall also find as to why there is no cancellation for the exaltation of planets on the analogy of the rule concerning the debilitation of planets.

	Sun Mercury	Venus Moon Ketu	
	CHART I (A Young Man)		Jupiter
Mars			
	Rahu Saturn	Ascdt	

Chart I belongs to a young man born in Libra Ascendant having Jupiter, Mars, Moon and Sun in exaltation, but he was not rich. He did not have good education. His family circumstances were not enviable. He remained unmarried for more than four decades. He was not much respected in his society. He was neither a political figure nor did he belong to any group where he could command any important status or leadership. Four planets in exaltation did not make him a king or a king-like, nor was there any prospect of his attaining that position.

Chart II belongs to another person with three planets, namely Jupiter, Mercury and Saturn in exaltation. Added to these, Sun and Venus are in their own signs. We cannot consider all those five planets as exalted, but even three planets in exaltation should have made him really royal or a person of high social status. He was a tempo driver and lived among the persons who were not socially eminent. The person was aware of his shortcomings, which made him psychologically depressed and suffer inferiority. He was married, and had several children. He was extremely self-conscious and desirous of living a good and respectable life. He was well-off financially, but he could not enjoy the privileges of affluence and of money that he earned because of the compulsions of his life.

			Ketu
	CHART II (A Tempo Driver)		Jupiter
Moon			Ascdt Sun
Mars Rahu		Saturn Venus	Mercury

Chart III is another interesting horoscope of a person who had two exalted planets but he has to struggle very hard in life. He had good education but there was nothing spectacular in that. His marital relationship had been extremely precarious. He had been in government service, but under special circumstances he managed to get a United Nations job which gave him much money, but life otherwise remained at the subordinate level. He suffered from psychological tension to a great extent. He did not move in the higher echelons of the society.

	Mercury	Sun	Venus
Ketu	CHART III (A Grown-up Man)		
Mars			Rahu
	Jupiter	Ascdt Saturn	Moon

Chart IV is still more enigmatic as far as the exaltation of planets is concerned. In this case, there are three planets in exaltation namely Moon, Mercury and Saturn. But his social life was very unsatisfactory. He had no family of his own. He did not rise very high in his professional career. He always had financial problems. Family responsibilities were enormous. He had to carry the burden of his parents, brothers and sisters, which put great strain on him. He was neither emotionally satisfied nor had he adequate financial comfort.

	Mars	Moon	Rahu
	CHART IV (An Unsuccessful Man)		
Jupiter (R)			Venus
Ketu		Ascdt Saturn	Mercury Sun

Chart V pertains to an Air Force Officer who had always been dogged by tension in his official career. Inspite of his being supremely efficient in his profession, he had to seek premature

Venus	Sun Mercury	Mars	
Ketu	CHART V (An Air Force Officer)		Moon
			Rahu
		Jupiter (R)	Ascdt Saturn (R)

retirement and finally settle down as a poultry farmer, where he had to struggle hard to maintain himself. In this horoscope, Sun is exalted and so is Venus. The Moon is in its own sign. The struggle of life so much affected his health that his hair became prematurely grey and he also lost his health untimely. Early in his life, he unexpectedly lost his wife.

The following horoscope (Chart VI) pertains to a person whose respectability in his society was not enviable. He was not very well-off financially. Educationally he was not very well qualified. He lost his father at a very young age and he was physically handicapped to a great extent. His present sources of income were not very satisfactory and only penny trickled down to him, Saturn's exaltation which also happens to be lord of tenth and eleventh has not mitigated his problems.

	Ascdt Mars		Rahu
	CHART VI (A Poor Astrologer)		
Jupiter (R)			Sun Mercury Venus
Ketu		Saturn	Moon

The above examples are given to indicate that the exaltation of a planet by itself does not lead a person to affluence. This, however, does not imply that the exaltation is an ordinary feature of a horoscope. As a matter of fact, exalted planets have a very special role to play in the life of a person. The exalted planets very intensely affect the concerned individuals. Their influence is to heighten the different 'principles'[1] which they govern. There is correspondence between the 'seven principles' in man, the 'seven sheaths' and the seven planets.

It is also stated that exaltation of a planet is linked with past incarnations of the individual. This is the fundamental consideration in the study of human principles which shows the level of evolution of the soul functioning within the various sheaths.

The physical form of an individual is merely the tip of the iceberg and is influenced by the quality of different planets in a horoscope.

The sheaths and the ensouling spirit within these sheaths react differently to different stimuli impinging upon the individual. All these combined together determine the course of various incarnations of the individual. Whenever any aspect of this integrated man attains maturity, that acquisition becomes a permanent part of the soul and that permanency is reflected in the exaltation (or even in the ownership position of a sign) of the planet.

The Sun functions at the *Atmic* level which is the seat of the primordial spirit. During the process of manifestation it gets immersed in various veils of *avidya*, spiritual ignorance. Represented by the Sun, this principle is designed to represent the supreme energy in the individual. It generates its own energy and provides warmth and vitality to all other planets representing other aspects of life. In the human being, it stands for his soul, the immortal. Those who have acquired maturity at this level would be very significantly aware of their primeval nature, the source of his inner energy and vitality and thereby, they would have tremendous confidence and the feeling of assuredness and as such, they would find it extremely difficult to yield to anyone else. Such a person with his *Atmic* principle very much unveiled, would have a glow on his face, initiative in his action and would be benign in temperament when it

---

[1]Fundamental life-essence differentiated to vitalise various aspects of one's personality.

comes to bestowing some favour to others. Sun's exaltation bestows the real regal grace.

The exaltation of Moon reveals the basic temperament of the person. The Moon is linked with primordial matter and cosmic ideation and it operates on *maya* containing within it the unmanifested design of the soul. The Moon receives the life-force from the Sun, radiates it to the Earth, generates the energy required for growth, that is, for change and progress towards the blossoming of the inner seed of potentialities latent in man. It is like water which in association with heat from the Sun nourishes and enables the plants to grow and bear fruit. For predictive purposes, Moon could be assumed as awareness, or consciousness which enables an individual to comprehend the implication of various forces impinging on the individual and to assist him in his decision-making process. This awareness is reached not as a result of mentation, but as a reflection of the Mind of the Supreme, that is, as a result of the maturity of one's *Buddhic* principle. It can be perceived in the great patience and serenity often felt in the presence of such noble souls.

Mercury is a link between the fourth and fifth principles, namely the *Mahat Principle* and the spirit vibrating through the *Anandmaya Kosha*. It enables the individual to develop his *Antahkaran* comprising his *Chitta*, *Buddhi* and *Ahamkara* as well as a sense of attachment.

Mercury's exaltation leads to superb intellect enabling the individual to articulate and express brilliantly his feelings and experiences. It is the energy which enables pliability, articulation, interpretation and comprehension. Anything coming in contact with Mercurial intelligence is able to project it to the external world with its own imprint.

Venus is often linked with *Kama Rupa* which is the vehicle of desires and passions; it enables creative impulses to traverse from centre to the circumference. For astrological purposes, Venus can be linked with the energy passing through Mercury in order to be expressed and given concrete shape in the material world. It is perceived as sensitivity, creativity and perception of divine purpose in every form of manifestation.

One receives intuitional flashes through Venusian radiation and this energy radiation through Venus leads to unity, harmony and the sense of fulfillment.

Mars is connected with life principle, *prana,* which vibrates through the *pranamaya kosha* and energises the individual and enables him to function energetically in the concrete world of manifestation. It represents the heat which enables all forms of creation to grow. It is life with externalisation as its basic nature: whatever is within it, is brought without under its impulse. Because it is related to the unveiling of the inner content of the entity which is intimately connected with the very expression of the life-force, it is expected to operate at all levels of existence from the physical to the supreme spiritual. The role of externalisation which is the essence of life principle does not only provide a vast expansion of the field of its operation, it also makes the planet intimately linked with the very purpose of manifestation and thus with the basis of all forms of creation. The well-being of the individual and fulfillment of his mission in life depends upon the evolution and maturity of the life principle vibrating through Mars.

Jupiter having very deep relationship with the Etheric Double of the human constitution which derives its elements from *Akasha Tattwa* is a much misunderstood planet. The existence of every manifested entity depends upon the wisdom contained within this planet. It provides the fuel for the Martian fire so that the growth and expansion of the manifesting entity is made possible. In predictive astrology, it enables the individual to reach near his goal, the impetus for which has been given by other principles of life.

Saturn linked with *annamaya kosha* has the gross physical body and physical forms of concretisation as its area of operation. It is the veil over the spirit thus concealing the true (spiritual) nature of the being. It is the principle which ultimately dissolves everything. The initial divine impulse which first found its basis in the *Atmic* principle gradually flows down to material planes and reaches its final state produced by Jupiter and then to the physical form under the sway of Saturn, but to complete the circle so that the Spirit again merges in the Ultimate, the gross physical form of existence becomes the last stage whose dissolution releases all bondages to enable the fragmented energy particle to merge in the Total, the Whole. This function of Saturn is its essential quality and in its exaltation, Saturn enables the ego to get a glimpse of its primordial nature. That glimpse of the reality is the spirit of disenchantment bestowed by Saturn.

How the various predictive characteristics of the basic planetary nature is modified is a very different subject with which we need not get ourselves involved at the present moment. Instead, we shall now revert back to the few charts which we mentioned earlier to see what the exaltation of various planets has actually done in the lives of the persons concerned. This exercise is expected to highlight the irrelevance, in the present context, of financial gain or social status.

The exaltation reveals some rare inner qualities of the individual which expose his inner nature.

Chart I with exalted Sun has given immense initiative and fortitude to the person who is extremely self-opinionated. He is very decided in his actions and in his heart he does not feel that his social status should stand against his being recognised on equal level with other individuals as far as his individuality is concerned. In Chart V also the exaltation of Sun gave the individual enough self-assurance and courage to stand completely on his own. His official and financial constraints did not deter him to take his own decisions about his life and to face whatever ordeals he had to face on account of this.

Both these individuals show distinct personality of their own. Chart I also shows that his education may not be of the required organised type, but his awareness of the various problems impinging on him, on his family members and on the society is very realistic. This has given him the capacity to take calculated steps with regard to his plans and programmes.

In Chart III we have illustration of the Martian exaltation. In his life, his doggedness in achieving his objective in life, namely money has been fulfilled. From a very ordinary status of his family, he attained an affluent position. His doctors had declared him incapable of having any child, but he got himself treated from the best physicians of the world and had a daughter. His marriage was almost on the rocks, but it was finally salvaged and in the end he became much interested in his wife, family and friends and his relationship developed warmth and affection. But his exaltation of Saturn made him recognise the futility of monetary affluence and at a later stage of his life began dedicating his time for philanthropic activities. Exaltation of Saturn is evident even in the case of Chart II. In his life also, the receipt of enormous amount of money did not turn off his head, rather it made him realise that money is not everything. He had a very happy married life with few lovely children and very loving parents. At one time he had the highest linkage with political power in the country. However, there had been certain deep psychological currents in his life which almost dissolved all these materialistic aspects of life to make him recognise that in life, there is something beyond physical attainments. Saturn's exaltation is found in Chart IV as well as in Chart VI. In both these cases, though led by different forces in life, the natives felt that there are certain transcendental forces which finally determine the quality of life and the happiness of the person. This cannot be acquired merely by human efforts.

Venusian exaltation is present in the case of Chart V. In his life, apart from personal dignity, he could perceive tremendous intuitive understanding of the inner forces of life. Having joined one of the most coveted services in the world, where, if he wanted, he could have earned much money, but he became intimately connected with several religious organisations. His penetrating insight revealed to him the inner shallowness of all such relationships; in his professional duties he could get an intuitive understanding of the motives and future manoeuvres of his enemies. Inspite of various blows of life, he did not become bitter. He finally achieved a kind of harmony in all his relationships which satisfied him and his cravings for worldly things almost ceased under the influence of this equipoise.

Jupiter's exaltation is evident in Chart I and II. Both of them by the dint of their own efforts progressed well and enlarged their personality by engaging themselves in activities which fulfilled their life's mission. Mercury's exaltation of Chart II and Chart IV very aptly resulted in their pliability and articulating what they wanted to express, which of course included concealment of their feelings and emotions as well as giving words to their thoughts and ideas. The Chart II individual was unable to use polished language and written words, but the basic undertaking of life is superbly under his command.

From the above, it is clear that the exaltation of a planet does not necessarily lead to affluence, but to maturity of certain basic faculties showing maturity of the soul in that direction.

The exaltation of planets is important for the individual irrespective of the fact whether they lead to financial prosperity and rise in his social status or not. The exaltation shows the acme of certain achievement. This implies that the planetary radiation is not coloured by association or placement of the planets concerned. The fact that the exaltation reflects the qualities and faculties acquired in earlier births does not assure that these qualities would have unrestricted facilities for their expression in every situation. It also does not imply that perfection was achieved in their regard. Complications arise due to their interaction with various conditions in a horoscope. These conditions are created due to one's karma and the ultimate destiny awaiting the ego.

The present incarnation of an ego is merely one of the many beads in the garland of births and deaths in which the qualities once acquired and developed become its permanent nature. But the soul has to traverse through many difficult as well as pleasant circumstances of life. During this period, the radiance of these exalted planets may be obscured to some extent, but it can never be obliterated. The ember will be there though the ash-layer may be thick to incapacitate its operation effectively; whenever the conditions become favourable, the glow will brighten again. Therefore, it is necessary that the predictions regarding the effects of an exalted planet are made, after giving due consideration to other adjoining circumstances as well.

Three points that arise in the present context are: first, the effect of exaltation of planet cannot be identical in all the houses, though the basic nature of the exalted planets indicated earlier may hold basically good.

Second, all the astrological texts have emphasised the importance of *Pancha Mahapurusha Yogas* in which exaltation of planets except Sun and Moon lead to very auspicious results. The implications of these *yogas* may have to be examined in the present context specially to find out the reasons for excluding the Sun and the Moon from them.

Third, the rationale of the presence of *Neechabhanga Raja Yoga* for the cancellation of debilitation of planets must be carefully understood.

The different houses indicate various aspects of one's life and the planets in their exaltation affect the subtler aspects related to those houses. For example, from the first house one would prognosticate dignity, tranquility, honour, and general nature of the person. Sun in exaltation in this house would make the person regal, ever vibrant with energy and very honourable. The second house indicates the basic attractions in the world of manifestation, the quality and tone of speech, modesty, and creative potential.

When Mercury is exalted in the second house as in the case of Chart II given earlier, there could be movement to the higher realms of spirituality, basic honesty as well as earnest desire for engaging oneself in worldly, social and material forms of activities requiring adaptability. Saturn in that house, as in the case of Chart V, would lead to indulgence in materialism though always having the basic pull towards disenchantment from such involvements.

The third house reveals courage either for materialistic movement of the ego or for the spiritual journey that is undertaken by it. Exalted planets in this house would show the related principle of life activating this movement.

The fourth house is concerned with wisdom, pure intellect and the deepest aspect of one's desire and aspiration. This is the house where the seed intended for germination is stored for incubation. Exaltation of any planet in this house shows how the radiance of the specific planet would produce the related urges in the man. Chart III has Mars exalted in the fourth house and the life struggle of the person was to externalise his innermost material cravings, which when realised enabled him to have disenchantment with the same due to Saturnian exaltation initially, but giving him a unique quality of tranquillity towards the later part of his life.

In the fifth house the exaltation of a planet would not operate much on physical creativity or progeny, i.e., for procreativity but the chanting of Vedic hymns (as symbolically mentioned in *Uttara Kalamrita*) would be expressed by it depending upon the planet concerned. Mars in this house would energise externalisation of hidden knowledge of Nature. Jupiter would enable the person to harness the Nature's creative energy by rituals, while Mercury will enable original interpretation of the forces of Nature. In this way, one can understand that the exaltation of planets in different houses would energise the subtler aspects indicated by the concerned houses.

Exaltation of Sun or Moon in the eighth house would enable the latent powers concealed in man to be activated. Moon will also give rise to tremendous insight in those hidden faculties while Sun will energise the positive forces to express that which lies in the individual. In the case of Chart I, the Venusian radiance shadowed by Ketu's association and the Saturnian aspect present there due to karmic forces, nonetheless, enabled the ego to have a great insight in working of the hidden forces on his life to establish close rapport with them. In Chart IV, Moon in exaltation with aspect of powerful Jupiter on it, gave rise to the expression of Solar radiance with ethical background by way of developing executive faculties which had been for long dormant in the person. He succeeded very effectively in the poultry industries and as a pilot trainer. Mercury in exaltation associated with Sun made his skill in imparting effective training exemplary. Mars in Aries, which has its positional strength only a little less than its exaltation, in the seventh house (specially under the influence of Saturnian aspect) enabled his perception of the inner laws of life to produce a kind of disenchantment from superficiality of mundane relationships.

Exaltation in the tenth house could be very deceptive. Basically, an exalted planet by its operation on the corresponding sheath in the individual would enable the individual to attain his destiny in this life. This is indeed a very powerful combination. Any planetary exaltation in the tenth house will certainly lead to attainment of the destiny earmarked for the ego in the present incarnation. But the determination of one's destiny is a difficult task.

The exaltation of planets plays an important role in constituting the *Pancha Mahapurusha Yogas*. These are auspicious combinations formed by planets in exaltation, in their trine signs or in their own signs; they should also occupy the angular houses, the *Kendras,* in the Chart. These combinations preclude the luminaries—the Sun and the Moon—from their scope, i.e. these planets do not come under the scope of these combinations. The result of the various planets vary only marginally as given in classical texts. When Mars under this combination produces *Ruchaka Yoga,* according to *Jataka Parijatam,* it produces a king or a king's compeer and the person gets knowledge of science and is well versed in sacred hymns. With Mercury in exaltation in these *yogas,* the person will be a king, high-spirited and diligently devoted to befriending the kingsmen. Jupiter leads to *Hamsa Yoga* which leads to the acquisition of every comfort at its command and the person enjoying *Hamsa Yoga* intent on acquisition of knowledge of the sacred scriptures. The exaltation of Venus makes a person understand the (inner) meaning of sacred scriptures, clever in the application of three regal powers namely energy, capacity and counsel. Saturn produces *Sasa Yoga* which makes the person a king, a minister, or a general, haunting woods and mountains. There are certain other minor characteristics of these *yogas,* but they are not very important in the present context. Essentially, all these planets when they are in strength make the person important, that is the main feature of making them all king-like, if not king himself. The results of exaltation of the planets arise from maturity of certain 'principles' of the personality which have already been indicated earlier. Each planet has relationship with a distinct principle, or the spirit energising the ego. When the planets are in exaltation, then these life-forces have attained the acme of perfection; in their *Moolatrikona* positions or in their own signs also, they are very powerful. Being in strength implies that those aspects of life which are controlled by them are well vitalised.

Sun and Moon are excluded from the *Pancha Mahapurusha Yogas.*[2] The Sun is connected with *Atmic Principle,* and it is related to the primordial spirit which ensouled the ego and gave its marching order. The Sun functions on an abstract plane which is generally considered as the higher-triad consisting of *Atma, Buddhi* and *Manas.* There is no evolution of these faculties and the ego perceives them in their purity only once. *Pancha Mahapurusha Yogas* are mainly concerned with evolution of the ego; the way it progresses to attain its destiny. It suggests that the individual under its impulse would succeed in completing the task assigned to it. The Sun and the Moon are therefore, in these *yogas,* out of the game. Only the five planets which are linked with Mahat principle, *Vijnanamaya kosha, Prana, Linga Sharira* and gross physical body i.e. Mercury, Venus, Mars, Jupiter and Saturn have to generate the evolutionary impulses for the individual; but the Sun and Moon are not connected in the process directly.

The four houses connected with these *yogas* are the first, fourth, seventh and the tenth houses. The first is the starting point for the ego wherein the marching orders for it are given. The seventh is the point wherefrom he begins to consider his homeward journey. The first is the apex of the Spiritual Grand Triangle, whereas the seventh

---

[2]*See, Sun and the Pancha Mahapurusha Yogas,* Chapter 18.

is the apex of the Grand Material Triangle and both combined together form the mystic hexagon. The first and the seventh are sensitive points for spiritual as well as material progress. Exaltation of planets in strength there would enable the individual to carry out his divine purpose effectively. In the first house the planet will lead the individual to strength and help him in his creativity and store merits so that his future course of evolution is smoothened. In the seventh house, these planets will induce the ego to have greater involvement in social and family relationships with usual problems of adjustment which will ultimately succeed in giving him strength and maturity. The fourth house is linked with *Hiranyagarbha* or the Cosmic Womb from which all have proceeded. It represents the nadir of the stellar course. A planet in strength which is capable of acting intensively and successfully here, will be able to bring forth the pristine qualities of the ego. And in the tenth house, which is the zenith, there is blossoming of those faculties, of the germ or of the pristine seeds, which began their flowering process from the fourth house. Thus, the placement of exalted or otherwise strongly positioned planets in these houses, makes the person extremely active, energetic and concerned with activating the specific principle with which it is concerned. Success in this process makes the person happy, lucky, and regal. But there are many more 'blinds' in the effect of *Pancha Mahapurusha Yogas* which one has to understand and interpret according to one's own insight and intuition.

An important astrological combination is related to the cancellation of debilitation of planets and bestowing auspicious results thereof. This combination is known as *Neechabhanga Raja Yoga*. The essence of this *Yoga* lies in the exaltation of the planet which owns either the zodiac in which the planet is debilitated or where it attains exaltation and the placement of such a planet in *kendra* position in relation either to ascendant or the Moon sign. If a planet is exalted, then debilitation of the planet owning this sign or the planet owning the sign where it is debilitated, does not seem to weaken it. Exaltation is a position which by itself bestows some kind of regal status implying thereby that nothing can deter its authority. If we approach exaltation of a planet from this standpoint, we shall recognise that a skill once acquired cannot be lost. One loses one's status, one forgets information, one is deprived of wealth and human relationships, but an understanding or insight once acquired is there forever for the individual. It may be out of practice but not lost. We have been told in Indian scriptures that the soul, when it is in its pristine state, knows everything and is almost like the Ultimate itself. During the course of manifestation, the veil of ignorance makes the ego forget its pristine nature and it is immersed in material sheaths. While in such a manifestative process, it undergoes various births and deaths and acquires knowledge. The main purpose of such an acquisition is to understand the inner forces of nature and the constitution of one's own self. The exaltation of planets refers to this kind of acquiring real understanding of the self. The different planets are linked with different sheaths which enforced ignorance pertaining to this subjective realisation. When the ego has gained maturity and has acquired understanding of that specific realm, this maturity is reflected in the strength of the planet working at that level. Once that maturity is gained, the weakness at other levels does not destroy this maturity. Therefore, there is no cancellation for the exaltation of planets. The debilitation of a planet showing some weakness at a particular level could to a great extent be mitigated and their inauspicious results restrained by exaltation of counterbalancing planet.

30

THE MYSTERY OF BHAVAT BHAVAM

Bhavat Bhavam is an ancient astrological dictum revealing one of the inner mysteries of celestial influence. The phrase is however very difficult to translate into English. The dispositor's dispositor is only obliquely related to it. In simple terms, it could mean that the disposition of a house (*bhava*) should be examined by considering it as an ascendant and finding the same relative house, as it is to the ascendant in the chart and analysing the nature of that house as related to it. For example, if one has to examine the third house, it is suggested that this house be assumed as an ascendant and since it is third from the original ascendant, one should find out the third house from it and examine the nature and disposition of that house, which in this case will be the fifth house. It is certainly a very involved approach to astrological prognostication, but it is certainly worth probing it deeper.

The diagram on the following page is expected to elucidate the doctrine. It presents the twelve houses of the natal chart in a different format. This consists of three parts, namely the area lying between the circle and the hexagon, the upward directed triangle and the downward directed triangle. For convenience sake, the first is called the Sea of Immutability which would contain within it the second, fourth, sixth, eighth, tenth and the twelfth houses. The second portion, namely the upward directed triangle can be named the Spiritual Triangle, and the downward directed triangle can be termed the Triangle of Materiality.

The Sea of Immutability is divided into two segments; one, consisting of only the second, sixth, eighth and twelfth houses, and another, only the fourth and tenth houses. The first group represents primeval life-impulse which during the course of cosmic evolution assumes various levels of manifestation. But by itself, it remains in its pristine state without any change. Death is an attribute of this state. In fact, it is not death as such, but death leads us to the realm where nothing exists which is not an imperishable reality. Several descriptions of these houses are given in astrological texts, which, in fact are references to this imperishable state of existence.

The fourth and the tenth houses are apportioned from the universal Sea of Immutability. Their basic nature remains the same as others, but they are of immediate significance to the incarnating ego. The fourth house indicates the universal womb in which all actions and karmas at different levels are stored, where these are processed under the Universal Alchemy and apportioned subsequently during several incarnations so that the incarnating ego may attain its destiny as contained in the tenth house. Though these

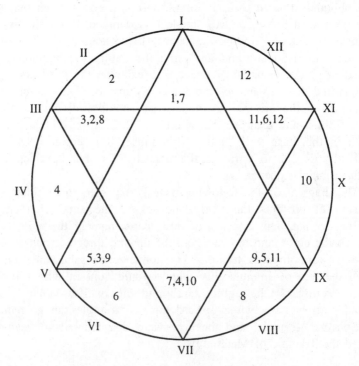

two houses are primarily related to the individual birth of the ego, they are parts of the Eternity and of the same nature as the earlier four houses.

The numericals indicated within each house division in the diagram indicate the houses which shall be related to it as per the dictum of *Bhavat Bhavam.* For example, the ascendant is not indicated anywhere else except in the first house because, the first house to the first house is the first house. Second to the second house is the third house, so in the third house we have mentioned two as well, besides three. In this way, we find that the houses represented by the Sea of Immutability contains only one numerical, thus they do not involve themselves with any other house except their own. In other words, they are so self-contained that they do not depend on others for their fruition though others are much dependent upon them. For example, the third house is related to the second and the eighth, and the eleventh house is concerned with the sixth and twelfth houses. Fourth and tenth houses, following the autocratic and aristocratic demeanour of the Sea of Immutability, do not concern themselves with any other house, while the seventh house is much concerned with both of them. The Sea of Immutability are not concerned with any other house except their own, while the three angles of the Triangle of Materiality are greatly concerned with themselves as well as with the houses of the Sea of Immutability. The Spiritual Triangles are concerned with themselves and only with the houses represented by the Triangle of Materiality. The dictum of *Bhavat Bhavam* suggests that there is a system by which the various houses are related between themselves and reveal the fructification of each other according to some design if considered carefully.

The ascendant has the singular distinction of being related to only one house namely the seventh house, otherwise every other house-division in a horoscope according to this dictum, is either completely unconcerned about any other house (as in the case of houses included in the Sea of Immutability) or is linked with three houses. It is only the ascendant which comes in contact with the seventh house only on the principle of *Bhavat Bhavam.*

Ascendant is very different from other angles of the hexagon. In essence, the ascendant reflects all houses of the horoscope. Under this situation, it must be something special if it is related to the seventh house which represents partnership whether in marriage or in business; the house is also concerned with death and dissipation of energy and with sexual pleasure. These are the basic impulses of the seventh house. But, according to the present dictum, the seventh house is also expected to reflect some of the features of the fourth house. The seventh house being tenth of the tenth house has also a similar relation with that house. The house will function as a secondary house to the fourth and the tenth houses. In that very sense, the first house should be related to the seventh house. The first house epitomises the entire horoscope, nonetheless there are certain basic features of the first house itself. The ascendant represents the life-essence ensouled in the persons. On its vitality and energy content depends the entire physical functioning of the person. On the temperament produced by this life-essence depends the emotional and passional nature of the person. The essential impulse of the seventh house can be considered sexual relationship and sociability whose fructification will depend upon the potency and temperament inherited by the person. In order to activate the tendencies of the seventh house, much energy received from the first house must be directed to it. Thus a kind of causal relationship is established between the first and the seventh houses. The later provides the basic urge which the individual wants to express, but the capacity to activate and to fructify that urge comes from the first house, which happens to be seventh from the seventh house. Thus the primary house provides the basic urge to actualise certain results, while the relative house-division considering it as the ascendant and the other representing the same relation to it as it has with the original ascendant, provides the energy required to fructify this basic urge. It seems as if the next house produces a kind of sieve through which the basic urge has to flow out in order to reach the world of externalisation. It can be illustrated as follows:

Let us assume that Libra sign of the zodiac constitutes the seventh house and Venus is posited there while the first house which will have Aries as the sign of the zodiac, has Mars in it. Under this combination, the individual will have lustful urges; he will have great desire to establish amiable social relationship with others. His business partners will be understanding, cooperative and very profitable. These possibilities however will not fructify to the desired extent. Mars in Aries will make this house so antagonistic to the seventh house that much of the individual's urges will be frustrated. The individual may expect a very presentable, physically desirable, and socially inclined wife. But Mars in Aries will not help the fructification of this possibility. The situation may deteriorate to such an extent that the married life may hit the rocks, business partners may shy away, and the individual may suffer so much psychologically that mental imbalance of the person cannot be ruled out.

On the other hand, if Scorpio is the sign of the zodiac of the seventh house, the first house will consist of Taurus and if Venus is in the ascendant, the situation will be radically different. The individual under this situation may feel repugnance to sex and the married life may seem an imposition, a kind of restriction intended to destroy his personal life. His general temperament will be isolationist; sociability will not be his strong point. Yet, the circumstances of his life will compel him to live differently. He will be squeezed in a very compromising situation. He may remain psychologically averse to what he is compelled to do physically, yet he will do that and on occasions will enjoy the same. A kind of contradiction thus will be very apparent in his life.

With Sagittarius as the seventh house, there will be little of both. He will not be much interested in others while he himself will be a self-centred person pursuing his own personal goal of self improvement. The actualisation in his life will also be supportive to his basic goals. The seventh house impulses under Sagittarius will not be very physical while Gemini ascendant will have weak life-essence to enable him indulge in physical activities. So his basic impulse and physical capabilities, both, will be synchronised; no contradiction will be there though he may fell less than a he-man.

Again, in the case of Capricorn if it becomes the sign of the seventh house, one will find that the basic urges of the person aroused by the Capricorn sign will not be very expansive; there will be some non-traditional element in those urges, much cruelty along with some influence of immorality could be there. Such basic impulses will be adequately encouraged by the sustaining and nourishing nature of Cancer which will be the sign in the first house. In this case, the actualisation of the basic urges will not remain merely on the mental level; the influence of seventh and the first houses combined together, will find the individual in a kind of immoral situation. Such individuals may be basically moral if other factors produce such conditions, but in actual life he will have the stigma of immorality, sensuality, and non-sociability. Such however will not be the case with Aquarius sign as the seventh. The denial being in this case the basic impulse of the seventh house, it will get reinforced by the Leo sign which will happen to be the first house sign.

We may approach the problem in a different way. Examining the four angles of the hexagon, we find that the third house is related to second and eighth houses as it is the second house counted from the second house, and it is eighth from the eighth house. The fifth house is linked with the third house as it is placed third from the third house, and the fifth house happens to be the ninth from the ninth house so it is related to that house as well. Thus, the fifth house has two roles to perform. First, it has to reflect its own basic impulses, and second it has to express some characteristics of the third as well as of the ninth houses. In deciphering the nature and disposition of the fifth house, one has to be very careful. For this reason, the examination of this house will be a little different from our earlier analysis.

The basic function of the fifth house is to express creative urges and creative actions at different levels of manifestation. That is its basic impulse. But it has also the role of actualising the basic urges of the third house because it is the third from the third house. It has also to actualise the basic impulses of the ninth house, there is an inter-relationship between the fifth and the ninth houses. The three houses are joined together in the fifth house. The basic urges of the third house are powers, courage, the will to actuate what the inner man has willed to do. These being the basic urges of the third house, they can be actualised only when favourable conditions for them are presented by the fifth house. The basic urge of the fifth house is creative action. Unless opportunities for action are presented to the individual to demonstrate his valour or courage, such outbursts which are contained in the third house will become still-born. But the opportunities for actualisation of creative actions as indicated by the fifth house require the support of the ninth house. The influence of the ninth house in this way flows indirectly to the third house. The fifth and the ninth houses relationships are considered auspicious, because the opportunities for actualising creative urges are provided by the ninth house, whilst the ninth house basic urges to transform the individual in order to spiritualise him can find fruits, only if the actualising possibilities provided by intelligence and creative actions produced by the fifth house impulse are also present.

The third house represents the thirst for life, that is the other aspect of prowess and courage. The second house provides the basic impulse of death, and so does the eighth house. A fortified and strong third house imparting powerful current of thirst for life will very much reduce the impulse of ill health and death. The ninth house also imparts the impulse of travelling to one's ultimate goal which greatly influences the individual's attitude to life. The earning of income and the process of socialisation for some ulterior purposes are some of the basic urges of the eleventh house. Any effort towards achieving these objectives will greatly depend upon the impetus given to it by the general attitude of life. Otherwise, one may remain a go-getter in mind only without translating the ideas in actuality.

From the above description, it can be seen that the dictum *Bhavat Bhavam* is vitally important in revealing the basic motivation of various house divisions in a horoscope.

This dictum also distinguishes between the basic motivation and the possibilities for their translation into actual action. The former represents the original *bhava* and the actualisation possibilities are expressed by the *Bhavat Bhavam*. In order to get fruits of the basic urges, it is necessary that those urges are translated into action. So it is necessary to consider both the related houses.

There is also a very important question as to the period when these qualities can surface. The *Dasha-Mahadasha* Systems when calculated to indicate the special rulership of a planet over the life-events of a person would indicate the period of fructification of the planet and the specific aspects of life related with the planet and the house-divisions related with it. Under the present dictum there are many planets and houses involved. Whose influence will surface at any specific period? This is a question about which considerable experience is still to be gained. One can only depend on one's intuitive flashes and experiences to prognosticate in their regard.

31

KALA SARPA YOGA:
Restriction Over Human Potential

Among the astrologers, from the ancient times to the modern investigational astrological age, the interest in *Kala Sarpa Yoga* has been mixed. Even the main constituents of this combination being the Nodes of the Moon, its existence itself for prognostical purposes is approached with some kind of reservation. When we talk of the planets being encircled by these planets, which necessarily occupy first-seventh positions between them, people often enquire whether the encirclement process starts with Rahu or with Ketu based on which the astrological influences of the combination are predicted. The nature of Rahu and Ketu itself has been shrouded in much mystery and many astrologers prefer treating Rahu like Saturn and Ketu akin to Mars, but the need for duplicating the framework reduces the God's expertise in managing his universe to the human level where two individuals are entrusted with a task as if it is very difficult to perform and so require 'Joint Admiral' or 'Joint Chief' or so on. In fact, there is distinct differentiation between the functions of all the nine planets. Our ignorance of these differences does not make the planets identical. By considering the Nodes as shadow planets, the ancient seers also displayed their great insight in the planetary mysteries. When all the seven planets are encircled between Rahu and Ketu, a special situation arises which certainly requires very careful consideration for assessing the realistic trend in the life of the individual.

Rahu and Ketu are karmic planets. This is a very enigmatic statement itself. As a matter of fact, all planets reveal certain karmic traits of the individual so this statement requires special explanation. When any planet represents the karmic status of the individual, it is different from stating that the specific planet is an agent of the law of karma.

The subject of karmic agents and karmic planets is very serious for a deeper understanding of the human personality specially in relation to astrological predictions. In the present context, it is suggested that Rahu and Ketu are karmic agents which convey the decisions of the Lords of Karma whereas other planets represent the abilities that the individual ego has already acquired. The difference between the two situations is very subtle. In the latter case, what is emphasised is the capability already acquired by the individual which is the result of the individual's own efforts. The Lords of Karma or any other Divine agency cannot reduce them unless the individual himself tampers with them. They are the permanent property of the individual ego. What the Lords of Karma can do is to provide certain circumstances, certain conditions and situations, certain problems and so on which the individual could possibly confront and tackle whereby utilising his skill and expertise earn greater merit and greater skill. The individual's freedom in the application of his expertise is very wide. When a planet becomes the karmic agent, specially in the present sense as it is being used, it becomes a regulatory force. Individuals put under the charge of a group leader may be very superior to the group leader himself, but they have to obey him; they cannot over-rule him. In a cricket team, the individual players may be much better than the skipper in various ways but they have to play the game according to the position provided by the skipper and directions indicated by him. In case, the individual player begins to show his superiority (leading to insubordination as it may seem) he has no place in the team. On the same analogy, the karmic planets are the skippers, or the supervisors, whereas other planets are the players in the team. Even the skipper is a player, but he has a greater role and some other responsibilities. The karmic planets are also players in the team. Even they have some functions as other planets, but they have something else also to perform. Rahu and Ketu being the karmic planets operate like other planets, but they have some added responsibilities as well. The added responsibilities on the Nodes of the Moon are responsible for the operation of the *Kala Sarpa Yoga.*

It is not without any purpose that the ancient seers attached so much importance to Rahu and Ketu. References to them have been made even in the Vedas. The allegory of the churning of the ocean revolves around the Serpent which was tied round the mount Meru and served as the churning cord. Even the gods could not protect their own design from the onslaught of Rahu-Ketu nexus: their killing of the demon only made them twofold, the one became two but always sticking together. The Sun and the Moon cannot escape their torture when the Nodes decide to inflict the same on them. The very Earth rests on the crown of the serpent. The Nodes have been considered *Mahaviryam* (very powerful), *Kiritinam* (the crown), and *Chandraditya Vimardanam* (devourer of Moon and the Sun). Astrologically, these two are subjective planets working on the inner realms of one's being. These allusions have been referred to in the present context merely to indicate that the ancient seers thought of these two subjective planets as something basic to our existence. Their existence precedes any other manifestation. As such, there cannot but be some kind of law, the basic sustaining principle which holds the world of manifestation together. One aspect of this eternal principle is expressed as the law of Karma. It is indeed a very mysterious principle of evolutionary process. At one level of manifestation due to certain decisions of the deities controlling the operation of this law, the individual inspite of his achievements on different planes thereby attaining various capabilities is conditioned merely to act in a particular manner keeping in abeyance his other capabilities. These capabilities, talents, and meritorious deeds which rightfully belong to him, are suspended for the time being and he is decreed to undergo certain experiences in a particular birth for certain special purpose. In horoscopic terms, it will be indicated by the individual having the affliction of *Kala Sarpa Yoga.*

This configuration does not imply any combination for poverty, ill-luck, bad health, theft, abandonment from relations, dishonour or any such circumstances of which the people in general are afraid. It only implies that the individual's life is earmarked for certain special purpose, while keeping his other qualities and capabilities in store for their fructification at a subsequent period of natural growth. As a result of this situation, it is possible that the individual may feel exasperated finding that his natural share in affluence or evolutionary gifts is not made available to him. What in ordinary course of events should have belonged to him, is denied to him. The moment he realises that his birth is primarily for certain special purpose for which restrictions imposed under *Kala Sarpa Yoga* are essential and in case he could understand his main purpose in life, his disappointment in life could be greatly eliminated. This would take the sting of this combination out him. He has however to realise that this *yoga* does not necessarily preclude or apply only to highly popular and renowned leaders of the community. To the Lords of Karma, the social status of a person is merely for a certain purpose and this denial of one's meritorious deeds and capabilities even at lower pitch could be put in suspense, if that individual who is not so high in the scale of social status, needs the same for his egoic evolution. *Kala Sarpa Yoga* will be present in all types of persons whose soul requires such restrictions either for karmic reasons or for the preparations which their life is intended to make for some special purpose.

The above mentioned principle, though it may seem a little unorthodox, could be demonstrated by a few examples. It is done so, not so much to prove the case, but to clarify the principle enunciated above. Let us at first, take the example of Margaret Thatcher, the former British Prime Minister. She was born on 13 October 1925 with ascendant as Libra.

Chart I gives the placement of various planets. In it, all the planets in the sky are hemmed by Rahu and Ketu, the former in the tenth and the latter being in the fourth house. Undoubtedly, Mrs. Thatcher is a very powerful force in the present day world. Her personal life, her married life, her social status, her capabilities and the faculties at her command do not make her a miserable, frustrated and indigent person. She is rich, happy, psychologically balanced, and essentialy a family person. One will therefore fail to understand the results of the affliction caused by *Kala Sarpa Yoga* in the traditional way of thinking. But should we not consider that the former Prime Minister of the United Kingdom had to completely abandon her own personal life for the sake of her country. She cannot dress as she likes, for even her dress has to speak some diplomatic language. She could not help her own son in enabling him to earn a few pence more without incurring the national wrath

	CHART I Margaret Thatcher	Rahu
Ketu		Moon
Jupiter	Venus	Ascdt Mercury Saturn	Sun Mars

and the charge of nepotism. She could not condone the marital infidelity of her colleagues lest it should upset the public morale of the country. She was a complete prisoner due to the high office assigned to her by the Lords of Karma which is amply demonstrated by a very powerful horoscope she possesses.

Let us take another example of Sardar Vallabhabhai Patel, the Iron-Man of India, who was responsible for giving unity and solidarity to the modern independent India.

Sardar Vallabhbhai Patel was one of the ablest sons of India without whose contribution to the Indian political development, the country would not have been today as it is so presently. He was born on 31 October 1875 and about his ascendant there is some controversy. But it does not deny the affliction caused by the encirclement of the planets by the Nodes. His Rahu is in Pisces and

Rahu	Ascdt	
Mars Saturn	CHART II Sardar Vallabhbhai Patel	
	Moon	Sun Mercury (R) Venus Jupiter	Ketu

Ketu in Virgo and all other planets are placed in between them. One group of astrologers put him under Capricorn ascendant and another under Aries. The present chart is on the assumption of Aries ascendant. For our present purpose whatever ascendant we assume, his planets are encircled by Rahu and Ketu.

The most important point in the present case is to consider whether Sardar Patel could be considered a poor person, or one dogged by poor health. By any standard of judgment, Sardar had been one of the most successful persons in his profession where money was no consideration for his affluence. About his eminence, every politician would agree that indomitable courage and intergrity of character had made him invincible even to Mahatma Gandhi and Pandit Nehru both of whom were upheld as the undisputed leaders of the Indian population. The personal merits of Sardar did not fructify for his personal enjoyment; he was given his present birth at great sacrifice to his own life of ease and comfort.

It is for the astrologers to find out the special disposition of *Kala Sarpa Yoga* arising out of the placement of the Nodes in different signs of the Zodiac in order to decide the special contribution and the manner of the contribution the individual is made to offer. Here we merely wish to suggest that the powerful disposition of the *Yoga* arose from the special purpose in which the individual's own personal conveniences were not taken into account or were put in abeyance. He was, if at all we wish to say so, made to suffer for an impersonal cause, and as he was in harmony with the cause for which the was suffering, he was not frustrated.

Another example in the present context could be taken of Abraham Lincoln who was born on 1 February 1809 but some uncertainty exists about his exact time of birth also. However, even if we give sufficient margin to the birth time discrepancy, the position of Mars and Rahu will not substantially alter to nullify the *Kala Sarpa Yoga.* On an assumption that President Lincoln was born under Aquarius ascendant, Chart III is given below to indicate the placement of various planets.

Who can deny that this great person inspite of his personal vicissitudes, was one of the greatest men ever born on the soil of the United States of America. His personal problems, as it is evident from the horoscope, were not necessarily accentuated by the existence of *Kala Sarpa Yoga.* They already existed there, but they

Venus Jupiter	Ketu		
Ascdt Sun Mercury	**CHART III** Abraham Lincoln		
Moon			
	Saturn	Rahu Mars	

were subordinated to the task of uphelding the cause of democracy and equality of men while holding together the emerging nation.

The problems of his marital pain, the problems of collective management and administrative inexperience or in fact, every problem that President Lincoln encountered in his life was there as a part of his karmic birth, but the presence of *Kala Sarpa Yoga* transcended all of these personal problems to enable him to discharge the special responsibilities entrusted to him. For this, he bore the cross of his personal life happily or unhappily as his physical and psychological constitution permitted. But, by and large, he could not be considered a poor person with personal problems arising from the constraints imposed by Rahu-Ketu nexus. From astrological standpoint, it is important to consider the fact that in the case of Margaret Thatcher, the *Kala Sarpa Yoga* arises between Cancer and Capricorn for Sardar Patel between Virgo and Pisces, whereas for President Lincoln it arises between Libra and Aries. This characteristic along with the house-divisions at which the Nodes are placed, will determine the special features of its operation, but its basic disposition of putting in abeyance the personal predilections of the individual remains in all the cases as the vital basic point. In many cases, when the purpose is consciously registered, there is a streak of martyrdom in the person arising as a result of this combination.[1]

---

[1]A detailed description of *Kala Sarpa Yoga* is available in author's *Fundamentals of Vedic Astrology*, Vol. I, pp. 220-224, Passage Press, Utah, U.S.A. Also see, *Shadow Planets: Rahu and Ketu*, Chapter 26, (Supra).

GLOSSARY

Adhi Deva	:	Guardian Deity.
Agni	:	Fire
Akasha Tattwa	:	Ether considered as the fifth element
Anahat Chakra	:	The heart or the Cardiac force-centre located near heart which when energised enables the individual to unify his consciousness with universal life
Angles	:	Quadrant houses or the *Kendras* in a natal chart
Antahakarana	:	The core of the being; the seat of thought and feelings
Ascendant	:	The first house in a natal chart; *Lagna*
Ashwatha Tree	:	The holy fig tree; it symbolises manifestation with its roots in the heaven world while its trunk, branches and foliage spread in the realm of matter
Aspects	:	Planetary glance. All planets cast their sight at the seventh house in a natal chart but Mars, Saturn and Jupiter have other aspects also
Atman	:	The Soul; Supreme Soul, Brahman
Atmic Principle	:	The life-essence vitalising the highest level of consciousness
Avidya	:	Ignorance; illusion under which material universe appears real
Benefic Planets	:	Auspicious planets viz., Jupiter, Venus, Mercury and strong Moon

Bhadra Yoga	:	See *Pancha Mahapurusha Yogas*
Bhagya	:	Destiny
Bhagyasthana	:	The ninth house in a natal chart
Bhauma	:	Born of the Earth; Mars
Bhava	:	Roughly corresponds with house divisions in a chart
Brahma	:	Creator of the universe
Buddhi	:	Comprehension, intelligence, identified with Mahat, the second of the twenty-four *tattwas*
Bhuta(s)	:	Literally a ghost, an element: the five elements viz., earth, water, fire, air and ether
Bythos	:	A gnostic term meaning "Depth" or the "Great Deep". It is equivalent of space before anything had formed itself in it from primordial atoms that existed in its spatial depths
Chhaya graha	:	Shadow planets, viz., Rahu and Ketu, the Nodes of the Moon
Chitta	:	The seat of intellect, the mind
Dasa-Bhukti	:	Main and sub-periods of planetary rulership
Debilitation	:	The fall; the position opposite to 'exaltation' of a planet
Demiurges	:	The supernal or the celestial powers which built the universe and supervise its activities
Descendant	:	The seventh house in a natal chart
Dharma	:	Righteousness
Dharmasthana	:	The ninth house in a natal chart
Durga	:	The goddess, as the saviour or rescuer from all difficulties; she rides a lion
Exaltation	:	The position of a planet when it attains its maximum strength
Fohat	:	A term used to represent the active (Male) potency of the *shakti* (the female reproductive power). The essence of cosmic electricity
Hatha Yoga	:	A practical mode of *yoga* discipline for practising abstract meditation consisting of severe body manoeuvrability
Higher Triad	:	*Atma-Buddhi-Manas* taken together

Hiranyagrabha	:	Shining, resplendent, the Golden Egg the nuclear matrix from which Brahma was born; Mother Nature in essence
Ida	:	A channel for *prana* on the left side of the spine through which the feminine force flows up
Indriya(s)	:	An organ for sense-perception. The five *karmendriyas* (organs of action) are speech, hands, feet, excretory organ and generative organ; five *jnanendriyas* (the sense organs) are nose, tongue, eye, skin and ears
Jnana	:	Knowledge, wisdom
Kalapurusha	:	The Cosmic Man, the universe or the manifestation conceived as the expression of Cosmic Man in time dimension
Kala Sarpa Yoga	:	The planetary combination formed by the seven planets encircled by the Nodes of the Moon in a natal chart
Kali	:	An aspect of Parvati, Shiva's consort
Kamadeva	:	The Indian Cupid
Karaka	:	Significator
Karma	:	Action, duty, fate, consequences of acts done in former lives; the law of cause and effect or ethical causation
Karmasthana	:	The tenth house in a natal chart
Kavi	:	Poet; the planet Venus
Kendra(s)	:	The Angles, the Quadrant houses in a natal chart
Kuja	:	Mars
Kuja Dosha	:	Affliction of Mars. Mars in second, fourth, seventh, eighth and twelfth houses in a natal chart is said to destroy marital happiness
Kumara(s)	:	Youthful ascetic sages born of Brahma, but who refused to partake in the process of generative creation considering it impure involvement. They, however, remain at subjective plane guiding and supervising the manifestation
Luminaries	:	The Sun and the Moon

Maha Kalpa	:	The great age; the period between two great Deluges; a *Kalpa* comprises 155,520,000 million human years
Mahat Principle	:	The first principle of cosmic mind and intelligence; the second fo the twenty-four elements of *tattwas* in Sankhya philosophy
Malavya Yoga	:	See *Pancha Mahapurusha Yogas*
Malefic Planets	:	Inauspicious planets viz., Saturn, Mars, Sun and weak Moon
Materiality, the triangle of	:	The triangle formed by third, eleventh and seventh houses in a natal chart
Maya	:	Illusion, enchantment, unreality; philosophically, matter, wealth and worldly attainments; another name of *Prakriti* (matter)
Mooltrikona	:	The position of a planet in a sign of the zodiac where it receives more strength than in its own sign but less than that of its exaltation
Naga Dosha	:	Affliction caused by the curse of serpent god, which usually results in denial of happiness from offspring
Neecha Bhanga	:	Cancellation of debilitation of a planet
Neecha Bhanga Raja Yoga	:	Auspicious combination formed by planets enjoying cancellation of its debilitation
Nirvana	:	Liberation from involuntary cycle of births and deaths
Pancha Mahapurusha Yogas	:	Auspicious combinations formed by planets (non-luminaries) in exaltation or in their own signs posited in Angles. Jupiter in such a position produces *Hamsa Yoga,* Saturn *Sasa,* Mercury *Bhadra,* Venus *Malvya* and Mars *Ruchaka Yoga*
Papakartari	:	Flanking of a house by malefic planets on its either side, it destroys any benefical feature of the house thus flanked
Pingala	:	The positive or right-hand (male) spinal force. (*See Ida*)
Poorvajanma Karma	:	Action generated in previous births

Prajapati	:	Lord of Creation, proprietor. An epithet of Brahma, but Brahma also creatred ten Prajapatis who superintend the creative processes of the universe
Prakriti	:	Mother Nature
Principles	:	Fundamental life-essence differentiated to vitalise various aspects of one's personality
Punyakartari	:	Flanking of a house-division in a natal chart on its either side by benefic planets which greatly enhances the potential of the house
Quaternary, Lower	:	It consists of physical body, etheric double through which vital airs circulate, the passional body with desires, and the lower mind which functions actively as rational mind (intellect)
Ray	:	The special path on which each individual has to finally attain his goal
Sakata Yoga	:	A planetary combination formed by Moon and Jupiter posited sixth-eighth to each other
Samadhi	:	Meditation
Sanyasa	:	Renunciation
Saptarishi	:	The seven seers superintending the cosmic manifestation represented by the Great Bear stars
Sattwa	:	Harmony
Sea of Immutability	:	The second, fourth, sixth, eighth and twelfth as well as the tenth house in a natal chart represent the Sea of Immutability, but fourth and tenth houses are exluded from it for predictive purposes, as they are actively involved in shaping the present life of the individual
Serpent Fire	:	Kundalini, one of the primary forces of Nature
Seven Channels of Human Temperament	:	The differentiated path on which the individuals have to proceed towards their ultimate goal of Nirvana
Siddhis	:	Accomplishments, six in number
Sige	:	A gnostic term meaning silence

Six Primary Forces of Nature	:	*Para-shakti* (the supreme power generating light and heat), *Jnanashakti* (the power of knowledge and wisdom), *Ichchashakti* (will-power), *Kriyashakti* (the power of thought and volition), *Kundalini-shakti* (the Serpent Fire), and *Mantrashakti* (the power of mantras aroused by letter, speech and music)
Sushumna	:	The central sexless vital air, aspect of Kundalini in the spinal column (See *Ida, Pingala*)
Tamas	:	Darkness, sloth, inertia
Tanmatra	:	Prime qualities of sound, touch, sight, taste and hearing behind the five elements (See *Indriyas* and *Bhutas*)
Tantra	:	A spell, a charm
Tapas	:	Penance
Tattwa	:	Element
Tau	:	The path to salvation and consecration
Transit	:	Passage of a planet
Triguna	:	The three basic attributes viz., *Sattwa* (Harmony), *Rajas* (Activity) and *Tamas* (Inertia)
Trikona	:	Trine Houses viz., Ninth, Fifth and First (Lagna) Houses in a natal chart
Vedanga	:	Limb of the Vedas
Viparit Raja Yoga	:	An auspicious combination formed by all or any of the planets owning the sixth, eighth and twelfth houses in a chart posited in any way in these houses
Yajna	:	Sacrificial observances or rituals for spiritual purposes
Yama	:	God of Death
Yoga-Maya	:	The magical power of a yogi. The power of God in the creation of the world personified as a deity. Name of Durga.

SELECT BIBLIOGRAPHY

Behari, Bepin. *Astrology Simplified,* Sterling Publishers Pvt. Ltd., New Delhi, 1999.

----------. *A Study in Astrological Occultism,* IBH. Bangalore 1983.

----------. *Solve Your Problems Astrologically,* Motilal Banarsidass 2000.

----------. *Myths and Symbols of Vedic Astrology,* Passage Press, USA, 1990.

----------. *Fundamentals of Vedic Astrology,* Passage Press, USA, 1992.

----------. *Astrological Biographies: Seventeen Examples of Planetary Insights,* Motilal Banarsidass, Delhi, 1998.

----------. *Revelations of Zodiacal Signs and Lunar Mansion,* Sagar, New Delhi 2002.

Behari, Madhuri and Bepin. *An Introduction to Esoteric Astrology.* Sagar, New Delhi, 1997.

Blavatsky, H.P. *Isis Unveiled,* Vols I & II. California 1976.

----------. *The Secret Doctrine,* Vols I-VI, TPH, Madras, 1923.

Braha, James T, *Ancient Hindu Astrology for Modern Western Astrologer,* Hermetican, USA, 1986.

Brihat Jatak, Original by Varaha Mihira*.

Brihat Parashar Hora Shastra, Original by Parashar Rishi*.

Frawley, David, *The Astrology of the Seers,* Passage Press, USA, 1990.

Mees, G.H. *The Revelation in the Wilderness,* Vols I-III, Kanvashram
    Trust, Tiruvanmalai, 1985.
Sankaracharya, Adi Guru, *Viveka Chudamani*.*
Subba Rao, T. *Esoteric Writings,* TPH, Madras, 1998.
Uttara Kalamrita, Original by Kalidasa.

---

*Many English translations of these works are available.

INDEX

HOROSCOPES OF THE FOLLOWING EMINENT PERSONS HAVE BEEN DISCUSSED IN THIS BOOK

Abraham Lincoln
Chengiz Khan
Chaitanya Mahaprabhu
Dr. Rajendra Prasad
Dr. B.V. Raman
Dr. S. Ramanujan
Duke of Windsor
Gautam Buddha
Guru Nanak
J. Krishnamurti
Jawaharlal Nehru
Lord Krishna
Lal Bahadur Shastri
Morarji Desai
Mrs. Margaret Thatcher
Raj Kapoor
Ramakrishna Paramahamsa
Smt. Rukmini Devi Arundale
Sardar Vallabhbhai Patel
Shivaji the Great
Swami Vivekananda